PERFORMANCE
WITH ECONOMY

BY DAVID VIZARD

PERFORMANCE WITH ECONOMY

EDITED BY
LARRY SCHREIB

PRODUCTION BY
LARRY ATHERTON

ISBN 0-931472-09-1
Part No. 09-1

DRAWINGS BY
BOB ROBE

S-A DESIGN BOOKS, 515 WEST LAMBERT, BLDG E, BREA, CA 92621-3991

TABLE OF CONTENTS

ON THE COVER: ONE OF THE LATEST INNOVATIONS IN PERFORMANCE TECHNOLOGY IS THIS GALE BANKS ENGINEERING TWIN-TURBOCHARGED SYSTEM. DESIGNED TO PROVIDE HIGH BOOST, INSTANT RESPONSE AND EXCELLENT PART-THROTTLE ECONOMY, IT IS AN OUTSTANDING EXAMPLE OF MODERN PERFORMANCE WITH ECONOMY.

PREFACE

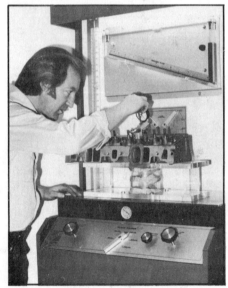

Fuel economy is boring! Ask any performance enthusiast and he'll tell you exactly how boring it is. But, don't for one minute believe that it isn't important. In times past we didn't think much about economy because the ultimate goal was power. The golden idol of every true performance enthusiast has always been horsepower. Virtually every backyard mechanic who modifies his engine spends time and money to gain more power. Power

equates to performance, and this is where the excitement lies. Unfortunately, the ever-rising price of fuel is making the financial burden of high-performance motoring a little less than bearable. Now, as a practical necessity and in view of the "permanent" fuel crisis, performance has taken on a new definition. In the foreseeable future the term high-performance will mean *more horsepower with more economy,* or at least, more power with no loss of economy.

Unlike previous performance books, this book gives power and economy an equal status. We will discuss each of these interrelated topics and try to guide the reader toward a realistic balance of power with economy. We're not about to tell you that we can return to the "good old days." Those days, be they good or bad, are gone forever. But, with carefully directed effort it's possible to build a modern "hot rod" that will provide blood-stirring performance and very respectable fuel economy. The mythical 500 horsepower, 50 mile-per-gallon gasoline engine is a fantasy and probably will remain so for many years to come. Within current technology, however, a very reasonable goal would be 300-350 horse-

power with 20-25 mile-per-gallon economy. We're going to show you various methods you might use to head in this direction. Make no mistake about it, though, building a modern performance automobile requires careful planning and a lot of dedication. But, it can be done! Performance is not dead. It just has a new face!

David Vizard

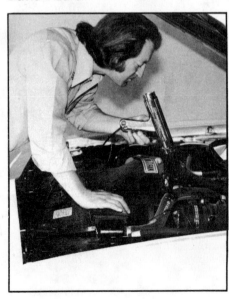

4

INTRODUCTION

Equating performance and economy is something the hot-rodder of yesteryear seldom considered, but the winds of change are here. From the Eighties onward, for however long hot-rodding may persist as a sport, the new generation of hot-rodders and performance enthusiasts must look at these two factors with equal concern. This is going to require a different approach to the traditional study of basic engine operation. The hot-rodder must now study these basics with a steady eye toward *a suitable balance between reasonable performance and reasonable economy!* So this is exactly where we will start.

In simple terms, the internal combustion engine is a mechanical device for converting heat energy into mechanical energy. The heat energy is derived from the burning of air and vaporized fuel that have been mixed in certain well-defined proportions. Generally, the greater the quantity of this mixture the engine can be made to burn in a given time, the more power it will develop. *The more efficiently it turns this heat energy into mechanical energy, the more powerful and economical it will be.* If these factors are kept in mind when building an engine for power with economy, the reader will at least be going in the right direction. However, to arrive at the intended destination, it is necessary not only to go in the right direction, but to choose the right road and then recognize the intended destination well in advance, so you can put on the brakes and arrive right "on the money."

Although this view of engine operation is indeed simplistic, it is applied to a device which functionally is anything but simple. An engine can best be viewed as a large collection of small components, each of which must functionally complement all of the others, in order for the whole to do what is required of it in the best possible manner. To achieve this end, the engine builder must *carefully select and individually test each component, assemble them with a specific operational goal in mind, and develop or fine tune the overall combination until this goal is achieved in the most efficient manner consistent with reasonable cost.* This functional harmony sounds disarmingly simple to achieve but, in actual practice, building a "totally efficient" engine is a very demanding task.

A good example of a highly developed combination is a Grand National stock car engine. A typical single four-barrel, 358cid Grand National Chevrolet will develop about 600 horsepower. In a Grand National superspeedway race car this engine will record a fuel consumption of about 5 miles-per-gallon at wide-open throttle. At first, this doesn't sound like a very economical engine but consider this: even though it takes a lot of brute horsepower to push a full-size sedan around a high-banked race track at speeds in excess of 190mph, the rate at which fuel is consumed in relation to the horsepower produced is relatively low. In fact, this rate is only 30-50% of the comparable fuel consumed per horsepower by the average street engine cruising down the highway at 55mph. The GN racer produces fewer miles-per-gallon because it is required to constantly develop huge amounts of power. However, it is a highly efficient engine because it delivers this extreme output from what turns out to be a proportionally smaller amount of fuel.

There is a good reason why a Grand National engine produces such impressive relative economy: incredible amounts of time, energy and money are spent by engine builders to de-

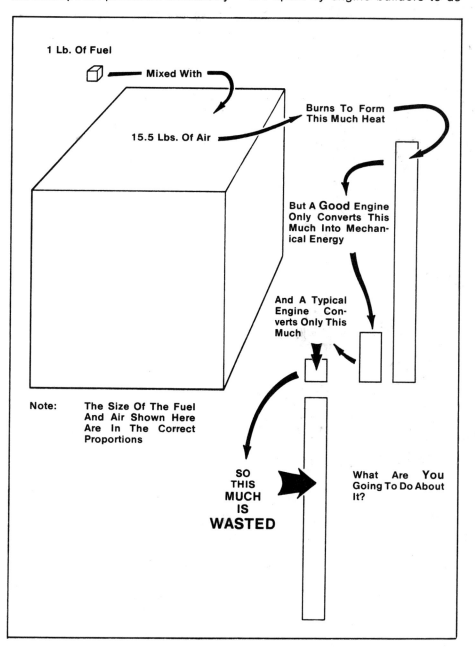

1 Lb. Of Fuel

Mixed With

15.5 Lbs. Of Air

Burns To Form This Much Heat

But A **Good** Engine Only Converts This Much Into Mechanical Energy

And A Typical Engine Converts Only This Much

Note: The Size Of The Fuel And Air Shown Here Are In The Correct Proportions

SO THIS **MUCH** IS **WASTED**

What Are You Going To Do About It?

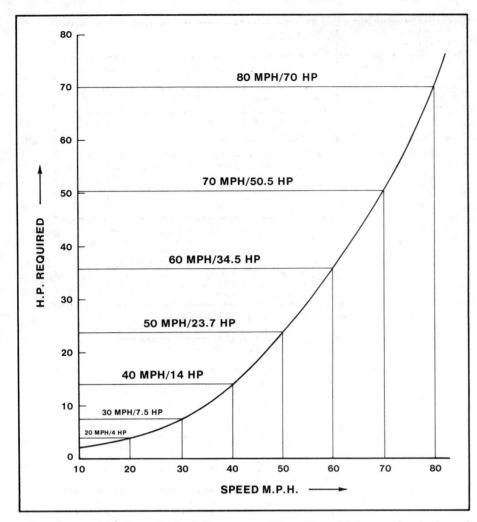

The accompanying graph shows about how much additional power is required as speed increases. This curve is approximately average for a V8-powered, automatic transmission-equipped, mid-size car. As can be seen from the graph, driving at 30mph takes typically 7.5hp, but to drive at 60mph requires 34.5hp. At 30mph the engine powering our average vehicle is probably burning about 1.1 pounds of fuel per hour for each horsepower the engine develops. If we run a comparable fuel calculation for the 34.5hp required to propel the car at 60mph, we find that even though there is a 20% improvement in fuel utilization, the miles-per-gallon have dropped to 11.6.

So, if driving fast isn't the answer, what can we do to get better mileage? We can build an engine and chassis to gain maximum efficiency in the cruise mode, while retaining high performance in the "foot-to-the-wood" mode. It is currently understood that *a great many of the alterations formerly accepted as strictly performance modifications also help fuel economy.* This is true to a greater or lesser degree, depending upon the specific type and method of modification. The kicker is that some modifications virtually destroy mileage. This means, if you intend to modify your engine, you should explore the full potential of the first category and carefully avoid modifications that fall into the second category.

To get horsepower from an engine we need concern ourselves only with full-throttle operation; but to get good full-throttle power and good part-throttle economy we have to consider many more things. For example, fuel distribution, fuel atomization, charge contamination, exhaust backpressure, and many other factors will influence overall efficiency, and the importance of these factors change as the engine moves through the operational mode from part- to full-throttle operation. Sometimes a component which is good for part-throttle economy may be way short of the ultimate for power, and the reverse is also true. Intake manifolds and cams are prime examples of components that can be biased one way or the other. To make a wise choice when such a situation presents itself, it is necessary to have some understanding of the situations involved. In the succeeding pages this book seeks to convey such an understanding.

THE WORLD'S FUEL SUPPLY BECAME LIMITED THE FIRST DAY WE STARTED USING IT!

velop a combination that delivers maximum power and maximum economy specifically at wide-open throttle. The key phrase here is "specifically at wide-open throttle." Since these engines operate within a relatively narrow rpm band, it is possible to tailor all of the individual components for maximum efficiency during a specific operational mode. Unfortunately, a street engine must function throughout a wide range of engine speeds and load conditions. This makes the job much more difficult, but no matter what the eventual use of the engine, if we are seeking high performance with a reasonable degree of economy, two factors must always be considered. *First, it is necessary to build a mechanically efficient engine that will operate as effectively as possible in the most appropriate rpm range for the specific application. Second, it is desirable to draw in the very minimum amount of fuel necessary to answer the demand placed on the engine at any specific time.*

Even if you aren't a theoretical wiz, you should be able to see the picture shaping up. To get mileage, the engine needs to generate the power as efficiently as possible in the first place,

and then the vehicle must be designed or modified in such a way as to utilize the minimum amount of power necessary to achieve the speeds desired. Essentially this means efficient engines and lightweight, aerodynamic cars rather than inefficient engines and heavy, high-drag cars.

Taking first things first, let's consider efficiency and speed. In the Grand National engine described earlier we noted that an engine could be efficient at very high speed. It is difficult for many people to accept that an engine can produce power more economically at full throttle than at part throttle. However it is generally true that an engine uses fuel more economically during wide-open throttle operation, at which time all engine systems are working at their peak design efficiency. It would seem, then, that we should all drive around at full throttle. However, the factuality and the wonderful simplicity of this view is upset by one thing: *the horsepower required to propel a car at ever-increasing speed goes up at a considerably greater rate than the comparable improvement in fuel efficiency.* The net result is fewer miles-per-gallon the faster the car is driven.

ITEM	EFFECT ON POWER	EFFECT ON ECONOMY	COMMENTS
Home tuneup	Depends on faults rectified	Depends on faults rectified	If your budget is limited, this is the very least you should do.
Dyno tuneup	Depends on faults rectified	Depends on faults rectified	Even with limited cash, this should be high priority. If you modify your engine, make a dyno-tune a top priority as it will make other modifications more cost effective.
Carburetion	Zero to substantial, depending upon the carb used and what it replaced	Zero to moderate depending upon the carb used and what it replaced	Don't buy a carb unless more cfm is needed or your old carb is in need of repair. Do not buy a new "economy" carb if your present carb is in good working order. An exception might be, if for performance reasons you need a carb that is easy to calibrate.
Intake manifolds	Moderate to substantial, depending upon manifold type	Moderate to substantial, depending upon manifold type	As far as performance is concerned, a good manifold will provide some of the cheapest power available. If you are looking for an economy manifold, be prepared to sacrifice a fair amount of power. Generally speaking, an intake manifold should be considered about the second item of hardware on the priority list.
Headers and exhaust systems	Moderate to good depending upon efficiency of original system	Moderate to good depending upon efficiency of original system	When the stock system is replaced with headers and a free-flow exhaust system, both mileage and power go up. Under most circumstances headers and exhaust systems should be the first modification made on the vehicle.
Cylinder heads	Good to very good	Effects can range from slight loss to reasonable gain depending on head specification	A good set of heads can add substantial amount of power but changes in mileage are generally marginal, unless the heads are built specifically for economy. On a cost effectiveness basis, heads should be about fourth on a hardware priority list.
Camshaft	On emission-regulated, late-model vehicles, good to very good	Marginal to moderate	Represents a good dollar-to-performance ratio, especially if cam is installed at the time a rebuild is done. On hardware priority list, it ranks about the same as an intake manifold.
Ignition system	Zero to marginal over well maintained stock	Zero to marginal over well maintained stock	Main saving is reduced need for ignition tuneups. Is expensive in terms of potential power and economy gains but more worthwhile if convenience factor is considered.
Turbochargers	Marginal to substantial	Depends on what the turbo replaced; mileage range can change from a marginal drop to a resonable increase.	High-boost, high-power system offers tremendous performance gains at reasonable cost. Many low-boost systems offer less potential power gain than that possible by more conventional engine modifications, i.e., headers, carbs, etc.
Nitrous-Oxide Injection	Good to substantial	No gains, no losses	Many, but not all, kits offer good power increase per dollar spent.
Synthetic oils	Marginal	Marginal to moderate depending on driving habits	Appears to be a good investment for long engine life and ususally, but not always, covers extra cost of oil with fuel saving. Provides greater mileage between oil changes.
Octane boosters	Indirectly leads to moderate gains	Indirectly leads to moderate gains	Should be considered a secondary economy measure. It leads to extra power and mileage only by allowing correct ignition advances and higher compression to be used. Possible economy gains, but usually does not cover the increased fuel cost, so must be looked upon as the price of power.
Water injection	Indirectly can lead to gains ranging from moderate to substantial, especially when used with turbocharging	Indirectly can lead to gains ranging from moderate to substantial, depending on compression	If an engine is modified to make full use of the potential of a water-injection system, the economy gains can offset the initial purchase cost relatively quickly. Indirectly, it can also lead to substantial extra power, especially when long-duration cams and high compression are also used.
Overdrive transmission	None	Good to substantial	A nice refinement for any vehicle that is used for long highway trips. Based on 20,000 miles a year and 15mpg, typical unit cost would be saved in a little over a year. Reduced noise and engine wear is a bonus.
Aerodynamic devices	Extra speed and road-holding possible	Marginal to moderate	Assuming proper function, aerodynamic devices generally take 3 to 5 years to recover costs in saved fuel.

CHAPTER

1

TUNEUPS

- IGNITION TUNING TRICKS
- CURING POINT BOUNCE
- TIMING FOR POWER
- VACUUM GAUGE MAGIC
- CHASSIS MODS

SIMPLE TUNEUPS

Low-emissions cars have been with us for quite awhile and many readers will have cars that have been built to strict emission standards. Some of the recommendations outlined in the following chapter may not be easily applied to these vehicles. (A

Because of strict emissions regulations, manufacturers are currently being forced to build "tamperproof" carburetors. Note that the idle screws on this Holley have only limited adjustment. On some carbs, such as the Rochester Q-Jet, the idle-mixture screws are hidden beneath hardened steel plugs to prevent indiscriminate tampering by backyard mechanics.

good example of this is the tamper-proof idle-mixture screw.) If your vehicle is a later emission-type vehicle, do what you can out of the tuneup procedures advised here, or skip this chapter entirely and go to a professional to have your engine dyno-tuned as decribed in the next chapter.

TUNING THE IGNITION

Spark Plugs

A survey taken by Champion Spark Plugs a few years ago showed that one out of every three cars in America had spark plugs that had passed their useful life. Spark plugs can cause less-than-satisfactory ignition long before they completely misfire. A practical rule for spark plug life expectancy is about 10,000 miles for a conventional, breaker-point ignition system, and 20,000 miles if a good electronic ignition system is used. Don't bother trying to stretch these limits. When plugs have passed their optimum useful life, throw them away and install new ones.

Spark Plug Wires

There are many types and varieties

of spark plug wires available. All plug wires, except those made strictly for competition, have to provide for the suppression of radio interference. The cheapest type is made from ordinary, inexpensive, carbon-string, resistive wire. For the high-performance engine, these plug wires should be considered barely adequate. Although they are satisfactory when new, they deteriorate very rapidly. When this happens the electrical resistance

When spark plugs are not changed or cleaned regularly, they can misfire and waste fuel. Believe it or not, the spark plug on the right came out of an engine that was still running...though it's difficult to understand how it could even start. The plug at left is an identical type in new condition.

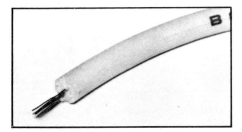

Metal-core spark plug cables, like this Belden cable, represent the best type of secondary (spark plug) wire to use when maximum spark energy and long life are required. If a plain, metal core is used, radio interference can be eliminated by suppressing the radiation from the wires. This can be accomplished through the use of either resistive spark plugs or radio-suppressed plug caps.

increases and the resulting spark quality is reduced. This can lead to the onset of misfiring. Probably the best type of wire to use is the wire-wound type, such as that marketed by Borg Warner. These wires suppress radio interference by an inductive method rather than a resistive method but do not cut down on the quality of the spark. As an added benefit, the life of these wires is almost indefinite.

If your engine is equipped with headers, you may find that the heat radiated by the headers can cause deterioration of the insulation on some types of wires. In this case it is advisable to change to silicone-insulated wires. Some of these use carbon string as a conductor. Although they withstand the heat, the carbon string will still deteriorate eventually. Figure on carbon-string wire having a peak-efficiency life of no more than one year. If your engine is currently equipped with this type of lead and the insulator is showing signs of cracking, they need replacing right now. Remember, without good plug wires you are not going to get an efficient spark.

Beware: most speed shops sell many types of fancy-colored plug wire. Some of these wires may be good and some may be less-than-optimum. Examine what you are buying. If they are the carbon-string type, then remember, they may need to be replaced every year. The spark plug wires are a vital link in the ignition system, and they are often overlooked. Buy the best wires you can get and know what you're getting before you lay down your money.

Distributors

Numerous minor faults can occur inside a distributor, and these will surely reduce power and economy.

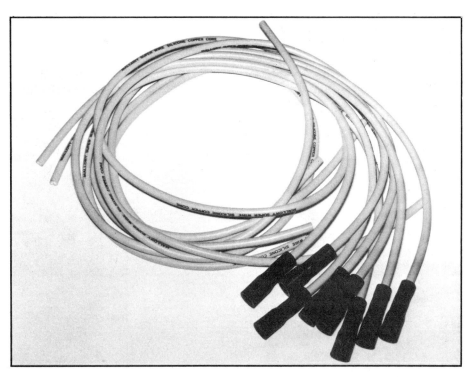

If an engine is equipped with tube headers or the plug wires are routed near the exhaust system, it is highly recommended that silicone-jacketed cables be installed. Silicone is much more heat resistant than the materials used in standard cable. Several brands of silicone-jacketed wire are currently available, as typified by the set of Mallory cables shown here.

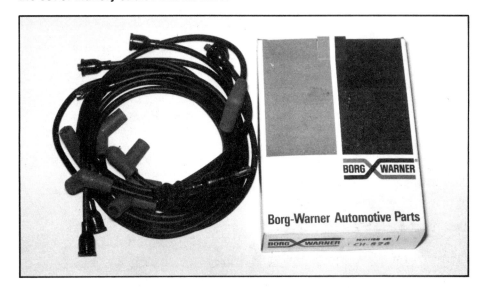

A Monel-type wire-wound cable is a worthwhile performance alternative to ordinary metal-conductor plug wire. This Borg-Warner cable set will provide all the benefits of a metal-core wire but will not radiate radio interference.

Most original-equipment plug cables are of the resistive type. The electrical conductor in these cables consists of a carbon-impregnated fiberglass or rayon cord. These conductors will deteriorate relatively rapidly (as compared to metal-core wires) and as they age, the resistance goes up. Eventually, the increased resistance may reduce secondary voltage delivery to the plug and cause misfire. The life of these cables can be as little as one year, and is rarely longer than three years.

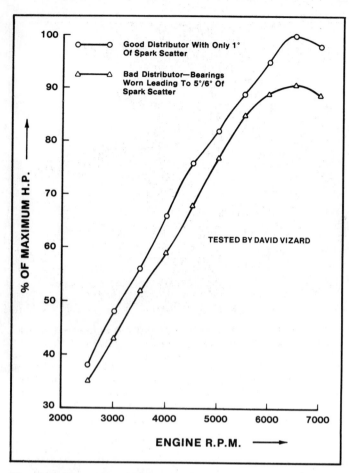

Legend:
- Good Distributor With Only 1° Of Spark Scatter
- Bad Distributor—Bearings Worn Leading To 5°/6° Of Spark Scatter

TESTED BY DAVID VIZARD

% OF MAXIMUM H.P. vs ENGINE R.P.M.

Worn distributor bearings can cause spark timing "scatter." This will adversely affect different engines to a varying degree, but as this graph shows, scatter can easily reduce power by as much as 10%. It can likewise reduce economy.

The centrifugal-advance weights (arrow A) and the vacuum-advance mechanism (arrow B) can be clearly seen in this GM Delco-Remy distributor. For the ignition system to give the correct ignition timing under various combinations of load and engine speed, both of these systems must be functioning correctly.

The first thing you should do is check that the distributor mainshaft bearings are not worn. To do this, remove the distributor cap, grasp the mainshaft firmly and see if it will "wobble" inside the distributor housing. Try forcing it in several different directions. The distributor bearings may wear just at one or two places, allowing play in one direction only. If the bearings are worn, remove the distributor and replace the worn bearings inside the housing, or replace the entire distributor. The maximum amount of play permissible is about .002-inch. This amount of clearance is barely perceptible to the naked eye.

If the bearings are worn, several distributor maladies may be created, all of which have a damaging effect on performance. First, and probably most important, is that play in the mainshaft causes the distributor timing to be erratic. In other words, if the correct firing point should be 20° BTDC at a specific engine speed, the wobble in the shaft may allow one cylinder to fire at 18°, the next at 22°, the next at 20°, the next at 19°, and so on. This phenomenon is often called "spark scatter." This inaccurate timing will obviously not help our search for power and economy.

Bad bearings in a breaker-type distributor can also cause the dwell angle (and dwell time) of the breaker points to vary considerably. This dramatically reduces the spark intensity at high engine speeds, bringing about high-speed misfiring. This may not directly affect economy because you rarely drive "economically" at full throttle, but it can seriously reduce maximum horsepower, as the accompanying illustration shows.

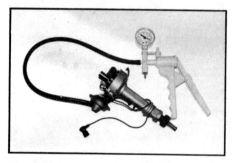

The Mighty Vac vacuum gauge and hand pump allows the pressure- or vacuum-operated components of an engine to be easily tested. Here it is being used to check the vacuum-advance mechanism of an ordinary ignition distributor.

The advance mechanism of the distributor should also be checked. Begin by testing the vacuum-advance diaphragm cannister. The easiest way to do this is to disconnect the line supplying manifold vacuum to the cannister. Use a hand vacuum pump to apply vacuum to this line. Look down into the distributor to see if the vacuum plate rotates slightly around the mainshaft when the vacuum is applied. This test should easily detect any leak in the vacuum-advance diaphragm. A replacement cannister must be installed if a leak is indicated.

Next, the distributor centrifugal-advance mechanism should be examined. The large advance weights are normally visible when the distributor cap is removed (in some cases they may be hidden beneath the rest of the advance apparatus). As these weights fling outward from centrifugal force, the breaker-point cam, or a corresponding component in a breakerless triggering system, rotates slightly about the mainshaft to advance the spark timing. Check to make certain the weights move easily and that the plate rotates freely about the mainshaft. Examine the posts on which the weights pivot to determine signs of wear. Check the counterbalance springs carefully while you're at it. There should not be any excessive slack in the system and there should not be any rough spots as it operates. If either of these faults exist, the ignition will not advance properly as engine speed increases. Normally, a very small amount of thoughtfully applied lubrication will prolong the distributor life substantially and cure most ills.

This may be obvious, but it needs to be said. If the inside of the distributor has collected a lot of dirt and debris, it must be thoroughly cleaned. Once the distributor is removed from the engine, most standard models are disassembled by removing a small roll pin that fastens the drive gear to the bottom of the mainshaft. When the pin is removed, the mainshaft and the advance mechanism can be pulled out of the housing. Reassembly is equally as easy. However, if you're going to go this far, you would be wise to consult a detailed rebuilding manual for specific details.

Breaker Points & Condensor

Since you are in the process of putting the distributor into good working order you should, with all breaker-type distributors, replace the breaker points, condensor, and rotor. You do this at regular intervals anyway (don't you?) and since the distributor is now being serviced, it makes sense to put in new service components.

Now you face the problem of getting the new points properly adjusted. This is one of the most important aspects of ignition system operation. The only sure-fire method for doing this is with a dwell meter. The dwell meter measures the amount of time, in distributor degrees, that the breaker points are closed. During the time the points are closed, 12-volt current flows into the primary windings of the coil, building a magnetic field around the windings. When the points open, this magnetic field collapses, generating a high voltage in the secondary windings of the coil. This high voltage flows through each plug wire to "fire" the plugs. If the dwell time (corresponding to the dwell angle) is reduced, there is less time available for the primary magnetic field to build. If this time is sufficiently reduced, there will be a drop in secondary voltage and spark intensity will be decreased. If the dwell is too long, another problem can arise. Excessive dwell time causes slow points separation during the opening phase. This allows the primary voltage to arc across the points, causing the face of the point contacts to deteriorate quickly. So, although more dwell than recommended might seem like a good feature, it isn't.

The best dwell setting for a distributor is always that recommended in the manufacturer's specifications. Usually these specs will give an upper and a lower limit for the setting. When new points have been installed in the

When properly tuned and maintained, a breaker-point ignition system will provide completely adequate service at normal engine speeds. However, the contact surfaces of the breaker switch (arrow) deteriorate rapidly. As the contacts move apart, primary voltage arcs across the gap, creating oxidation and increased resistance. Also, during operation the heel of the cam follower will gradually wear down, causing the ignition timing and dwell angle to vary. As a result, to insure economy and performance these systems must be tuned quite often.

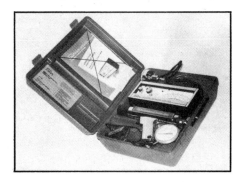

There are many cheap tuneup instruments on the market. Beware of inferior products. Some of the less-expensive stroboscopic timing lights have very feeble light output. If the light is weak, it is necessary to work in almost complete darkness to see the timing marks on the crankshaft damper. If you are serious about performance and economy, it is much smarter to use quality equipment, as typified by the universally respected Sun brandname.

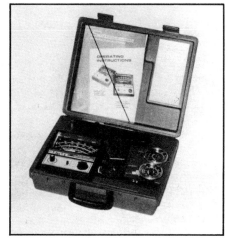

Even if you don't want to spend a lot of money you can still buy excellent hobby-oriented tuneup equipment. This Sunette kit (again from Sun) may fit your wallet better, yet it can do as much as a more expensive professional kit.

distributor, the heel that rubs on the point cam will initially wear a small amount until it beds in. In such a case, it is best to adjust the dwell setting to the lower limit specified by the manufacturer. As the heel wears slightly, the dwell setting will increase. If you are resetting used points, set them to about the mid-point between the limits.

Point Bounce

After breaker points have undergone considerable usage, the spring controlling the moving contact point

will lose tension. In some cases, the spring tension may have been inadequate in the first place. When this tension drops below a certain level, point bounce can occur earlier in the engine speed range. This prevents the primary side of the ignition system from sufficiently "charging" the coil. This has much the same effect as reducing the dwell time, and power and economy may be reduced.

Detecting point bounce is difficult. If you have a dwell meter, the onset of point bounce can be detected by a relatively sudden reduction of dwell angle when the engine is revved to

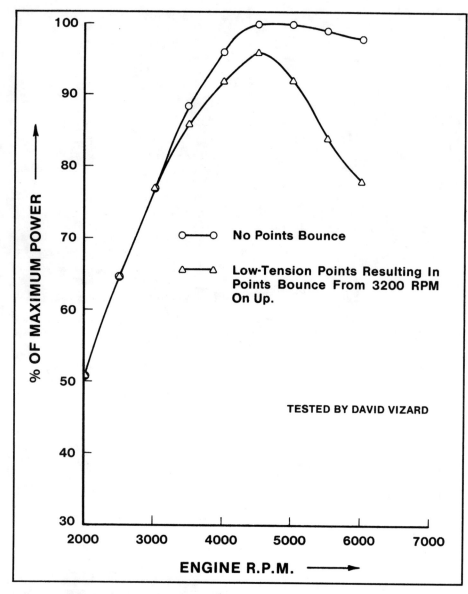

% OF MAXIMUM POWER

○——○ **No Points Bounce**

△——△ **Low-Tension Points Resulting In Points Bounce From 3200 RPM On Up.**

TESTED BY DAVID VIZARD

ENGINE R.P.M. ——▶

Proper ignition functioning is all-important. A simple thing, such as a set of points with too little spring tension, can substantially reduce power. When "point bounce" occurs the dwell angle is reduced, spark energy delivered to the spark plug declines dramatically, and the ignition malfunctions. In the early stages, inadequate spark energy causes the engine to misfire at high engine speeds. In the extreme, it can even cause misfire at idle and cruise speeds.

high rpm. Also, if the engine misfires notably at high engine speeds, this should be one of the first things you suspect.

To avoid point bounce, use a high-quality, brand-name set of breaker points with adequate spring tension. Often the high-performance models will provide increased spring tension. If your engine has sufficient valvetrain gear to allow very high engine speeds, these high-tension points will be a necessity. However, be aware that this increased spring tension will also cause the rubbing heel of the moving contact to wear more rapidly. High-tension points will, therefore, require more frequent adjustment and more frequent replacement. They will also lead to increased mainshaft bearing

wear, due to the increased load the heavy spring tension places on the shaft. If you don't really need them, don't use them.

Ignition Timing

There are numerous ways to set the timing of a breaker-type ignition system. Some of the popular "backyard" methods can be accomplished without any fancy equipment. However, all of these methods are a hassle and, in view of the fact that many modern ignitions are of the transistorized-type and must be adjusted with a timing light, it is best to dispense with old-fashioned techniques and only consider setting the timing with a timing light or strobe. If you don't have

a reliable timing light, it is worth investing in one, but make sure you buy one that has a sufficiently bright light. There are some cheap units that won't give enough light to make a glow worm jealous. These timing lights are barely worth what you pay for them.

In addition to a good timing light, you will need a tachometer. Often a dwell meter, as described earlier, will also have a tachometer built in. In such a case, it is called a "dwell-tach." With all this equipment in hand, start the engine, allow it to warm up sufficiently, then attach the dwell-tach according to the instructions provided with the instrument. Disconnect the manifold-vacuum hose leading to the distributor. Leave the hose connected to the manifold and plug the other end to prevent a manifold vacuum leak. Now, use the dwell-tach reading to set the engine idle speed as recommended in the specifications. If you don't have the specs, just make certain the idle is below the point at which the centrifugal advance begins to occur. On most engines centrifugal advance starts between 800 and 1000rpm, although many 4- or 6-cylinder ignitions do not provide centrifugal advance until the engine speed is well above 1000rpm.

Connect the timing light to the number-one spark plug according to the instructions provided with the light. Point the timing light at the index tab on the front of the engine. The flashing light will illuminate a timing mark on the spinning balancer. The relation between this mark and the index tab will indicate the amount of "initial" ignition advance. If the timing is not within specifications, loosen the clamp securing the distributor into the cylinder block and advance or retard

Setting the correct ignition timing into the engine is important. The most common and accurate way of setting the ignition timing is to use a stroboscopic timing light.

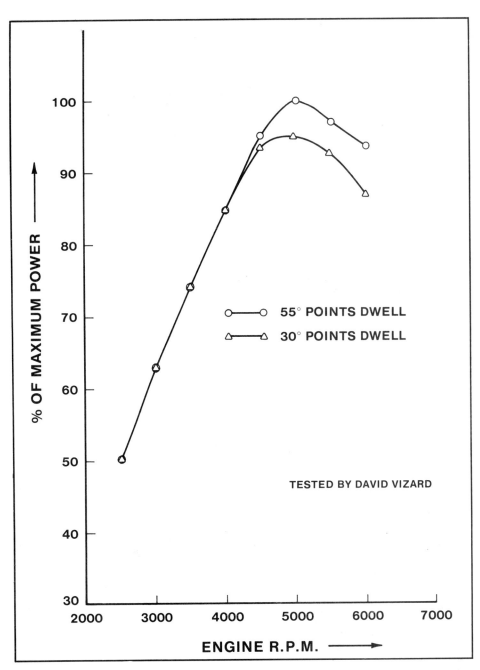

This graph shows power and economy losses created by improper breaker-point dwell angle. The dwell must be checked and properly adjusted to the manufacturers' recommendations at regular intervals. If the breaker-point rubbing block is worn (due to abnormally long periods between tuneups or before replacing the points) or if the distributor bearings are badly worn, the dwell will vary and ignition efficiency will decline.

(rotate) the distributor slightly until the timing light indicates that the timing mark and the index are aligned properly. Once this is achieved, the distributor clamp should be firmly tightened.

A point worth noting here: this procedure is fine if you already know what the initial ignition timing should be. On a modified engine, the stock timing figure may no longer be applicable. If this is the case, read the section on ignition systems, as this will detail how the ignition system should be retailored to suit a modified engine.

CARBURETION

The following recommendations assume that the carb is in perfect working order. This may or may not be the case. In many instances, a car may have been driven for several years without any suitable servicing of the carburetor. Under such conditions the carburetor will be in less-than-perfect condition. If it is suspected that something is wrong with the carb, it must be replaced or rebuilt.

For many people, rebuilding a carb is like jumping into the deep end of the pool. A carburetor is not the simplest piece of equipment, however, the task is not as serious as it would first appear. Most carburetor overhaul kits have adequate instructions. If you follow these directions carefully, the job is not difficult.

Bearing in mind the aims of this book, one brand of rebuilding kit worth mentioning is produced by Mike Jones Carburetion (see Appendix). This company sells kits for most of the popular brand carburetors. These kits can be obtained with spare jets, power valves, etc., to tune your carburetor for either economy or power. Unlike most carburetor kits, these are customized as much as possible to suit the specification of your engine. This unique procedure begins by writing to Mike Jones Carburetion to obtain a special order form. You fill out a general description of your vehicle and your performance or economy goals, and return the form. They, in turn, assemble a kit specifically aimed at fulfilling your requirements.

Air Filters

Air filters can cause a loss of both power and economy. A dirty filter element can typically account for a 5% drop in both areas. If the element was too small or too restrictive in the first place, power could be reduced by a total of 10%. A good free-flowing air

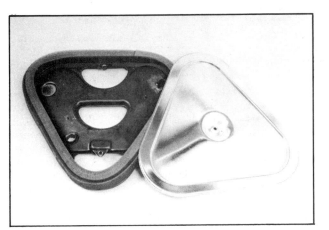

Dirty air filters waste horsepower. At best, a dirty filter element will cause a small reduction in mileage, at worst it can reduce mileage by a large percentage. To avoid lost power and economy, read the detailed discussion of air filters in chapter 3.

filter that really cleanses the incoming air is a must. Read the section in Chapter 3 concerning air filters to help you make a decision on what to use.

Tuning The Carb

Assuming that you have the correct carburetor and that the specifications of your carburetor are correct for the application, that is, it has the correct jets, correct accelerator pump, etc., then it is only necessary to adjust such things as idle mixture and idle speed. Many modern carburetors for emission-regulated vehicles allow only limited adjustment of the idle mixture. If you have an emission carb and, even with the limited adjustment, it falls within the correct setting, you're in luck. If it won't adjust to the desired setting because of other changes you have made to the engine, it will be necessary to remove the idle-mixture adjustment stops so that the mixture can be correctly set for minimum emissions. To accurately set these adjustments you will need an exhaust analyzer of some sort, otherwise you will be relying on nothing more than guesswork.

There are numerous exhaust analyzers on the market, some expensive, some medium priced and some relatively cheap. One that springs to mind is the mixture analyzer kit available from Heathkit. This company, incidentally, offers a lot of excellent, modestly-priced test equipment in kit form that can be assembled by any enthusiast.

The procedure for adjusting the mixture to obtain the best "lean idle" condition is relatively simple when you have an exhaust analyzer. You will generally be searching for the leanest idle mixture obtainable before distribution-induced lean-misfire occurs. And, you will find that these adjustments are extremely fine, but an analyzer will show you exactly how the carb/engine is responding to even the smallest nudge of the mixture screw. Virtually every exhaust analyzer is furnished with detailed instructions for hooking the analyzer to your engine and how to go about adjusting the mixture.

Another device that is well worth consideration, in view of its very low price, is the Colortune. This device allows you to look into the cylinder while the engine is running. You can then make carburetor adjustments until the color of the combustion flame indicates that the mixture is where it should be. One of the advantages of the Colortune unit is that it can be

plugged into any cylinder to get some idea of the cylinder-to-cylinder distribution at idle.

One last piece of advice. As the mixture is adjusted leaner or richer, as the case may be, the engine idle speed is likely to fluctuate up or down. While adjusting the mixture, it is a good idea to go back and forth between the mixture screws and the idle-speed screw to make certain that the idle speed is kept reasonably close to the desired rpm while zeroing in on the mixture adjustment.

Using A Vacuum Gauge

On pre-emission vehicles or vehicles with idle-mixture screws that do not have limited adjustment, satisfactory settings of the idle mixture can also be obtained by using a sensitive-type tuneup vacuum gauge (not a dampened-type dash gauge). To use this method, connect the gauge into a manifold vacuum source. Do not fall into the trap of connecting the gauge

The vacuum gauge has long been used by experienced mechanics as a tuning aid, as well as a means to tailor driving habits for maximum fuel economy.

to a "ported-vacuum" source. A ported-vacuum source does not provide vacuum at idle; it only provides a vacuum when the engine rpm is above the idle speed. This will not give a true indication of what's happening in the intake manifold at idle. Perhaps it is obvious, but we should say that the best way to tell a ported-vacuum source is to just see if it gives a normal idle vacuum signal when you hook the gauge to it.

After correctly coupling the vacuum gauge, set the engine idle-speed

On this conventional vacuum gauge from Auto Meter the scale is divided into "economy" and "power" segments. Best economy is achieved by driving in a manner so as to keep the needle in the economy range (high vacuum).

adjusting screw to obtain the desired idle rpm. Next, alternately adjust each of the idle-mixture screws in and out until the highest stable vacuum gauge reading is achieved. During the setting of the idle-mixture screws, the idle speed may go up. If it does, reset the idle speed back to the desired rpm, then go back to adjusting the idle-mixture screws until the highest stable gauge reading is achieved at the selected idle rpm.

CHASSIS TUNING

At this point you should have your engine running about as well as could be expected without any major modifications, but this is only part of performance-with-economy planning. The engine works to propel the chassis of the car down the road. If there is excessive rolling resistance created by improper chassis alignment, fuel consumption and performance will suffer.

The very first thing you should do is check tire pressures. Tire pressures don't need to drop far below the recommended level before you feel it in your gas tank. Regularly check these pressures with an accurate gauge, but don't worry about putting in extra pressure in an attempt to decrease rolling resistance. As far as fuel consumption is concerned, the pressure recommended by the manufacturer of your tires is probably close to optimum. Adding 5-7 psi to the tires will not make any measurable difference in economy but it may make a noticeable difference in road holding, ride quality and durability, usually a reduction in one or all of these areas.

If your car has acquired a lot of

Incorrect front suspension alignment will not only cost performance and mileage, it will also add considerably to your tire bill. The results pictured here are due to long-term operation with excessive toe-in adjustment. A proper frontend alignment would have extended tire life as much as 300 to 500%.

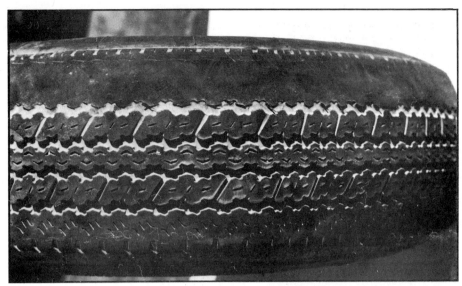

miles, it's a good idea to check some additional chassis components. Jack the car up and rest it on solid axle stands. Go around to each wheel and check the amount of brake drag. This is difficult to detect on the rear wheels because, of course, you are also turning a portion of the driveline, but rear brake drag is usually still detectable if it's more than a very minimal amount. On disc brake cars, it is common for the pads to be continually in contact with the discs, so there will always be some drag on the front wheels, but again this should be minimal. In these cases the wheels may not spin freely, but they should turn with only modest effort. When you find that the wheels turn only with a great deal of effort or not at all, take the car to a reputable brake mechanic to have the brake system checked thoroughly.

At the same time you are checking brakes, check the wheel bearings. Grasp each wheel and rock it back and forth vigorously to see if there is a lot of play in the bearings. If the wheel bearings are loose, follow the instructions in a good rebuild manual to reset the bearing preload. When they have been loose for a long time, there's a good chance that the bearings have been damaged, so give them a good visual inspection before you go any further.

If the bearings are properly adjusted but there is still excessive play in the front wheels, it could be that the upper or lower ball joints are worn. This may indicate normal high-mileage wear or, when the chassis doesn't have a lot of miles on it, there may be a problem with the front-end alignment. At this stage you either need to replace all the worn suspension components (again, follow a good rebuild manual) or have your local front end alignment shop do the job for you.

When misalignment is the problem, there are usually some obvious indications in the tire wear pattern. If the tires wear faster on the inside edge, it's a sign that the front wheels are tracking outward (excessive toe out). If the tires are wearing faster on the outside edge, this is a reasonable indication that the wheels are tracking with too much toe in. Not only does such misalignment add to your tire bill, it also does the same for your fuel bill.

Alignment and suspension geometry are important for long tire life and the minimum amount of rolling resistance, especially when wide-section tires are used. Extensive equipment is required for proper alignment and the average enthusiast should have a reputable shop check and adjust frontend camber, caster and toe-in. Here the shop supervisor at Suspensions Unlimited in Tucson, Arizona, is installing the equipment necessary to check camber and caster settings.

12 DYNO TUNING

- SELECTING A DYNO SHOP
- ENGINE PREPARATION
- GET YOUR MONEY'S WORTH

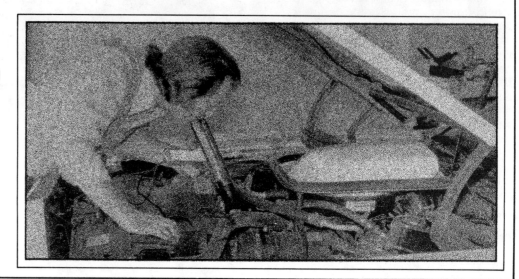

DYNO TUNEUPS

Doing a tuneup as described in Chapter 1 may be simple, but it does have limitations. It is assumed that you know the tuneup specifications for your particular engine and that these specs are correct. Modern emissions standards have caused manufacturers to carefully calibrate the carb and ignition for specific applications but, even so, manufacturing tolerances still mean that standardized settings may not be perfect for every engine that comes off the assembly line. And, when you modify your engine, the factory specs may be even more removed from ideal. If your engine has undergone three or four fairly radical changes you can, at best, only hope to find a reasonably adequate ignition curve and carb calibration through extensive trial-and-error testing. After modifying the engine to this extent you are likely to have a lot of time and money invested and *if the fine-tuning is not right on, all is wasted!*

Earlier it was stated that a successful engine was one in which all the components complemented each other and worked in harmony. The final "harmonizing" of any engine should be

the calibration of carb mixture and ignition timing to perfectly match the specific engine and application. Ordinary seat-of-the-pants testing will never get you to this position. This is where a chassis- or rolling-road dyno becomes a necessity. This device measures the horsepower developed at the driving wheels. In conjunction with an electronic engine analyzer, it makes a powerful tool for fine tuning performance/economy engines. It allows the engine and drivetrain to be analyzed for faults or miscalibrations that can be recognized and remedied.

The importance of a chassis dyno session cannot be emphasized too strongly. When working out the budget for your performance/economy vehicle, be certain to allow for the cost of a dyno tune. Generally you will find this effort as valuable as a cam change or a new four-barrel carb. Just remember, a carb fitted with jets only two sizes away from optimum can easily offset the potential economy gain from a good economy manifold swap or any similar performance-with-economy modification.

Not all dyno-tune shops are prepared to spend the time and effort required to adequately custom tune a modified engine. Many shops are

strictly "quick turnaround" deals. They prefer to set a stocker to factory specs, do a quick power run, relieve you of $39.95 or so and get you on your way. Choose your dyno tuneup shop carefully, *because in the final analysis it is the talent and ability of the dyno operator that will determine how well your engine will perform.*

DYNO SHOP EQUIPMENT

The equipment you can expect to find in a well-equipped dyno shop is about the same wherever you go. The dynamometer takes the form of a set of rollers set into the floor of the shop. Coupled to these rollers is a power-absorption unit and instrumentation that gives a readout of the power applied to the rollers by the rear wheels of a car. By adjusting the absorption unit, the "resistance" of the rollers (also called "the load") can be varied over a wide range. This permits the operator to place different levels of stress (load) on the engine and drivetrain by simulating various road and operating conditions. (Some dynos also have an inertia simulator. This adjusts the dyno load to simulate the weight of the car.) As long as the tires have sufficient traction to grip the rollers, acceleration and steady-state tests can be performed right in the confines of the shop.

Apart from the obvious asset of being able to check the actual horsepower developed by your modified engine and/or driveline, the chassis dyno has a less obvious advantage. A dyno is rarely used alone. It is often used in conjunction with an electronic engine analyzer. The dyno allows the simulation of on-the-road operation and the analyzer can be used to study the suitability of things like the spark plug heat range, the advance curves, carb jetting, power valves and idle calibration. (The "state-of-tune" is normally determined by electronically analyzing the ignition system and the chemical makeup of the exhaust gas.) *This permits the overall effect of a specific combination of engine components to be studied under actual operating conditions.* This makes it relatively easy to focus on what is wrong or incorrectly calibrated, and gives the dyno operator the means to fine tune the engine far closer than could ever be done by seat-of-the-pants road testing.

Because of the rising demand for maximum economy some dyno shops have taken this one step further. They have installed an "economy meter"

This Sun diagnostic computer represents the latest technology in engine analyzing equipment. Once the computer has been programmed with specific engine operational (tuneup) specifications, the printout console (far left) will, after the test cycle, give a written indication of malfunctions or improper adjustments.

along with the rest of the instrumentation. This gauge reads out in miles-per-gallon, so the dyno operator can tune for the best combination of economy and power.

PRELIMINARY PROCEDURES

You can save the dyno operator some time (and yourself some money) if you make a few preliminary preparations and are aware of what is going to happen when you arrive at the dyno shop. Install new spark plugs in your engine just before driving to the shop. You should probably use the stock heat range or, if you are not sure what heat range you should be using because the engine has been substan-

A chassis dynamometer can be used to duplicate road conditions inside the workshop. The rear wheels of the vehicle are positioned over a pair of large rollers in the shop floor. The car can be "driven" in place, the rear wheels turning the rollers, and different road/load conditions are simulated by varying the amount of resistance the dyno feeds to the rollers. The Sun engine analyzer in the background is used to monitor engine functions during the test and will detect any maladjustments or faults.

tially modified, opt for plugs about two ranges colder than stock.

Unless your plug wires are in perfect condition, replace them with new top-quality wires. If you have a traditional breaker-type ignition system, put in new points, condensor and rotor and adjust the dwell and timing to stock specs.

If you have a late-model car with a catalytic converter in the exhaust system, you must have a hole drilled in the exhaust pipe, ahead of the catalytic converter, and have a short, capped pipe brazed into the hole. This will allow access for the exhaust analyzer probe to sample the exhaust gas before it enters the catalytic converter. Remember, the function of the catalytic converter is to cause the decomposition of hydrocarbons and carbon monoxide. If the exhaust goes through the catalytic converter before getting to the sampling probe, it will not register the true constituents of the exhaust leaving the engine. (If you have a dual-exhaust system, be sure to put an access tube in each pipe, so each side can be analyzed independently.)

If your engine is equipped with a mechanical cam, set the valve lash according to the specs on the timing card supplied with the cam. Check that the oil and water are up to the mark, and before you arrive at the dyno shop, fill up with fuel. If several tests are required, a full dyno session can use quite a lot of fuel. It is not uncommon to use 1/4 to 1/2 a tank of fuel during an extended session. It can be irritating and time consuming to run out of fuel in the middle of the testing.

DYNO PROCEDURES

The tuneup procedure will follow a general pattern. The car will be positioned on the rollers and the electronic ignition and exhaust analyzers will be coupled to the engine. The first test is usually a thorough check of the ignition system to eliminate any possibilty of misfiring. By observing the oscilloscope patterns on the engine analyzer, the operator can ascertain whether or not the ignition, be it an electronic or a conventional breaker-type system, is functioning as it should. Any problems will have to be corrected

before the testing can continue.

After any possible faults have been eliminated, an initial power run will be made to determine the air-fuel ratio that the carburetor delivers to the engine. If the mixture proves to be too lean, the test will be stopped to prevent an excessively lean full-throttle mixture from damaging the engine, and the main metering system of the carb will be enriched to provide a sufficiently rich mixture to prevent any damage during the testing. From this point onward, the fine-tuning of the carburetor will start in earnest. This may require a few simple changes; on the other hand, it could mean going completely through the carburetor to recalibrate every circuit. If the carburetor calibration was way off base, getting these circuits correctly adjusted may take an hour, possibly two or more.

Once the carburetor has been adjusted to deliver the correct air-fuel ratio at both part- and full-throttle, attention will be turned again to the ignition. The reason the mixture should be calibrated first is that different air-fuel ratios burn at different rates in the combustion chamber. Therefore, the optimum ignition timing (the point when combustion begins) for a chemically-correct mixture is different than the optimum timing for a slightly rich or a slightly lean mixture. At this stage the dyno operator will be trying to adjust the ignition timing and distributor advance characteristics to give optimum performance and economy for the specific operation of the engine.

The first move is to ascertain the timing at regular points in the rpm range with the engine at wide open throttle (against the dyno load). This simply involves checking the advance at 2000, 3000, 4000rpm and so on, up to the rev limit of the engine, to determine the existing ignition curve. At this point the distributor would be removed from the engine and moun-

The oscilloscope pattern (arrow) of an electronic engine analyzer can quickly show an experienced operator the condition of the ignition system. When the ignition is correct, the trace on the oscilloscope will form a certain well-defined pattern. Different types of ignition problems will cause the pattern to change in certain ways, allowing the operator to find specific faults.

If peak performance and economy are to be achieved, the ignition timing advance provided by the mechanisms inside the distributor must be optimized for specific conditions. The distributor advance curves can be checked and tailored with the aid of a machine similar to this Sun distributor tester.

ted to a distributor testing machine. The machine is used to duplicate the operation in the engine (it spins the mainshaft of the distributor), and it gives a direct readout of the centrifugal advance provided by the mechanism inside the distributor. The experienced operator can easily determine when the advance begins, what the rate of advance is (how quickly additional timing is added in relation to the increase in engine speed), how much total advance is provided throughout the rpm range, and when the distributor has reached full advance.

At this point the knowledge of the operator becomes an important factor. Through experience he must select a theoretical advance curve to give the best performance and economy for the specific engine and chassis in question. Once he knows what sort of curve he wants, he can substitute various sizes of advance weight and different strength counterbalance springs until the curve fits the shape (i.e., the advance starts, increases at a specific rate and reaches a total amount) that he desires. Often this takes several trial-and-error fittings until the combination of weights and springs give the desired effects.

This ignition curve now ensures that the engine has the best full-throttle (fully loaded) power throughout the rpm band because the combustion is starting at the optimum time. *However, this does not guarantee that the ignition is correct during part-throttle operation.* Part-throttle operation creates higher manifold vacuum because the airflow to the engine is being restricted by the partially closed throttle plates. When the airflow to the engine is restricted, the compression pressure created just prior to ignition is lower. This lower cylinder pressure means slower flame speeds, thus necessitating more advance at part throttle.

Enter the vacuum advance. All modern ignitions utilize the vacuum conditions in the manifold to signal the distributor to provide additional ignition advance during part-throttle, light-load conditions. *This simple mechanism will provide considerable economy gains with virtually no loss to performance. Every modern performance must be fitted with an efficient vacuum-advance mechanism.*

Of course, the trick is to choose a vacuum-advance control "can" with correct advance characteristics for the engine. Some distributors, in particular those used on most late-model Ford engines, have an adjustable

The primary components of the centrifugal advance of a GM Delco-Remy distributor are shown on the left. On the right a double exposure shows how the advance plate and cam are rotated (advanced) when the weights are thrown outward by centrifugal force.

vacuum-advance mechanism. These can be readily adjusted to gain the optimum vacuum advance. However, the only way to adjust the vacuum advance on most distributors is to replace the vacuum control with one that is calibrated differently. There are, unfortunately, many different vacuum controls available. Each one provides a different amount of vacuum advance and the amount of vacuum required to activate the control will also vary. *The trick is to find the control that will give the right amount at the right time.* Once again, there are no magic formulas to follow. It requires experience and knowledge to determine the best control for a specific engine. You'll have to rely on the expertise of the dyno operator, so you better find one that knows his stuff.

In the now-distant past the "hot setup" was to disable the vacuum advance. If the dyno operator sug-

gests this, hit the road and find another shop. The vacuum-advance mechanism is critical if maximum economy is to be achieved. Time spent on the vacuum-advance system is as important, if not more important, than time spent on the centrifugal advance. Quite simply, it means more money in your pocket.

This is the basic rundown on dyno tuning. Don't underestimate what a good dyno tuneup will do for your car. No matter if it is nearly stock or if the only thing stock on the engine is the paint, a good dyno tune is one of the simplest and surest paths to performance with economy.

Optimizing the centrifugal advance is important for maximum economy at cruise speeds. Changing the vacuum advance, however, can be a problem because many distributors do not have an adjustable vacuum mechanism. Ford distributors are a notable exception to this general rule. A screw inside the vacuum cannister allows adjustment of the rate of advance. Delco-Remy GM distributors do not have an internal adjustment, but may be altered by replacing the cannister with one having a different calibration. Finding the best cannister for a specific application can be troublesome but, fortunately, an adjustable vacuum cannister for GM distributors is currently available from Crane Cams (see Appendix).

CHAPTER 3

CARBURETORS

- CHOOSING AN AIR CLEANER
- TRICK CARB MODS
- USING EXOTIC CARBS
- CALIBRATE FOR POWER

CARBURETION

There is no performance or economy topic that suffers from more deeply rooted misunderstanding than the subject of carburetion. A typical example is the persistent "rumor" of a 100mpg wonder carburetor produced in a garage workshop by some backyard inventor. These many devices (several have been discovered over the past 50 years) have supposedly been suppressed by oil companies that buy the rights to the patents and then refuse to let them be manufactured. The murky logic behind this theory supposes that by keeping these wonderful gadgets off the market they force us to buy more gasoline and they make more money (possibly they've found a better method to increase profits than by suppressing carburetor patents).

It is fact that a workable 100mpg automotive carburetor cannot exist. Consider this: many modern carburetors can be calibrated to give virtually any ratio of air-to-fuel desired, so these carbs can, theoretically, provide 100mpg performance. All you have to do is keep leaning the air-to-fuel until you have as much economy as you want. But, and this is a big but, unfortunately there isn't a gasoline-combustion engine currently in existence that can operate on such incredibly lean induction mixtures. Since the carb is so accommodating, we have to look elsewhere to find the

After the engine has reached operating temperature, feeding cold air to the intake is always worth more top-end power. The hood scoop on this Trans-Am normally has a false opening that has been blocked off to prevent air entry. Cutting out the opening so it can draw cool, high-pressure air from the base of the windshield added between 10 and 12hp to the engine output.

Opening the false scoop on this turbo Mustang and raising the filter-case lid with a .250-inch taller-than-stock element produced instant power and performance gains.

problem and we need go no further than the basic laws of physics.

If you are not convinced, consider this: it takes about 30 horsepower to propel a typical 3800lb car along the highway at normal speeds. If this car was actually able to travel 100 miles on a single gallon of gasoline, the fuel-to-work conversion efficiency would be about 150%. Conversion efficiencies above 100% defy irrefutable physical laws. So, as much as we would like to dream about "getting even" with 100mpg economy, within current workable technology it's not possible to build an ordinary passenger car engine that will fulfill this promise.

This doesn't mean there aren't fuel consumption differences between one carb and another, but at most, the differences are of a small order. No carb is perfect, but the existing carburetors are not as far from perfect as imaginative advertisements for economy "gadgets" would have us believe.

To get good economy, a correctly calibrated carb must excel in four areas: it must consistently produce the proper air-fuel ratio, the fuel must be thoroughly atomized and evenly diffused into the induction air, the resulting mixture must be delivered into the manifold in such a way as to provide all of the cylinders with a uniformly equal charge, and this must be done equally efficiently throughout the entire operating range of the engine.

As far as producing power is concerned, a carb needs to have as much airflow capacity as possible without compromising any of the qualities listed above. Carburetor "sizing" has long been controversial but the modern trend is toward selecting a carb with relatively small flow capacity (as rated in cfm, cubic-feet-per-minute). This is done largely to ensure good driveability, especially under part-throttle, low-rpm conditions. Therefore, if you are looking for maximum wide-open-throttle power, most stock engines can benefit from a carb with more capacity. Greater airflow, or more specifically a "denser" charge of air, is what we are looking for and the search for this must start right at the top with the air filter.

FILTERS & CASES

There are two general categories of air-filter cases: original-equipment cases (those provided on stock engines when they leave the factory) and the specialty or aftermarket cases (those designed to fit in place of stock, original-equipment cases). Although this may sound like a subtle distinc-

One of the most sophisticated performance inductions currently available is the solenoid-operated system on 79-80' Z/28 Camaros. Under part-throttle conditions, heated air is supplied to the engine to gain maximum fuel vaporization and economy. When full throttle is applied, a solenoid opens the air flap at the back of this hood scoop, allowing cold air to be drawn into the engine for maximum power.

If there is insufficient room to mount an air filter directly on top of the carburetor (due to hood clearance problems), this K&N low-profile adapter allows a remote air filter to be used.

A functional and efficient filter case is as important as a free-flowing filter element. This Moroso filter case allows a large element to be installed in a confined space. Flow bench and dyno testing have shown excellent results with this case and a high-flow element.

If hood clearance is not a problem, a specialty filter case with a generous floor radius into the carburetor, as shown here, will get the job done effectively. This filter case, in conjunction with a flat lid and a 2.5-inch high, 12-inch diameter K&N filter element, showed no power drop during dyno testing of a 356hp smallblock Chevy.

tion, there are differences between the two which separate them in many areas.

Let's look at the original-equipment cases first, as this is the type you are most likely to have. An original-equipment filter case is designed not only to hold an air filter but to also serve many other functions deemed necessary by the manufacturer. First of all, it must act as a silencer to muffle the intake roar of the carburetor. Second, it must assist toward quick engine warm-up by supplying heated air (generally from the vicinity of the exhaust manifold) to the carburetor immediately after initial start-up.

This second factor is also an emission-related function. Carburetors are calibrated to give the correct mixture when air of "average density" moves through the venturis. But, as it happens, when the temperature of air changes, so does the density. As air is heated, it becomes less dense, and although the same volume of air (in cubic feet) may go through the carb, the less-dense air will weigh less because it contains fewer oxygen-bearing molecules. However, a carburetor cannot sense density changes in the incoming air and the amount of fuel passed through the metering circuits may remain substantially the same, even though the density of high-temperature induction air (and the resultant amount of combustion-sustaining oxygen) is reduced.

It's very difficult, if not impossible, to sufficiently cool the vast quantity of air needed for sustained operation of a high-speed induction engine, so engineers take an alternate approach. They heat all of the air going into the carb and calibrate the fuel metering to match this low-density air. In such instances, the filter case will have a temperature sensor to regulate the amount of hot air drawn from an outside source, so that the carb is supplied with air at relatively constant temperatures of around 120-140° F. This, in effect, keeps the air-to-fuel ratio more accurate throughout the normal operating conditions of the engine and, in turn, helps the manufacturer to meet emission standards.

Unfortunately, hot air, being less dense and with less oxygen relative to volume, is not conducive to horsepower, but it does help economy. It causes the fuel to vaporize more readily, and this is especially important for part-throttle driving (and part-throttle operation is where the economy battle is won or lost). Some filter cases (and you should check your unit for this), have a cold-air bypass. With this type of filter case, full-throttle conditions (low manifold vacuum) cause a flap somewhere in the induction system to bypass the hot air drawn from around the exhaust manifold. Under these conditions, the engine is fed cooler air from an outside source and not from the vicinity of the exhaust manifold. On the face of it, this sounds like an ideal filter case. It would be but for one small point: the airflow capability of most original-equipment air filters falls substantially below what

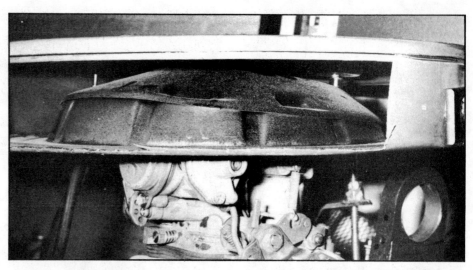

Here we see a typical original-equipment filter case. When the filter case is lowered around the carb to gain clearance for low hood lines, note that the filter case cover is positioned very near the mouth of the carburetor. This is generally not a problem at low engine speeds (rpm) but it can create a flow restriction at high engine speeds.

is needed for high-speed operation.

So, what to do. The first thing that springs to mind is to junk the stock filter and get a good high-performance specialty filter. The emphasis here is on the word good, because some fancy-looking, chrome-plated filter cases are not designed for flow efficiency. Many are intended only to dress up the engine compartment. Filter cases falling into this category are not designed to enhance either power or economy. They don't even equal the stock filter case for functional efficiency.

If you are going to purchase a specialty air filter, be sure you get one with a 360° peripheral feed. Also, be sure you purchase one with adequate diameter and adequate height. You are now going to ask what is adequate. We could get very technical here but there is no need. It's easy to restrict airflow with a filter that is too small but you can't go wrong with one that's too big. If you must use a specialty filter and case, simply get the biggest one you can fit under the hood.

When you only think about power, a top-quality specialty filter case is the way to go, but under certain circumstances it may compromise fuel economy. If the car is to be driven during cold weather, drawing hot air from near the exhaust manifold, as the original-equipment filter cases do, is a definite asset. This arrangement gives a quicker warm-up, and a shorter "choke on" time. As a result, bore wash and oil dilution caused by insufficiently atomized fuel entering the engine during cold-start is reduced, and cylinder wall and ring life is extended.

If you live in the warmer climes of the U.S., such as the Southwest, the

preheat facility of the original-equipment air filter is not nearly as much of an asset. Under these conditions, a specialty 360° peripheral-feed filter case provides the benefits of extra horsepower with little loss due to the slightly longer warm-up from a cold start.

It would appear that if you are in the market for improvements in the air filter area, you will have to make a choice of: staying with the stock case and living with the loss in performance that it may cause, or going to a specialty air filter to get some extra performance but losing out on economy. There is a way to get around this situation. If you live in a cold climate, stick with a hot-air, stock-type system. When the weather is cold it will be a definite asset and when summer comes you can make a simple change to get some extra performance. During

With some air filter cases it is possible to increase intake breathing potential by using a slightly taller air filter element in place of the stock filter. The cover will seal against the top of the filter element, but a small opening will be left around the edge of the filter case. This allows more air to enter the filter case and filter. Additionally, the larger element has more filtering area and is less prone to become clogged with dirt.

the winter use a stock-height filter but when the weather warms up install a filter element that is 1/4- to 1/2-inch taller. This allows a great deal of air to enter the filter case through the peripheral gap that's formed when the lid is raised by the taller element. Generally speaking, this extra intake area will allow airflow nearly equal to a good specialty air filter.

An old hot-rod trick that works in a similar way is to try turning the air filter lid upside down. In some cases, depending on the design of the filter case, this forms an annular gap between the lid and the sides of the case, and allows extra flow to the filter element. Unfortunately this trick fails as often as it works, principally because the case lid is usually of a dished form, and turning it upside down may put the lid closer to the mouth of the carburetor and create an airflow restriction at this point.

FILTER ELEMENTS

Not unexpectedly, the filter element plays an important role in determining how much air enters the carburetor. Essentially there are three types of elements currently available. The most common is the conventional, replacement-type, paper element that is available over-the-counter at any auto parts store. The next most popular type is the foam element that has become very common in hot-rod shops. And the most unique is the cotton-wire element produced only, at the moment, by K&N Engineering (see Appendix).

When selecting a filter, you have to remember that it has two primary tasks. The first is to clean the air going into the engine. The second is to allow the air to flow freely into the engine. If the quality of either of these two factors is reduced beyond a certain level, the air filter becomes a detriment.

If the filter element does not clean the air properly, engine wear will be accelerated. In dry climates this can reduce engine life dramatically. It is entirely possible to increase the rate of wear by 400-600%. And, an engine with worn rings, valve guides, valve seats and other parts, is not going to give good economy or good power. The point here is simple: you must use a filter and you must use a good one.

If you are going to install a non-stock filter, avoid the open wire-mesh filters. Such filters don't have a replaceable element. Instead, they use a wire mesh, approximately as coarse as ordinary window screen, to "filter" the

This foam-topped ram stack exemplifies a typical shortcoming of many badly designed filters and filter elements: it has insufficient area for the filtering media and will restrict high-rpm airflow to the carb.

As far as airflow is concerned, this particular ram stack and paper element filter was a disaster. When installed on a carb capable of flowing a maximum of 648.9cfm, it reduced the flow to 496.1cfm. This is an efficiency of only 76.4%.

A tall filter element worked fine with this turbo Mustang. The filter is about .250-inch taller than stock and with the false opening in the air scoop cut out to allow entry of cold air, an additional 6-8hp was gained at the rear wheels.

The filter dilemma: which do you choose. They all claim to be good, but manufacturers often tend to be overly optimistic! The only way to be certain is to perform careful testing.

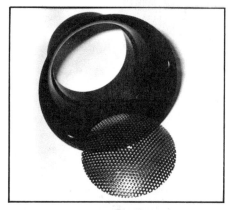

Don't kid yourself into thinking that this setup is a filter. The wire strainer will not remove airborn dust and dirt and, surprisingly, it will not allow air to flow into the engine easily. If you want performance and reliability, this type of "filter" is best left on the shelf.

air. They are effective at keeping airborne objects larger than low-flying ducks out of your carburetor, but they do little else. They certainly look trick but, surprisingly, most of them don't flow very well.

An increasingly popular hot-rod trick is to operate an engine on the street with no air filter. This is a good way to wear out an engine very rapidly. If you are looking for power and economy, remember, economy is not only how many miles you get per gallon, but also how many miles per engine. If you're smart, when you choose a filter you'll settle for nothing less than a large, thick sponge foam or similar paper or cotton-wire (K&N-type) element.

The second factor to consider when buying a filter is airflow. The accompanying graph shows the results of a flow test conducted on several types of filters. You will notice the paper filter does very well when it is fresh, but performance drops off rapidly as fine particles clog the pores in the paper. On the other hand, foam filters and cotton-wire filters do not clog as quickly. The cotton-wire type filter can be used effectively (without

If you are replacing a paper element with a plastic foam element, try to increase the size of the element. Even the best foam element will restrict airflow slightly more than a good paper element. If possible, increase the filter area by 10-20%.

cleaning it) for as long as 50,000 miles, under typical conditions, without developing excessive airflow restriction.

In the world of high-performance automotive air filters, the K&N filter may be considered as the Rolls Royce of the market, but it is also one of the highest priced filters (as is the Rolls). A K&N should be your first choice if your budget will allow, but if you can't afford one, buy yourself a good, big, foam filter. Either of these types of filter can be easily cleaned. With careful maintenance you may not have to buy another filter element for the life of the vehicle. It is also worth noting that because foam and cotton-wire filters can be cleaned regularly (and easily), they are more likely to be serviced regularly. The cost of doing so is zero and it will maintain performance and mileage.

AIR FILTER FLOW COMPARISON TESTS

TESTED BY DAVID VIZARD

FILTER TYPE	
TYPICAL PAPER ELEMENT AFTER 12,000 MILES IN DUSTY CONDITIONS	2.9 CFM/SQ.INCH
WORST PAPER ELEMENT TESTED (FRAM)	3.2 CFM/SQ.INCH
TYPICAL PAPER ELEMENT AFTER 5,000 MILES	4.0 CFM/SQ.INCH
SYNTHETIC FOAM: UNIFILTER, FILTRON, RAM FLOW, ETC., NEW	4.5 CFM/SQ.INCH
TYPICAL PAPER ELEMENT, NEW	4.9 CFM/SQ.INCH
K & N FILTER AFTER 500 MILES OF BAJA OFF-ROAD RACE *	5.1 CFM/SQ.INCH
BEST PAPER ELEMENT TESTED (MOTORCRAFT), NEW	5.2 CFM/SQ.INCH
NEW K & N FILTER (COTTON/WIRE CONSTRUCTION)	6.5 CFM/SQ.INCH

AIRFLOW IN C.F.M. PER SQ. INCH OF OUTSIDE AREA OF FILTER MEASURED AT 1-1/2-INCH H2O PRESSURE DROP

* THIS FILTER WAS LOADED WITH 3/16-1/4-INCH THICK LAYER OF DIRT OVER ENTIRE FILTER ELEMENT.

Most "reusable" air filters are saturated with an oil-based fluid to help trap airborn dirt particles. Periodically they must be washed, to remove the trapped dirt, and re-oiled. Follow manufacturers directions to the letter, as over- or under-oiling can adversely affect the efficiency of the element.

The ability of a filter to flow air even after it becomes loaded with dirt is important. Even packed with as much dirt as shown here, this K&N filter flowed as well as most brand-new paper filter elements.

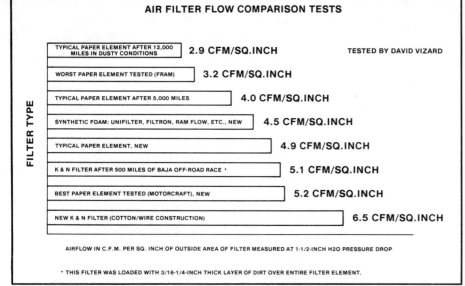

This close-up shows the difference between a conventional paper element and the highly respected K&N cotton-wire element design.

Exactly how much performance and mileage is gained by attention to the air filter will vary from vehicle to vehicle. Our chart shows the average gain when measurements are taken from several vehicles. In each test zero restriction is determined by removing the air-filter element, but leaving the filter case (with lid) in position. In all instances, installing a less-restrictive filter element caused the carburetor mixture to become leaner. Under some circumstances a less-restrictive element may cause a lean-misfire condition on emissions-type vehicles. If this situation occurs, it may be necessary to rejet the carb to compensate. A dynamometer test session, as discussed in Chapter 2, may be required to recalibrate the carb accurately.

The McCoy Racing filter installation has been designed with the circle-track racer in mind. The lid and base are similar to the Moroso unit, but are moulded in high-impact plastic. The filter case is also supplied with a shield to prevent damage to the filter (in this case a K&N element) from flying dirt-track debris.

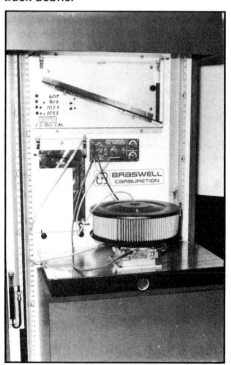

EFFECT OF FILTER FLOW EFFICIENCY ON POWER AND ECONOMY

(AVERAGE TAKEN ON 3 VEHICLES OVER TOTAL OF 6000 MILES)

Y-axis: % OF MAXIMUM HORSEPOWER MEASURED AT REAR WHEELS

X-axis: ENGINE R.P.M.

○——○ Clean High-Flow, Low-Restriction Filter

△——△ Paper Filter With Restriction Equivalent To 10,000/12,000 Miles.

% MILEAGE CHANGE WITH HIGH EFFICIENCY FILTER

CITY DRIVING	+ 1.8%
URBAN DRIVING	+ 2.1%
FREEWAY DRIVING	+ 2.0%
HIGH SPEED (CLOSED COURSE)	+ 4.2%

NOTE: Although Test Vehicles Had Internally Vented Carb Float Bowls, Restrictive Filter Always Caused A Mixture Enrichment To Some Degree. Emission Figure Reflected Such A Mixture Change.

TESTED BY DAVID VIZARD

CARBURETORS

There is an old saying that a penny not spent is a penny saved. This is economy. Due to the fact that most modern carbs have approximately the same economy potential, it takes many miles of driving to recoup the investment of buying an economy carb. If a fuel-saving carb increased your vehicle mileage from 18mpg to 19mpg, a realistic possible gain, it would take about 20,000-25,000 miles before the fuel savings equaled the cost of the carb.

If your current carb needs to be replaced, however, you should think

Flow bench testing at Braswell Carburetion has shown that the Moroso Performance and McCoy Racing filter cases (they are identical), in conjunction with a 4-inch high K&N filter, will flow enough air to produce induction efficiency greater than 99% on engines producing 650-700hp. With this type of flow efficiency available, there is no excuse for running any engine without an air filter.

carefully before you proceed. Because we are considering power with economy, the selection of a carb with suitable airflow capacity becomes easier. Unlike a horsepower-only engine, a power/economy engine must be able to operate efficiently at low engine speeds, as well as at high rpm. Because of the flexibility of combustion engine operation, any specific part-throttle power requirement can be developed at many different engine-speed and throttle-opening combinations. However, *the most fuel-efficient way to operate an engine is to use as low an engine speed (rpm) as possible, together with as wide a throttle opening as possible.*

This means that gear ratios, cams, manifolds, etc., must be selected to meet such criteria. If an engine is expected to operate at relatively low engine speeds and wide throttle settings, it must have a carb with venturis sized to give reasonable air velocity through them at the required low rpm. If there is insufficient velocity through

This view of a disassembled Rochester Quadra-Jet shows the small primary and large secondary venturis. Such an arrangement produces high air velocity through the primary bores, resulting in good fuel atomization and excellent part-throttle economy and response.

When good low-rpm performance and mileage and reasonable top-end power are required, a vacuum-secondary carb, such as this Holley Model 4150, makes a good choice.

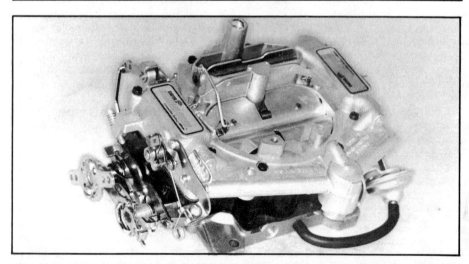

The Carter Thermo-Quad main-metering system can be accurately calibrated by varying the size of the main jet and the size and shape of the metering rods that fit inside the main-jet orifice. The tapered metering rods are controlled by manifold vacuum and move up or down to vary the overall area of the orifice. This permits precise metering according to manifold conditions (load). When correctly calibrated, the Thermo-Quad can deliver excellent mileage and power.

the venturis, a weak booster signal is developed, as a result fuel will not be drawn from the main metering system in sufficient quantities. In addition, the fuel will not be properly atomized as it enters the manifold. This all adds up to inefficient operation.

Selecting a carb that is too big (an airflow rating that is too high) for a specific engine and chassis combination inevitably causes a low-speed "bog" that will hinder performance, especially on an automatic-transmission vehicle. Because of the low-rpm considerations required for efficent operation, it is possible to develop some relatively simple guidelines for selecting a carb with the correct flow rating.

When power takes a slight priority over economy, a good performance/ economy four-barrel carb should be rated at about 1.8-2cfm per cubic inch of engine displacement. If your engine is equipped with a Rochester Q-Jet carb or a similar carb with an air valve to control secondary airflow, up to 2.3cfm per inch of displacement is acceptable. On an engine where economy is preferred slightly over power, a good figure is about 1.5cfm per inch of displacement.

If your engine is already equipped with a four-barrel carb that is in pretty good condition, think long and hard before buying a replacement. Remember, if a carb flows air and prepares the induction mixture correctly, it will perform as it should. Replacing one correctly calibrated 650cfm carb with another is not likely to produce any extra power or economy.

For the applications we are considering, four-barrel carbs with vacuum secondaries or with air-valve secondaries are preferable to those with mechanical secondaries. With a vacuum-type carb the primaries are generally small enough to provide good low-rpm efficiency. And, when the secondaries come into action, the combined airflow of the primaries and secondaries is usually adequate to give good high-rpm power.

FOUR-BARREL CARBS

The most popular four-barrel carbs currently used on domestic V8's are: Rochester Quadrajets, Holleys (of one sort or another), Carters and Ford Autolites. *Any of these carbs will give good power and economy when set up correctly, i.e., by an expert using a chassis dyno.*

Of the four, the Holley is probably the simplest to calibrate. It is an extremely easy carb to fine tune and generally it only takes a few jet changes to dial it in. Replacement parts for nearly all Holley models are readily available at most auto-supply stores and hot-rod shops.

The Carter Thermo-Quad is not as popular as the Holley for conventional performance and racing applications but it is, nonetheless, an excellent street performance/economy carb. Main fuel metering is accomplished by means of a tapered needle that is centered inside of a metering orifice. The tapered point of the needle is free to move up and down inside the orifice and is controlled by engine vacuum and a counterbalance spring. In effect, this provides a variable-area main metering orifice.

Calibration components (jets, needles, etc.) are available from Carter dealers or from Chrysler dealerships (Carters have been standard equipment on Chrysler products for many years). There is a major problem with trying to obtain calibration or replacement parts from a Chrysler dealership. The Chrysler parts book does not list small replacement parts by a standard Carter number or calibration rating but, instead, by a Chrysler part number. If, for example, you want a specific replacement jet or metering needle but you don't know the Chrysler number of the part, the counterman is probably not going to be able to help. The book will list several numbers, all with the general identification as "replacement metering jet" and not a single clue as to the size of each. And, one part number up or down in the list may not necessarily be the richer or leaner jet you are seeking.

This same general lack of access to replacment parts is also common for Rochester, Quadra-Jet and Autolite carburetors. On the other hand, the ease of obtaining Holley parts, plus the very reasonable price tag, have made the Holley an overwhelming favorite among mechanics and hot-rod enthusiasts. But don't believe that because they are so popular they will provide more performance and/or economy. It seems unlikely that any carburetor will ever supplant the Holley Model 4150 for professional racing applications, but *any of the well-known four-barrels - Carter, Rochester, Autolite or Holley— can provide suitable street performance and economy if you learn how, and take the time, to fine tune them properly.*

TWO-BARREL CARBS

When driven at normal highway cruise speeds, a vehicle equipped with a two-barrel carb rarely shows any worthwhile economy gains compared to a four-barrel counterpart. A two-barrel carb can be best viewed as a cost-saving item that allows the manufacturer to build a lower cost vehicle. As such, a two-barrel carb should be regarded as a limitation to horsepower rather than an aid to economy.

Buying a two-barrel carb for the sake of pure economy doesn't make much sense but if your engine is already equipped with a two-barrel and you have a tight budget (and economy is the only consideration), you might consider a two-barrel "economy" manifold like the Edelbrock SP-2P. If you use your existing carb with such a manifold, you can expect to gain more low-rpm torque and a significant, though modest, mileage improvement.

When you approach the situation from the power angle, you might want to stay with your existing two-barrel manifold and use a 350 or 500cfm Holley Model 2300 two-barrel carb. These carbs are close brothers to the Holley racing carbs and they can provide excellent wide-open-throttle

power, while retaining a conventional two-barrel configuration. (This author has had sufficient experience with Holley Model 2300's to know that they perform surprisingly well—both from the mileage and emission standpoint, as well as power output—for such a seemingly simple carb.) On a mundane street vehicle, replacing a Rochester 300cfm two-barrel with a 500cfm Model 2300 Holley can increase wide-open throttle power by 10% without any apparent mileage penalty.

If you anticipate buying a new carb and manifold, there isn't much justification for selecting a two-barrel carb and intake manifold. If you are buying both items, get a reputable four-barrel manifold and a vacuum- or air-valve-secondary four-barrel. When properly installed and calibrated, this setup will give you all the mileage of a two-barrel carb, plus a lot more top-end horsepower.

EXOTIC & UNUSUAL CARBS

The carbs mentioned so far by no means represent all the possibilities that could be used. They are only those

Many original-equipment, two-barrel carbs can easily be replaced with the Holley Model-2300 two-barrel. This carb is virtually a Model 4150 cut in half and can flow up to 500cfm. It will deliver Holley performance without requiring a swap to a four-barrel manifold.

Another import brand capable of excellent all-around performance is the Japanese-made SU carb. This type of design is known as a constant-depression carb. It is almost impossible to over-carburete an engine using this type carb, as it only opens far enough to satisfy specific engine air demand. This particular installation is on a Toyota Land Cruiser.

that are conveniently available, are of known capabilities and represent good value for the money. If you are in the market for something different or "exotic" there are many less well-known alternatives, some of them practical and others a little less so.

One of the best economy carbs available anywhere is the S.U. carb or its Japanese-built equivalent, the Hitachi carb (commonly fitted to imported Datsuns). These carbs are best suited to small 4- or 6-cylinder engines but a few manufacturers, notably Rover and Rolls Royce, have used S.U. carbs on V8 engines.

So far, all the carbs we have considered are designed primarily to be used on conventional plenum-type manifolds. However, independent-runner manifolds (each bore of the carburetor feeds into only one separate or independent manifold runner, which, in turn, feeds to only one of the cylinders of the engine, and there is no shared or "common" plenum chamber where all the runners join together, as on conventional manifolds) with multiple carburetors can be made to work very well on V8 engines. Carbs for such applications include the sophisticated Weber and Dellorto side-draft designs. Both of these carburetors have low-, mid- and high-speed circuits that can

The European-made Weber carburetor and it's near-twin, the Dellorto carb (also European), are recognized worldwide as sophisticated and reliable carburetors. Such designs are ideally suited to individual-runner induction systems used on small engines, and when correctly calibrated, carbs of this type will give good mileage and power on small engines.

be easily adjusted to give very accurate fuel metering throughout the normal rev range of most engines.

Independent-runner systems are good for producing torque at low engine speeds, usually more than can be developed on the same engine by a plenum-type manifold. At the same time, these independent-runner systems provide increased breathing ability and can cope with the flow requirements of the upper speed ranges with ease.

The main drawbacks with independent-runner systems is that they cost a lot of money and, since multiple carbs are generally required, you are faced with the prospect of calibrating each carb. If they are not calibrated properly, they can use exorbitant quantities of fuel. A calibration error, multiplied by four carburetors, is likely to put the overall calibration much further off base than a similar calibration error on only one carb. On the other hand, when correctly calibrated, they need not suffer any mileage penalty compared with a more conventional carburetion setup.

There are many other brands of carburetors that we have not mentioned here. Some of these lesser-known brands may be useful, but you should be wary of buying a carb from a company that does not have a well-established reputation. Designing and building an efficient performance and economy carb requires a great deal of knowledge, money and work. Be especially wary of exorbitant mileage claims. As mentioned in the opening segment of this chapter, we all live within the narrowly structured confines of the laws of physics, and though we can all look forward to future improvements, there is virtually no possibility of a "miracle breakthrough" in carburetor design.

CALIBRATION

When a novice learns about calibrating a carburetor, he often places too much emphasis on the main metering circuit and he spends a lot of time changing the main jets. In fact, the main jets determine the maximum allowable fuel flow through the main circuit. They, to a large extent, only affect the air-fuel ratio at operating conditions near wide-open throttle. It is important that the main jets are correctly selected to insure the proper mixture when you need wide-open throttle, such as when you must pass another car on the highway, but they play only a small role in overall economy.

One of the principal advantages of the Holley carb, apart from the low cost, is the minimal number of calibration components that are needed to fine tune the fuel metering. Because of the popularity of the Holley, components such as those shown here are readily available nationwide.

If we are considering performance with economy, the most important carburetor calibration for mileage and, for that matter, driveability at normal highway speeds, is the idle and transition circuit. If this circuit is too rich, you will be using too much fuel virtually all the time. If it is too lean, driveability will be affected and you may have to use more throttle than necessary to move the vehicle in a satisfactory manner. Also, if the idle and transition circuit (the transition portion of this circuit actually provides most of the metered fuel during normal cruise conditions) is improperly calibrated, you may have to hold the throttle open just a bit too much during cruise. This could activate the main circuit and lead to excessive fuel delivery when the engine does not need it. Under these conditions, the main jets may also have to be calibrated slightly rich to compensate for a lean condition in the idle and transition circuit. All this boils down to one thing: unnecessary fuel consumption.

Generally speaking, the best calibration for the idle-transition circuit is one that gives you the highest manifold-vacuum reading at normal cruise speeds. We should amplify that a little: if you can get your engine to idle at 17 inches of vacuum instead of 15 inches, all other things being equal, it is burning less fuel because the engine is drawing in less air (when vacuum at idle is higher, the throttle blades are closed more tightly, so less air is able to enter) and less fuel is being atomized into this air. Likewise, if you can increase the vacuum reading at cruise speeds, the engine is probably consuming less air and less fuel.

Virtually all modern production carbs are manufactured to high production and calibration standards, but for specific non-standard applications they can occasionally be improved. Here, David Braswell of Braswell Carburetion is checking the various circuits of a custom-modified Holley carb.

29

This all sounds terrific but there is a big problem. Most carburetors do not have provisions to easily change the calibration of the idle-transition fuel calibration. Often this calibration is provided by a fixed fuel orifice and a fixed air orifice that admits bleed air to the circuit. This circuit is not designed to be easily modified because it is rather difficult to determine the best possible calibration unless you have a lot of experience and some very spec-

The accepted procedure for tuning a new carb usually starts with a check of the idle and idle-transition circuits. A vacuum gauge is an invaluable tool for testing these circuits.

ialized tools. This is not to say, though, that it can't be done. (Those interested in studying this in greater depth should refer to a service manual for the specific carburetor in question.) But, if you don't want to get into the carburetor this deeply, there is an alternative solution. *Make absolutely certain you use a carburetor that the manufacturer has designed and recommended for your specific engine and application* (they probably know more about carburetor design and selection than you do).

Once the idle-transition circuit is operating satisfactorily, it's time to turn your attention to the main metering circuit. There is a portion of the

engine operating cycle when the main circuit does provide almost all of the fuel requirement. As the throttle is opened more (with a load on the engine) the idle-transition circuit will be deactivated and the main delivery through the booster venturis becomes the primary source of fuel. This occurs largely during light acceleration and when more-than-usual throttle is required, perhaps as when climbing a slight grade. At wide-open throttle the main circuit will be flowing to the maximum capacity allowable by the main jet, but the power-valve circuit (sometimes called the economizer circuit) will also be adding extra enrichment fuel. So, it is possible to lean

Proper adjustment of the idle mixture is important for both economy and power. With a vacuum gauge properly connected to the manifold the mixture screws should be adjusted to gain the highest vacuum reading possible at the specified idle speed (rpm). The mixture screws on the Holley 4150/4160 are located for easy access.

the main circuit in order to gain an added measure of economy during light acceleration, as long as there is enough compensating enrichment in the power-valve circuit. If you lean the main circuit too much without making certain you have adequate enrichment for wide-open throttle operation, you will be risking engine damage.

This balancing act between the

Here is a before-and-after shot of a modified Holley main body. note that the choke extension has been removed in an effort to increase airflow into the carb. This is a common racing mod but should not be attempted in street carbs used in colder climes. This will eliminate the choke and make cold-starting difficult.

In an effort to skew delivery curves for highly specialized applications, some racers will modify the Holley main body to accept replaceable air bleeds (arrow). This modification will affect the delivery "timing" of the idle-transition and main fuel circuits and is a very tricky game if you don't have a wet-flow bench to check the results. Carefully select the right carb for your specific application and leave these "fancy tricks" to the fast-talkers.

The throttle blades and throttle shaft are precision components and should be handled carefully during carburetor maintenance and rebuilding. The throttle blades must be correctly aligned inside the bore to insure proper idle and low-speed fuel flow. Do not remove them unless you have had experience with this type of rebuilding.

spark plugs. If you don't know how to read spark plugs, learn, or realize that you are risking possible engine damage if you lean wide-open throttle fuel delivery too much.

When all the previously mentioned circuits have been finalized, attention can be turned to the accelerator pump system. In the old days of hot-rodding it was quite popular to have as much accelerator-pump "shot" as possible. This probably created more piston ring problems (due to excessive raw gas in the cylinders) than any other single cause and, even for maximum performance, it's not necessary. In the interests of performance and economy, the accelerator pump should only discharge enough fuel to avoid acceleration "flat spots." This calibration must be made by trial-and-error road testing. You will need to decrease the amount of pump shot (follow an appropriate service manual) in gradual steps, and after each alteration, test the full-throttle acceleration from a slow roll. When you finally note a definite hesitation as the throttle is pushed wide open, back up a step. Leaning the pump shot can help a great deal in overall economy, so don't be in too big a hurry. Sometimes a small hesitation at a slow roll will hardly be noticed during normal driving cycles. Drive the car for a few days to become familiar with it, perhaps a very small loss in performance can be more than justified by a noticeable increase in economy.

The "Black Magic" carb from Internal Combustion Engineering is a modified version of the ever-popular Holley 4150. This carb is modified for maximum top-end performance but when dyno tested by the author it produced a gain of 31 hp with no loss of mileage or low-rpm torque.

main and power-valve circuit is rather difficult to achieve without some experience and it can only be nailed down with great accuracy through the use of a chassis dynamometer and an exhaust analyzer. It is possible to put the engine in a loaded state on the chassis dyno and continue leaning the main circuit until the exhaust analyzer shows signs of lean misfire. And, as long as the power-valve activation point and delivery volume is enough to prevent wide-open throttle detonation, you'll be in good shape. If you don't have this sophisticated equipment, it's possible to do some trial-and-error testing, but as you lean the main circuit watch for signs of wide-open throttle (manifold vacuum below about 4 inches of mercury) detonation on the

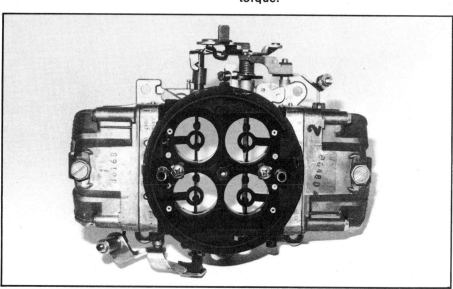

CHAPTER 4 INTAKE MANIFOLDS

- BUY OR MODIFY?
- MORE POWER—LESS GAS
- THE SECRET OF SPACERS
- CARB MATCHING

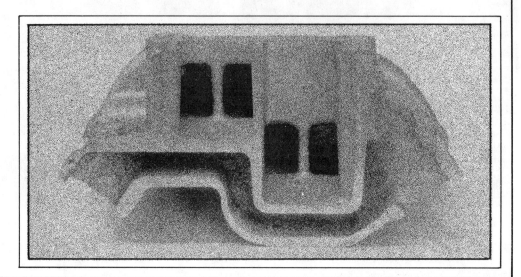

INTAKE MANIFOLDS

Over the years every imaginable combination of carburetor(s) and manifold has been used on combustion engines. However, since our primary interest is to gain both power and economy, we will ignore exotic combinations. There are some unusual manifolds that may provide a suitable balance between performance and economy, but any special design almost always requires a great deal of tuning expertise to gain the full potential it may offer. *It would be wise for the novice tuner to stick with proven combinations.* We can, therefore, rule out the use of multiple carburetors and

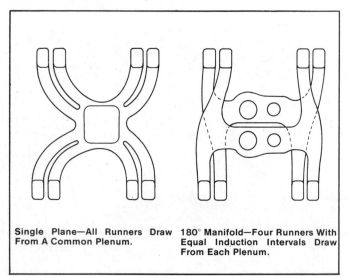

Single Plane—All Runners Draw From A Common Plenum.

180° Manifold—Four Runners With Equal Induction Intervals Draw From Each Plenum.

There is a distinct difference between the plenum and runner configurations of dual-plane and single-plane manifolds. In the single-plane design all of the runners join in a single common plenum beneath the carb, and are routed directly from the plenum to the port openings in the head. In the dual-plane design there are two small plenums and the runners are routed so that the cylinders draw alternately, according to the firing order, from each plenum.

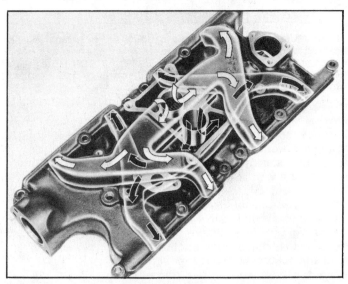

This phantom view of a typical dual-plane manifold shows the airflow patterns through the runners. Because each subsequent cylinder in the firing order draws from a separate plenum, this type of manifold design provides very good low-speed torque. But, note that the routing of flow in each runner is fairly long and the flow must make several turns. This reduces high-rpm flow capability and maximum power.

This smallblock Chevy Quadra-Jet manifold is typical of factory 180° manifolds. It provides good low-speed torque and with the proper cam will produce peek power at 5000-5500rpm.

concentrate on practical street-type setups, namely those designed for a single two- or four-barrel carb.

There are many different manifolds available for all of the popular engines. At first the choice seems staggering, but the picture is less complicated if you categorize them. (We will not consider the exotic types of carburetion mentioned in the previous chapter. If you choose an unusual carburetion setup, you will probably have to use an uncommon manifold and we'll leave it to you to solve the equally uncommon problems that are certain to result.) When you decide to use a commonly available two- or four-barrel carb, your choice of manifolds will fall into one of two broad categories: a single-plane manifold or a 180° manifold (often called a dual-plane manifold).

A single-plane manifold is one in which the carb feeds into a common plenum chamber below the carb. All eight runners draw their charge of air and fuel from this common chamber. A 180° manifold has a dividing wall in the plenum that separates it into two chambers. This, in effect, operationally divides the carb into two separate two-barrel units (one primary and one secondary barrel for each chamber). The manifold runners are routed from the plenums to the cylinders in such a way that air-fuel is drawn alternately from each plenum and, subsequently, from each half of the carb. As a result, an intake pulse is experienced by each half of the carb every 180° of crankshaft revolution. (A look at our drawing will quickly illustrate the difference in these two fundamental types of manifolds).

Manifolds must be designed to operate within specific engine-speed ranges (rpm limits). The 180° design favors low- and mid-range torque (approximately 2500-4500 rpm), but it generally delivers less flow and power at higher engine speeds. The open-plenum manifold generally develops less low-end torque but can be made to produce good mid-range and much stronger top-end performance (approximately 4500-6500 rpm).

The exact torque and power production of either type manifold will be greatly affected by individual differences in the specific manifold designs and differences in the type of engine on which they are installed. The design of the manifold can affect performance through factors such as runner length, runner cross section, runner volume, plenum shape, plenum volume, etc. As a very basic rule, it can be said that the larger the runner and plenum are, the more the manifold will favor power at the top end of the rpm scale. The smaller the runner size and plenum volume, the more it will favor low-end torque.

You cannot, however, just decide you want high-rpm power, install a racing manifold and go for it. The rest of the engine components must also be selected to support high-rpm operation. When selecting an intake manifold, the trick is to determine a realistic point for the engine to reach peak power. Then, you must select a coordinated "package" of intake and exhaust components that will operate optimally at this peak. To make a proper manifold choice for the combination you must understand why there can be such a difference in the power and torque capabilities of a 180° manifold and a single-plane manifold.

In the carburetor chapter it was stated that two functions of the carb were to meter the correct amount of fuel into the incoming airstream and to atomize and disperse this fuel uniformly into the induction air. These

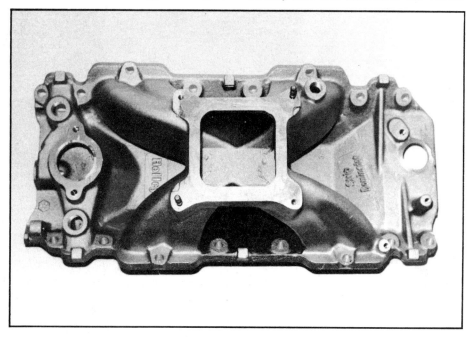

This Holley Strip Dominator for the small-port, big block Chevy is a typical single-plane manifold design. Note how all barrels of the carb feed into a single plenum and that all runners join this common plenum.

major functions are markedly influenced by the manifold design.

In a 180° manifold the enclosed volume between the carb venturi and the intake valve is substantially less than with a single-plane manifold. This volume becomes important when the intake valve opens and the piston moves down on the intake stroke. As the runner begins feeding the cylinder, a pulse is generated in the runner. This pulse is more intense in a 180° manifold because of the reduced volume in the runner and small plenum. The result of this sharp pulse is a high momentary gas speed through the carburetor venturi. This provides positive fuel metering and better atomization of fuel dispensed at the booster venturi than if a relatively less powerful pulse had been generated in the runner. The intake pulse has the same effect on the idle-transition fuel because it creates a sharp signal for the circuit to read. As it turns out, this is just what is needed to make a manifold work at low rpm.

In a single-plane manifold, the situation is slightly different. When a cylinder induction pulse in created in the runner, much of the intensity of this pulse is diluted because of the large plenum volume associated with these designs and because the plenum is directly coupled to the volume of the other seven runners. As a result, the pulse strength at slow engine speeds is vastly reduced and spread over the relatively greater area of two or four venturis, depending on how many are open at the time. As engine rpm rises, the situation changes. At higher levels the engine needs greater induction volume and the gas speed through the carb increases. At this point atomization is already pretty good and the large plenum volume becomes a help. At wide-open throttle, as each cylinder needs fuel it has four venturis from which to draw. In a similar situation with a 180° manifold, the cylinder has only two barrels available to it. With more venturi area available to each cylinder, the engine as a whole, can produce more peak power.

As a result of this not-so-subtle difference, the 180° manifold will give good torque at low speeds and the single-plane manifold will produce better power in the upper rpm ranges. Not unexpectedly then, the single-plane manifold is often the choice for pure racing-type high-rpm power. *However, when it comes to economy, the 180° manifold definitely has the edge.* This is why many, if not all, factory single four-barrel manifolds are of the 180° design.

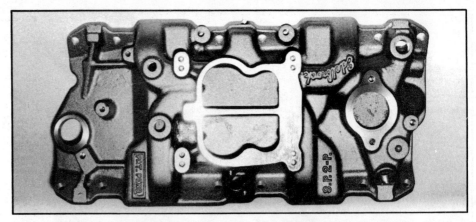

The Edelbrock SP-2P design is currently considered one of the best low-rpm, street-type, economy manifolds. It is based on the traditional 180° (dual-plane) configuration and features unusually small runners to maintain good port velocity at low engine speeds.

The Edelbrock designers have carefully contoured the entry from the plenum to the runners and the shapes of the runner legs of the SP-2P design to minimize flow losses inside the manifold.

As the runner legs of the smallblock Chevy SP-2P manifold approach the cylinder-head port entry, the size of the runners gradually increases. At the cylinder-head mating surface the runner opening is sized to match the smaller ports found on standard Chevy street (non-performance) cylinder heads. This maintains relatively high flow velocity during part-throttle cruise.

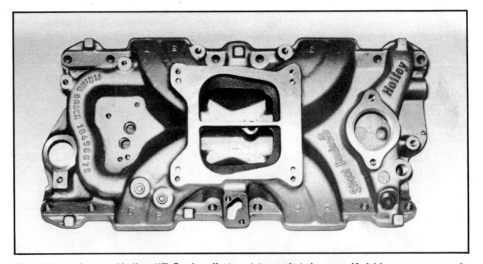

The relatively new Holley "Z-Series," street-type, intake manifold is very unusual. The runners are routed like a single-plane design but there is a divider in the plenum, separating the right and left sides of the manifold. It also features a unique "resonant" passage joining #7 and #8 port runners.

The selection of your intake manifold is going to depend a great deal upon how much personal importance you place on economy or power and, as a consequence, what maximum rpm limit you intend to impose on the engine. Basically, if you are going to have your engine produce maximum power at approximately 4500-5000 rpm, undoubtedly a 180° manifold is the ideal choice. During part-throttle conditions, you may expect to use about 10% less fuel than with a deeper breathing, single-plane manifold.

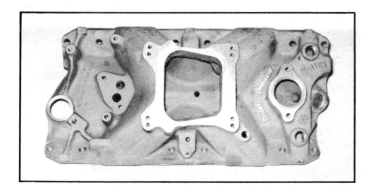

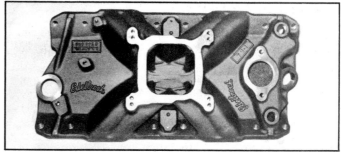

The Holley Street Dominator manifold is equipped with all the necessary vacuum tappings, passages, etc., required by current emissions equipment. Flow-bench testing has shown that this manifold has highly efficient flow characterisitics. It works best on engines that have modified heads, a performance cam and headers.

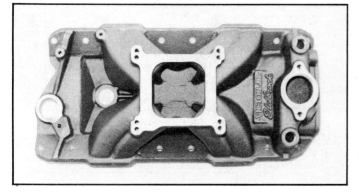

This Edelbrock TM1 design will give strong mid-range torque and good top-end power when used on a high-compression engine with a strong performance cam.

Although this Edelbrock Victor Junior is designed primarily for competition, it can, under certain circumstances, be used as a performance street manifold. When used as a street manifold, it has proved to work best on engines around 350cid. Since it is designed for fairly high engine speeds, it should be used with a high-flow carb, modified heads, a performance-type cam, and headers.

When you're thinking of economy, this isn't the only advantage of a 180° manifold. If the engine is cammed to operate in the range that is compatible with the manifold, the throttle response is much sharper. As a result, normal acceleration away from a standstill is much better than would be obtained with a single-plane manifold. (We assume, of course, that you don't put the tach on seven grand and side-step the clutch at every stoplight.) If you are selecting pieces to build an engine with peak power in the 5000-6500 rpm range, or maybe even a little higher, a single-plane manifold is going to be the way to go. The penalty can, depending upon the manifold chosen, be a slight loss in part-throttle, low-rpm fuel economy.

Not all single-plane manifolds are the same. By varying the size of the runners and plenum, a single-plane manifold can be made to operate optimally at any level between 4000 and 7000 rpm (higher if it is strictly a racing manifold). Some single-plane manifolds produced in the last few years have been designed specifically for mid-range operation. They may be considered for some power/economy applications, but realize that these manifolds must be carefully matched to a suitable, carefully-calibrated carburetor if they are to provide even minimally acceptable economy. The more performance-oriented models, the sort designed to operate in very high rpm ranges, are not practical for any street power/economy engine.

There is another fact that you must

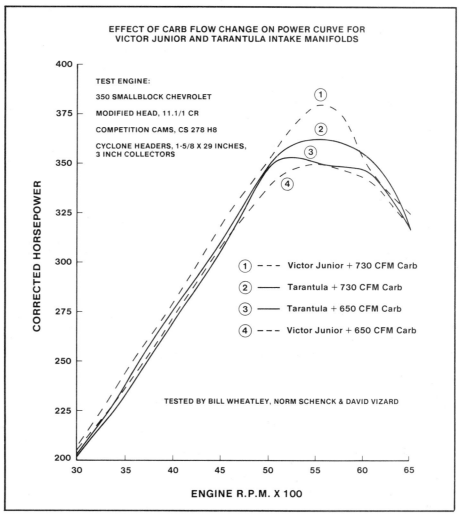

EFFECT OF CARB FLOW CHANGE ON POWER CURVE FOR VICTOR JUNIOR AND TARANTULA INTAKE MANIFOLDS

TEST ENGINE:

350 SMALLBLOCK CHEVROLET

MODIFIED HEAD, 11.1/1 CR

COMPETITION CAMS, CS 278 H8

CYCLONE HEADERS, 1-5/8 X 29 INCHES, 3 INCH COLLECTORS

① --- Victor Junior + 730 CFM Carb
② — Tarantula + 730 CFM Carb
③ — Tarantula + 650 CFM Carb
④ --- Victor Junior + 650 CFM Carb

TESTED BY BILL WHEATLEY, NORM SCHENCK & DAVID VIZARD

CORRECTED HORSEPOWER

ENGINE R.P.M. X 100

consider before choosing a manifold: the carburetor. If you choose a manifold that operates at high engine speeds, to make this manifold "work," you must also put a large carb (high cfm rating) on the engine. This may bring about carburetion problems in the lower rpm range. On the other

Even specialty manifolds are compromised by manufacturing requirements. This aftermarket manifold can be marginally improved by rounding the entrance to each runner, in the areas indicated by the arrows.

hand, if a high-rpm manifold is used with a small carburetor, the engine will not produce suitable maximum power and the mid-range response will be reduced because of the relatively large runner volume and the small carb. You may be tired of hearing this, but once again we have to say: the name of the game is to select all of the components so they match and work in harmony.

The chart included here illustrates the working range of two of the most popular brands of manifolds: Holley and Edelbrock. If you consider carefully and use this chart as a guide, the job of selecting from the many manifolds available should be easier and the manifold you choose should, hopefully, fulfill your requirements.

The final efficiency test for any induction system, prior to installation on the engine, is to see how well it performs on the flow bench. This modified, big block, Chevy head, with a Holley Strip Dominator manifold, a modified 850cfm Holley and a large K&N air filter, flowed more air than the original, bare cylinder head!

Not only does a specialty, aluminum intake manifold help power, it also provides a considerable weight reduction. The factory, cast-iron manifold shown here weighs 36lb, as opposed to the 14lb weight of the Edelbrock Scorpion.

ORIGINAL OR SPECIALTY?

Most stock engines are equipped with a four-barrel carb on a 180° cast-iron manifold and the immediate question is usually whether it's worthwhile changing this manifold for a specialty manifold. There are many good reasons for swapping manifolds but think twice before spending money on just any specialty, aluminum, four-barrel manifold. If you are working on a tight budget, the $100 or so you will spend might be better invested in other areas to produce more performance/economy improvement per dollar invested. On the other hand, if your budget is not too tight, a specialty manifold does give a substantial weight reduction over a cast-iron man-

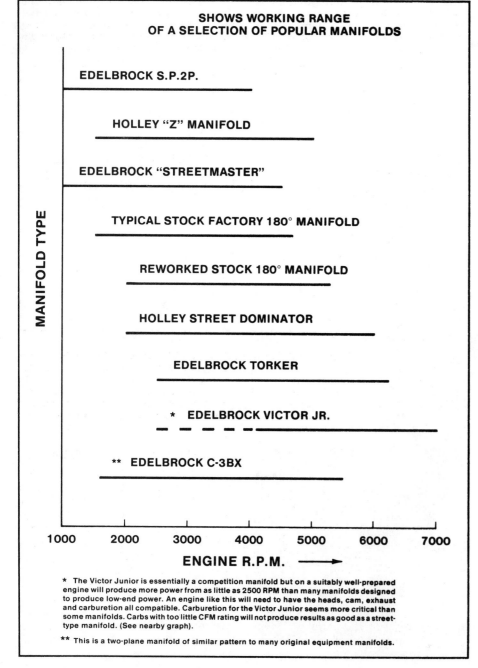

SHOWS WORKING RANGE OF A SELECTION OF POPULAR MANIFOLDS

MANIFOLD TYPE

EDELBROCK S.P.2P.

HOLLEY "Z" MANIFOLD

EDELBROCK "STREETMASTER"

TYPICAL STOCK FACTORY 180° MANIFOLD

REWORKED STOCK 180° MANIFOLD

HOLLEY STREET DOMINATOR

EDELBROCK TORKER

* EDELBROCK VICTOR JR.

** EDELBROCK C-3BX

1000   2000   3000   4000   5000   6000   7000

ENGINE R.P.M. ——▶

* The Victor Junior is essentially a competition manifold but on a suitably well-prepared engine will produce more power from as little as 2500 RPM than many manifolds designed to produce low-end power. An engine like this will need to have the heads, cam, exhaust and carburetion all compatible. Carburetion for the Victor Junior seems more critical than some manifolds. Carbs with too little CFM rating will not produce results as good as a street-type manifold. (See nearby graph).

** This is a two-plane manifold of similar pattern to many original equipment manifolds.

ifold, as well as offering some extra performance. If you decide to go to a single-plane manifold, you have no choice but to opt for a specialty manifold.

There is another alternative to consider before making up your mind. Some work with a high-speed hand grinder inside the plenum and runners of an original-equipment manifold can often increase the performance potential quite considerably. The worst restriction in most stock manifolds (especially General Motors manifolds) occurs at the bottom of the two plenum chambers. At this point the plenum makes a sharp right-angle turn and joins the port runners. The sharp inside edge formed at this juncture causes a substantial flow restriction. Rounding off this edge and enlarging and smoothing the inside contours of the runners can add breathing efficiency without any notable sacrifice in other areas.

If you are on a tight budget, a stock 180° manifold can easily be reworked for more performance. Flow-bench testing has shown that flow gains as high as 15% can be achieved with only minor rework.

One of the biggest impediments to smooth airflow on original-equipment, four-barrel manifolds is the sharp corner between the carb opening and the plenum. The airstreamer indicates that the airflow wants to take a gentle turn between the plenum and the runner. Rounding the sharp edges along the airpath can help flow considerably.

This manifold has been reworked by the author. About four hours of grinding and the addition of this modified carb spacer produced considerable flow improvement. It will flow more than the stock, factory manifold but not quite as much as a good specialty, single-plane, street manifold.

The design, size and shape of the plenum are also important. The ribbing in the bottom of this original-equipment manifold contains excess fuel that drops out of the intake mixture (during cold starts) until heat from the exhaust crossover can evaporate it.

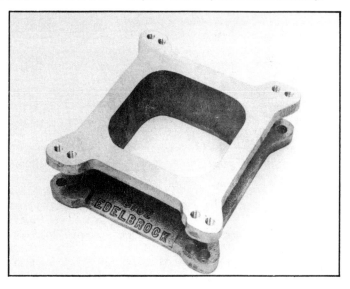

Stock manifolds often show notable high-rpm flow gains when a spacer is used between the carb base and the manifold flange. The spacer increases the volume of the plenum and, more important, if an open spacer is used (as shown), the plenums are no longer isolated from each other. This permits each plenum to share high-rpm flow from both primary and/or secondary barrels of the carb.

EXHAUST CROSSOVER

All original-equipment manifolds are built with an exhaust-heat passage in the floor of the manifold, directly beneath the carburetor. This passage joins an exhaust port in one cylinder head with an exhaust port in the other. As hot exhaust gas flows through this passage it heats the plenum area of the manifold to help atomization of fuel. In particular it tends to reduce fuel puddling on the floor of the manifold, and is especially important during start-up when the engine is cold and during low-speed conditions in cold

weather.

Unfortunately, though heating the intake mixture helps cold and low-speed operation, it is a deterrent to high-rpm, peak power. Here again we face a compromise between performance and convenience. Just how helpful the crossover is depends on the type of manifold you have, how you drive and where you live.

The effect of the crossover will be different if the manifold is cast iron or aluminum. Because cast iron conducts heat at a slower rate than aluminum, it takes a long time for a cast-iron manifold to warm up. This can affect the driveability of the vehicle. If the crossover is removed or blocked off in a cast-iron manifold, the carburetor choke will have to be engaged much longer before good driveability is achieved during the warm-up cycle. On the other hand, an identical manifold made of aluminum will conduct heat more quickly and, generally, the time the choke needs to be engaged will be shorter.

If you want to achieve maximum power and retain suitable driveability, you can often vary the effectiveness of the crossover to suit your specific circumstances. When the vehicle is used in a cold climate, such as the northern states, and it is equipped with a cast-iron manifold, the crossover should not be altered. If you want to go to the trouble of removing the manifold at the beginning of the winter and summer seasons, you could block off the crossover during the warmer months, but you will need to recalibrate the carburetor choke to keep it from staying engaged too long and wasting fuel. If you choose to do this though, you should realize that the power gains to be had from blocking the crossover are very small and the work required to remove and reinstall the manifold is very large.

If you live in the hotter parts of the country, such as the Southwest, the amount of exhaust fed through the crossover passage can be reduced without substantially affecting driveability. The easiest way to do this is to use a special gasket with a crossover block-off plate between the manifold and the cylinder head.

If you are using an aluminum manifold in the colder climates, one side of the crossover passage can be blocked off as described above or restrictor plates can be installed in both of the manifold gaskets. These restrictor plates have a small hole in them to reduce the size of the crossover opening. This will reduce crossover heat somewhat while still allowing some manifold preheat. In hot climates, under most circumstances, the crossover passage can be completely blocked. The only exception to this is

In cold climes, engines with cast-iron manifolds will warm up more quickly and use less fuel if the exhaust crossover passage (arrow) is not altered. In warmer climates, warmup is less critical and high-rpm power will be slightly improved if the heat crossover is reduced by installing restrictor plates (shown below the gasket).

when economy is considered much more important than maximum power. Under these conditions, some exhaust flow in the crossover is desirable.

SPACERS

One of the most popular and inexpensive performance tricks invented in recent years is to place a spacer plate between the carburetor and the intake manifold. This modification is largely considered a way to improve power in the higher speed ranges, but it also has some benefits for economy.

When a spacer is used on a 180° manifold, the manifold is partially converted into a single-plane design. The spacer raises the carb away from the

Sometimes a "four-hole" spacer will improve the transition of flow from the carb to the intake manifold plenum. However, this trick doesn't always increase power! For maximum effect, each carb, manifold and engine combination must be individually tested under operating conditions.

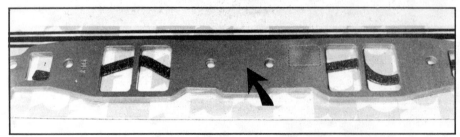

When aluminum manifolds are used in warmer climates, they rarely need crossover heat to provide adequate part-throttle fuel vaporization. Under these conditions, manifold gaskets with completely blocked exhaust-crossover passages can be used.

opening in the manifold and the small open area below the carb becomes a common mini-plenum. This increases plenum volume and provides some shared breathing for each cylinder.

The amount of spacer that is optimal will vary from engine to engine. A spacer between 5/8-inch and 1.5-inches thick will be most effective when applied to a 180° manifold. On single-plane manifolds, spacers as thick as 2 inches or more can be considered.

In addition to increasing plenum volume, mounting a spacer on a manifold with a very low profile is, in effect, also an effort to raise the carburetor and give the high-speed air-fuel exiting from the bottom of the carb more room to turn toward the runners before hitting the floor of the plenum(s). This will aid mid- and high-rpm power. However, before such an installation is considered, you should verify that you have adequate clearance beneath the hood to allow the carburetor and air cleaner to be raised by the thickness of the spacer.

Spacers also come in different types. The most common type, and the type we have generally been discussing to this point, has a single large opening between the carb and manifold. The second major type has four individual holes, each matching the bottom of one of the carburetor bores. The effect of a four-hole spacer can be considerably more pronounced on some engine and manifold combinations. They are obviously intended for single-plane manifolds and they really shouldn't be considered unless you are prepared to undertake a lot of trial-and-error testing.

There are some unique four-hole spacers that have recently become popular and though they are designed for special applications, they should be mentioned here. One is a four-hole spacer that flares out from the individual throttle bores to a single, square hole at the other end to match the manifold opening. This design increases the plenum volume and extends the bottoms of the throttle bores. It isolates the throttle bores and the venturis from turbulence in the manifold. Such a configuration can help airflow and power, especially on high-winding engines but at normal engine speeds it does not offer a substantial advantage over the much simpler single-hole spacer.

Another model used on very-high-rpm racing engines is really not a spacer as much as it is a simple bore extension. This is a thin plate that fits between the carb and the manifold,

Lack of hood clearance may prohibit the use of a tall spacer. Under such circumstances, a thin spacer may still help, but don't expect miracles. Generally, the improvement will be only 3-4hp, and then only at the very top of the speed range.

and four individual tubes are welded to the plate, each matching one of the carb bores. In some applications this can isolate the carb bores from plenum turbulence but it does not enlarge the volume of the plenum. Usually these are used on high-rise, single-plane manifolds that already have relatively large plenums. It is an effort to somewhat improve the mid-range response from a carb and manifold combination that is basically intended for unusually high engine speeds.

Either of these spacers can help cure a fuel stand-off problem (fuel that is forced backward through the carburetor because of intense pulsing in the intake manifold) on high-rpm engines. If they do cure such a problem, they will inevitably lead to more power, but don't expect them to give you any more horsepower if such problems don't exist.

Though the effect of a spacer is aimed at power, it can be used to assist high-rpm performance without sub-

stantially hurting the low-range economy. When you make more power, you use more fuel, but the point to remember is that we are looking for power "on demand" without losing reasonable economy during normal cruise modes. This is exactly what a spacer does. However, it is difficult to predict how a particular engine, manifold and carb combination will respond to a specific spacer. Sometimes varying the thickness of the spacer by as little as 1/4-inch can dramatically affect the performance of the engine. To find the best combination you will have to do some experimenting but, fortunately, spacers are usually pretty cheap and with some ingenuity you can fabricate them yourself. The money you save or spend here will not make you wealthy, on the other hand it may make a difference.

An engine dynamometer can be used to check the effect various carb spacers have on engine power, but the acid test is always a careful track or road test. Spacers will often affect engine "response" more than absolute power. (The driver may feel that the engine responds more quickly to the throttle.) However, even if you can't do extensive testing, a simple open spacer may slightly improve high-rpm power.

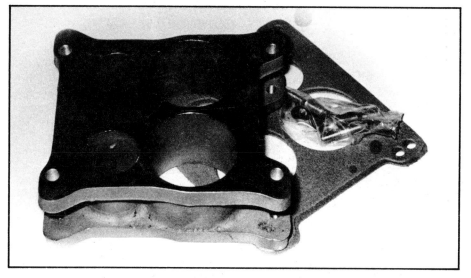

Spacers for spreadbore carb designs, like the Rochester Quadra-Jet, are less common, but they are available. The sample shown here is from Offenhauser.

CHAPTER 5 CYLINDER HEADS

- STREET PORT MODS
- POWER PORTING
- FLOW BIAS
- CHAMBER SCIENCE
- COMPRESSION RATIOS
- THERMAL COATINGS
- GRINDING YOUR OWN HEADS

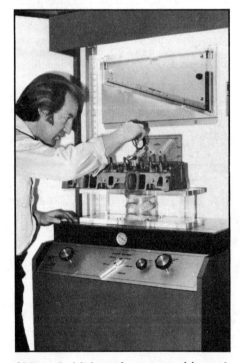

Although high-performance, big-port, cylinder heads are available for most popular engines, if you are on a tight budget, a well-prepared standard head will work very effectively on nearly any street engine. Here author David Vizard checks a standard smallblock Chevy head prior to installation on one of his test engines.

CYLINDER HEADS

Of all the things that influence power and economy, the most important and the most overlooked is cylinder head design and preparation. If the cylinder head does not allow the engine to "breathe" effectively, the engine will not operate efficently either in the mid-range, where economy is important, or at the top end, where we look for power and performance.

Generally speaking, the average hot-rodder neglects to tap even part of the cylinder head potential. It is tempting to view cylinder head preparation as black magic, practiced by high-dollar witch doctors. Buying a set of professionally reworked heads is expensive and after you spend this kind of money, you want to believe that something ethereal has been accomplished. Don't believe it. All-out racing cylinder head prep is incredibly expensive because of the enormous amount of hand labor required. We don't mean to imply that you can achieve the same level of performance by carving up a set of heads on your kitchen table, but anyone who is handy with a high-speed hand grinder can make worthwhile improvements to

stock heads.

At first, it may appear that achieving extra power from cylinder head work goes hand in hand with extra economy. This is only partially true. Some modifications performed on cylinder heads are good for power but are not conducive to economy, and the reverse is equally true. Before you can intelligently modify a set of cylinder heads you must decide what is most important: power or economy. More than likely you want both and you can, to some degree, achieve a suitable balance between the two, but you can't have everything, all the time. In this chapter you will find the basic factors affecting each of these criterion. Read the contents carefully and use the information it contains to build heads to suit your specific needs. *There are considerable benefits available at very reasonable cost, but don't expect miracles.*

INTAKE PORT

If you want an intake port that will produce maximum economy, the good news is that you have very little to do. You need a port with a small cross section and a rough surface texture. This almost perfectly describes most

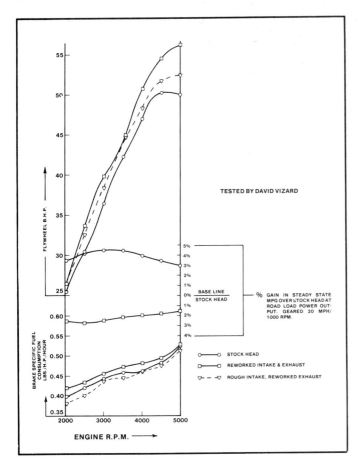

TESTED BY DAVID VIZARD

% GAIN IN STEADY STATE MPG OVER STOCK HEAD AT ROAD LOAD POWER OUTPUT. GEARED 20 MPH/1000 RPM.

○—○ STOCK HEAD
□—□ REWORKED INTAKE & EXHAUST
▽---▽ ROUGH INTAKE, REWORKED EXHAUST

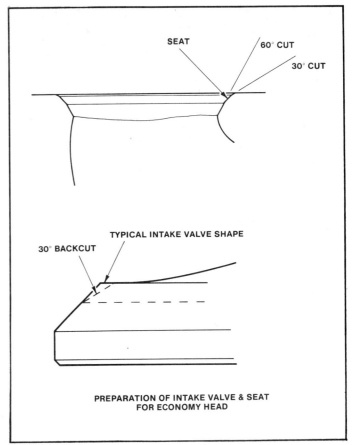

PREPARATION OF INTAKE VALVE & SEAT
FOR ECONOMY HEAD

This graph shows what typically happens to power and economy when a cylinder head is modified. With the intake and exhaust reworked for max flow, the engine makes more power. Note that the biggest power gains occur at higher engine speeds (rpm). However, the fuel economy declines, though the maximum loss is only 2.2%. (In this test the valve sizes and compression ratio remained stock.) When the head was reworked for max economy, the intake remained as-stock but the exhaust port was reworked and a larger exhaust valve was installed. Exhaust flow was increased about 30%. As a result, power was also increased, but not by as much as produced by the head with modified intake and modified exhaust. Moreover, note that overall fuel economy was improved by a very satisfying .5-4%.

stock intake ports.

The accompanying graph shows how the intake port finish and flow efficiency affect economy and power. These tests were done on a four-cylinder engine (to avoid reworking two heads for every test), but they are valid for any type engine.

You will note that, generally speaking, the most important increase in economy is obtained with nothing more exotic than a three-angle valve job and a 30° chamfer cut on the backside of the intake valve (see accompanying drawing). You may also note that this relatively simple "mod-

The valve seat is the most important part of any intake port! This Neway tungsten-carbide cutter is a handy tool for finalizing the size of the seat prior to hand lapping.

ification" also produced an identifiable increase in maximum power.

A proper valve job is among the most important features of any cylinder head. Always take as much care as possible to insure the job is done correctly. If you want maximum economy and maximum power, accept nothing less.

HIGH-PERFORMANCE STREET PORTS

Although preparing the intake ports for maximum economy sounds pretty simple, if you take this simplistic approach, you may be cheating your-

Increasing exhaust flow, no matter what the means, helps economy. Generally, a 6% increase in exhaust-valve area produces about a 1% increase in part-throttle economy. One of the most effective and simple modifications of the exhaust valve is to backcut the valve at a 30° angle (arrows).

self out of a lot of power. The question is: if you go for that power, how much economy will be lost. The answer is: *if the port is reworked sensibly, the amount of loss in economy will be minimal, but the power gain will be substantial.*

The trick to building a high-performance street port is to make certain that once the air-fuel mixture leaves the carb (hopefully, you have chosen the right carb) it is not restricted by a port that is too small or it does not lose velocity because the port is too big. A high-performance street port should have minimal cross-sectional area consistent with maximum airflow. In other words, material should be removed only from points where substantial airflow gains result. When the job is done right, a flow test will show that the volume of air able to move through the port is larger and the velocity of this air is substantially the same as a stock port.

Let's look at an example to illustrate the point. The people at C&G Porting of Tucson, Arizona, have what they call an "econo-power" head. A version of this head is intended for the smallblock Chevy and is based on the popular and widely available original-equipment performance head (based on a head casting with a 291, a 461 or a 462 number cast on the underside). They modify this head specifically to give street performance with economy. The primary emphasis is on crisp

No matter what the intended purpose, cylinder head development is a painstaking job. Here, Carl Schattilly of C&G Porting is utilizing a typical airflow bench to test one of his modified econo heads.

low-rpm engine response.

They remove metal only from areas that will give a substantial increase in airflow. As a result, the port opening is not the traditional rectangular shape found on many custom ports. Instead, it has a trapezoidal shape (see photos). The unusual shape developed from testing that indicated airflow on the port floor is minimal, and widening the port near the floor does little to help flow in the valve-lift ranges normally available from street cams. The top of the port is a high-flow area and widening the port here produces more flow volume.

In passing, it is worth mentioning that the most critical area, as far as total flow volume is concerned, is not the entry but rather the area close to,

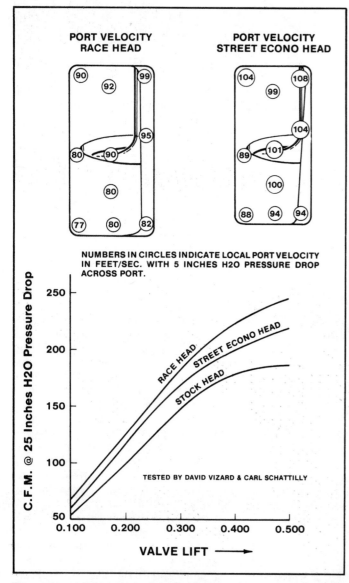

PORT VELOCITY RACE HEAD

PORT VELOCITY STREET ECONO HEAD

NUMBERS IN CIRCLES INDICATE LOCAL PORT VELOCITY IN FEET/SEC. WITH 5 INCHES H2O PRESSURE DROP ACROSS PORT.

C.F.M. @ 25 Inches H2O Pressure Drop

RACE HEAD
STREET ECONO HEAD
STOCK HEAD

VALVE LIFT

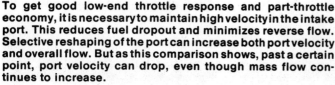

TESTED BY DAVID VIZARD & CARL SCHATTILLY

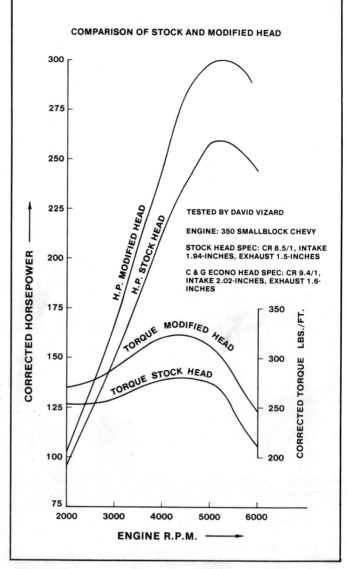

COMPARISON OF STOCK AND MODIFIED HEAD

CORRECTED HORSEPOWER

H.P. MODIFIED HEAD
H.P. STOCK HEAD

TORQUE MODIFIED HEAD
TORQUE STOCK HEAD

TESTED BY DAVID VIZARD

ENGINE: 350 SMALLBLOCK CHEVY

STOCK HEAD SPEC: CR 8.5/1, INTAKE 1.94-INCHES, EXHAUST 1.5-INCHES

C & G ECONO HEAD SPEC: CR 9.4/1, INTAKE 2.02-INCHES, EXHAUST 1.6-INCHES

CORRECTED TORQUE LBS./FT.

ENGINE R.P.M.

To get good low-end throttle response and part-throttle economy, it is necessary to maintain high velocity in the intake port. This reduces fuel dropout and minimizes reverse flow. Selective reshaping of the port can increase both port velocity and overall flow. But as this comparison shows, past a certain point, port velocity can drop, even though mass flow continues to increase.

The performance capability of a cylinder head is often related directly to the size of the valves. In this test the diameter of the intake valve was increased from 1.94 to 2.02 inches and the exhaust was increased from 1.5 to 1.6 inches. Note that both torque and horsepower were increased substantially. Not all heads respond as readily as the smallblock Chevy, but when power is the goal, larger valves help a lot.

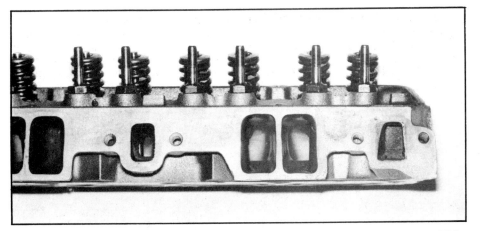

Note the top of this C&G econo port is wide and the bottom is narrow. This maintains good port velocity without any loss of maximum airflow, and will produce both economy and power.

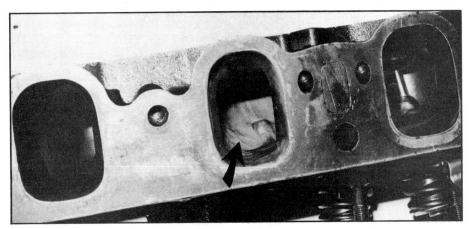

All big block heads have either big or small intake ports. This is an example of the small-port design. Although the term "big-port" generally denotes performance, the shrewd hot rodder can build a high-powered engine using these cylinder heads. Over 500hp is possible in street form, and the small ports will help part-throttle economy.

and right at, the valve seat. For maximum flow at high engine speeds the flow through the ports has quite a head of steam and it's hard to get this high velocity flow to "turn the corner" and enter the chamber smoothly. However, for a practicable street port, this area does not have to be reworked because we don't have to worry about the very high flow rates needed in racing heads. (This is fortunate because recontouring this area is difficult and expensive.)

It is also worth noting that the C&G econo-power port is rough ground, not polished. As it happens, a polished intake port looks pretty, but it does virtually nothing for power, and it can hurt economy. And, for the applications we are considering, the rough-ground finish does not hurt power.

By comparison with an as-cast stock intake port, a C&G trapezoidal econo-power port loses virtually nothing in fuel economy, but it gives an 8-10% power increase. Incidentally, these figures assume no change in the exhaust port; they are just the effect of changing the intake port. Reworking the exhaust raises the power increase to 12-15%.

POWER PORTS

When you are less concerned about economy and yearn for acceleration that threatens to hemorrhage your eyeballs, it is tempting to go for a set of super-trick, "humongous-port," high-buck heads. If this urge comes frequently, there's little we can do to help, but we will offer some cheap advice (cheap compared to what you'll pay for the heads). There is no point in buying a set of heads with ports built to work at .700-inch valve lift because you are not likely to use a cam with this much lift on the street (at least it seems unlikely but, of course, you may love

These are heads from a Ford Boss-Mustang engine. The gargantuan ports were designed to produce maximum high-rpm, wide-open throttle horsepower. It is difficult to get good part-throttle fuel economy from an engine having very large intake ports. The clay insert is a flow-test experiment to see if port volume can be reduced without significantly affecting the high-rpm flow properties of this port.

In contrast with the normal production heads, the ports on this Brownfield, aluminum, smallblock Chevy head are enormous. These racing heads have proven capable of developing very good power above 5000rpm. But, at low engine speeds they can be less effective than standard cast-iron heads.

replacing your valve springs every week).

Cylinder head science has become very sophisticated in recent years and many head porters can deliver heads with ports big enough to feed a Saturn Five rocket motor. When you have money almost anything is possible, but realize that there is a distinct cross-over between practical and impractical port work. It is relatively easy to modify most intake ports to produce enough flow to match a cam with as much as .550-inch valve lift. When you put a bigger cam in the engine and you demand more from the port, the amount of effort (and money) required to gain the added flow goes up like a lunar rocket.

Again, let's take a smallblock Chevy head as an example. To get better flow numbers, head porters will typically widen the port entry as much as possible. However, the pushrods pass through the head casting on either side of the port openings. This would normally limit the width of the port, but when flow is all-important they just

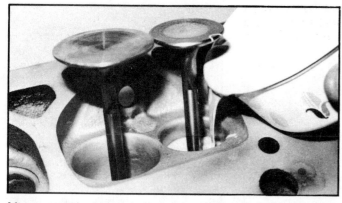

After a series of tests is completed, many head porters will make a silicone rubber mold of experimental ports and chambers to keep a permanent record of the size, shape and volume. This is often useful for future development and comparisons.

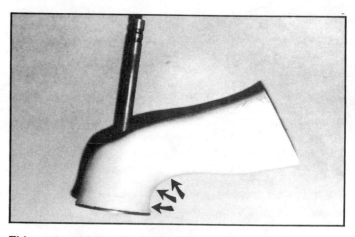

This port mold clearly shows all important surface contours. In nearly all ports, one of the most critical areas for maximum flow is the shape of the short-side radius (arrow).

move the pushrods over. Sounds simple, but you also have to redesign the rockerarms and almost everything else in the vicinity. After all of this work (and money) you have a port that gives only slightly increased flow at enormously high valve lifts, but it isn't going to do any good on a street engine.

Current Grand National stock-car Chevys deliver almost 600 horsepower at engine speeds near 8000 rpm without ports that require pushrod relocation. There is no reason why a street port should be any wider, even with the biggest cam and the best valve springs you can buy (high-lift cams can, and generally do, cause valve spring trouble).

INTAKE VALVE SIZE

Installing a larger intake valve (if there is enough space between the valves and between the valve and the chamber or cylinder wall to do so) is a good way to increase the power potential of the head. The point of putting in a bigger inlet valve is simple: a larger valve increases intake flow. There are, however, more than a few pitfalls for the unsuspecting hot-rodder to fall into when he attempts this modification.

The problem that is most often overlooked is that, on many vertical-valve engines, a larger intake valve can cause more valve shrouding (this problem occurs when the edge of the valve is near the combustion chamber wall and flow around the valve head is cut off by this restriction). Almost all vertical-valve engines have some valve shrouding and it almost always has a bad effect on intake flow at mid and high lift (though heads which have an open type of combustion chamber and more valve angle don't suffer from this problem as much as as those with less valve inclination).

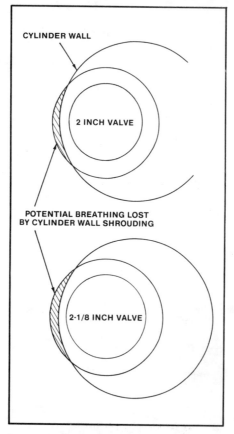

Increasing the valve size does not guarantee more flow. As the valves are made larger, the edge of the valves must come nearer to the chamber walls. (This is especially true on an engine with inline valves.) The resultant "valve shrouding" causes a portion of the valve area to become ineffective, and if the shape of the chamber creates a lot of shrouding with the bigger valve, the available breathing area will actually be reduced. The outer circle represents the minimum space required to prevent shrouding. Note how the small valve has less shrouding than the big valve. In our example the small valve loses 8.2% of the effective breathing area but the large valve loses 12.8%. As a result, even though there is more breathing area with the large valve, the shrouding offsets this advantage.

No matter if you are using stock or specially-made valves, a little time spent blending the back of the valve into the seat face is a cheap way to gain power.

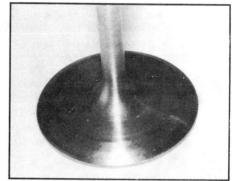

Cylinder heads on engines with pushrod-operated valves typically have a low approach angle to the chamber. In such cases, a valve with a relatively flat underhead area can improve both low- and high-lift airflow.

When a larger valve is installed it is often possible to grind the combustion chamber to give about the same clearance around the new valve as existed with the original valve. If the shrouding factor is not reduced to at least the original level, the larger intake valve may not flow any more air than the original one. Therefore the point of installing the larger valve is lost.

If a larger valve is installed successfully, i.e., it increases flow, the advantage is that it can give greater airflow at the lower lifts as well as possibly more flow at higher lifts. If low-lift flow can be increased, it achieves the same effect as a cam that opens the valve faster. However, a bigger valve does not increase the mechanical stress on the valvetrain, while a cam with a high flank-acceleration rate (it opens the valve more quickly) can greatly increase valvetrain stress and wear. Big valves and good low-lift flow are essential to the type of cam a power/economy engine should have, namely a cam with relatively short timing.

Generally, the proper installation of a larger intake valve into a stock port and chamber can increase power without any notable penalty in fuel consumption. Some heads, however, simply won't respond to a larger valve unless other complementary modifications are also undertaken, and developing a full "set" of modifications for a head can require a lot of time consuming flow-bench testing. A good example is the early Chevrolet performance head with 1.94-inch intake valves. The installation of larger Chevrolet 2.02-inch valves in nearly any of these heads, without any other changes, will reduce flow. It usually takes a considerable amount of grinding, both in the combustion chamber and in the port pocket, to regain the lost flow, and it's not just a question of grinding, but knowing where to grind and how much to grind.

EXHAUST PORTS

One of the easiest ways to throw away both power and economy is to have a restrictive exhaust system. By the word "system" we mean the total length of the exhaust tract, from the exhaust valve to the tip of the tailpipe. Any resistance to flow along this path reduces power and economy. Any back pressure in the system pushes down on the piston while it is coming up on the exhaust stroke. This downward pressure on the piston is negative work. It effectively subtracts from the power stroke. From any point of view, exhaust flow out of the engine must be as easy as possible.

This means the best exhaust port is the port that flows as much as possible.

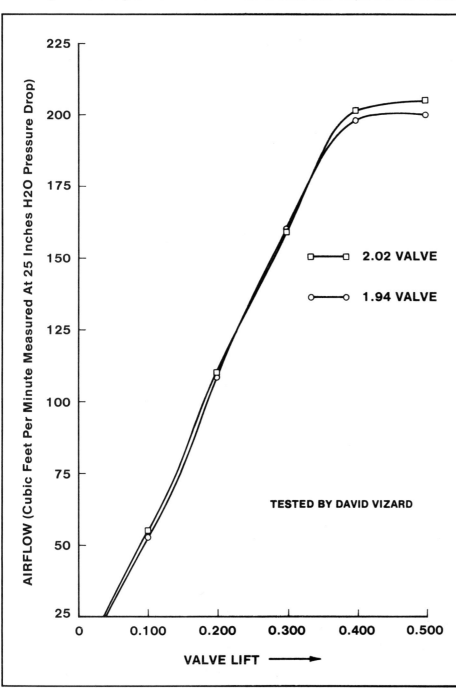

This is a flow comparison between 1.94- and 2.02-inch intake valves in a smallblock Chevrolet head. Apart from cutting the seat to suit the larger valve, no other changes were made. Note the minimal flow increase with the large valve, even though the valve area has increased 8.5%. Flow with a 2.02-inch valve can be improved beyond what is shown here but the chamber wall must be cut away to reduce the shrouding.

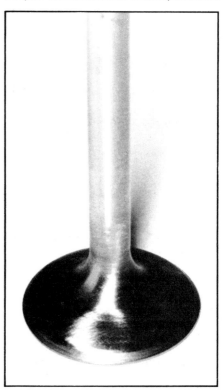

The shape of the exhaust valve is dictated by flow requirements and the fact that it absorbs a lot of heat from escaping combustion gases. As a result, most exhaust valves must have a relatively bulky head shape to maintain durability.

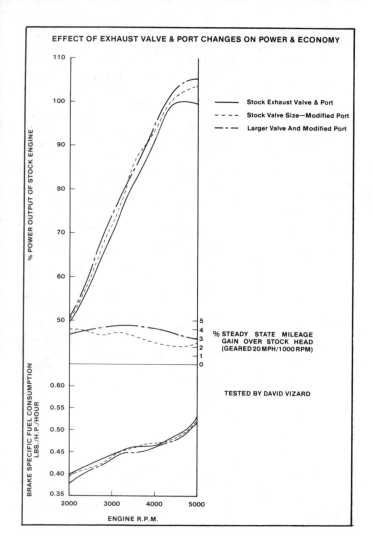

EFFECT OF EXHAUST VALVE & PORT CHANGES ON POWER & ECONOMY

— Stock Exhaust Valve & Port
--- Stock Valve Size—Modified Port
-·- Larger Valve And Modified Port

% STEADY STATE MILEAGE GAIN OVER STOCK HEAD (GEARED 20 MPH/1000 RPM)

TESTED BY DAVID VIZARD

% POWER OUTPUT OF STOCK ENGINE.

BRAKE SPECIFIC FUEL CONSUMPTION LBS./H.P./HOUR

ENGINE R.P.M.

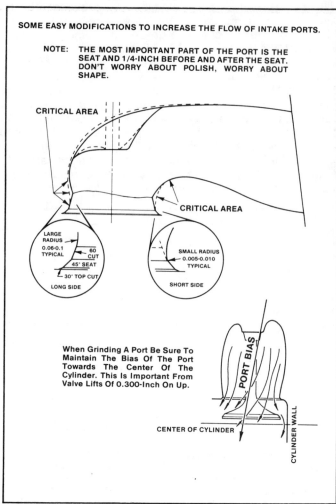

SOME EASY MODIFICATIONS TO INCREASE THE FLOW OF INTAKE PORTS.

NOTE: THE MOST IMPORTANT PART OF THE PORT IS THE SEAT AND 1/4-INCH BEFORE AND AFTER THE SEAT. DON'T WORRY ABOUT POLISH, WORRY ABOUT SHAPE.

CRITICAL AREA

CRITICAL AREA

LARGE RADIUS 0.06-0.1 TYPICAL
60 CUT
45° SEAT
30° TOP CUT
LONG SIDE

SMALL RADIUS 0.005-0.010 TYPICAL
SHORT SIDE

When Grinding A Port Be Sure To Maintain The Bias Of The Port Towards The Center Of The Cylinder. This Is Important From Valve Lifts Of 0.300-Inch On Up.

PORT BIAS

CENTER OF CYLINDER

CYLINDER WALL

We have included a graph that compares the effect on power, part-throttle economy and full-throttle economy of three different exhaust ports: stock, modified and modified with a big exhaust valve. *You will note that power is not affected quite as dramatically as a similar modification to the intake port, however, reworking the exhaust port does have a greater effect on economy than the intake port.*

FLOW BIAS

When developing heads for maximum power, the primary objective is maximum flow potential. This inevitably means using the largest valves that can be physically installed into the space available in the combustion chamber. A subsequent decision is just how much room should be allotted to the intake valve and how much to the exhaust. In other words, what's best: a very big intake and a small exhaust, both valves the same, or a bigger exhaust valve than intake?

Years of experimenting and experience have shown that, generally speaking, the exhaust valve needs to be about 75% of the size (or more precisely 75% of the flow) of the intake.

The big block Chevy responds well to exhaust work. The biggest increase is found by using the 1.88-inch exhaust valve, as opposed to the 1.72-inch valve used in the standard big block head. Additionally, increases can be gained by intelligent port contouring.

This rule applies when the combined valve sizes (the diameters) equal the total available space in the chamber, as would be the case when maximum power is the priority. If less-than-maximum valves are used, power is obviously not the overriding consideration, and the balance between intake and exhaust valve size is less critical.

When economy, not power, is the principal object, the exhaust valve size can be increased, even at the expense of intake size. As the exhaust valve is increased from the classical 0.75:1 ratio, mileage will improve. However,

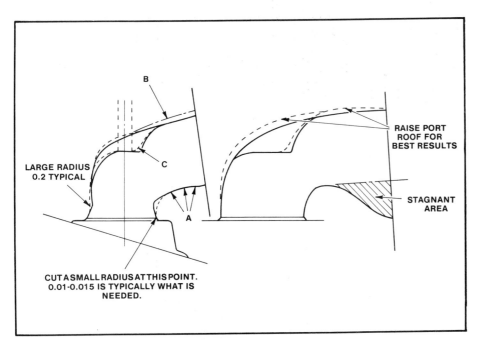

LARGE RADIUS
0.2 TYPICAL

B

C

A

RAISE PORT
ROOF FOR
BEST RESULTS

STAGNANT
AREA

CUT A SMALL RADIUS AT THIS POINT.
0.01-0.015 IS TYPICALLY WHAT IS
NEEDED.

In many respects, techniques similar to those used on the intake port can be applied to the exhaust port. The left drawing shows a typical smallblock Chevy port. Note how the long-side needs a large radius from the seat, but the short-side utilizes only a small radius. Cutting adjacent to the seat, in this fashion, helps flow in the low- and mid-lift ranges, without affecting the flow at higher lifts. Since a large change-of-direction is made on the short-side, it is very important to produce a smooth radius, just after the seat. On many heads with this general port shape, the area indicated by arrow A should not be touched, except to remove any large casting irregularities. Improper modification in this area can cause the flow to detach itself from the port floor. A general loss of port performance results. It is often beneficial to raise the port as indicated by line B, but this will only pay off when relatively high lift cams are used, i.e., 0.500-inch or more. In some instances, the gases spilling off the valveguide boss can also be critical. A good radius is required, as indicated by arrow C. Some exhaust ports, such as the 429-460 Ford in the right drawing, are very difficult to improve. There is such an acute turn on the port floor that a stagnant area is formed. Reworking the port in the stagnant area is a waste of time, as it won't help flow one iota. In such a case, it is best to lead the flow away from the floor and up toward the roof, by giving it additional area along the port roof, as indicated by the dotted lines.

as in all things, there's a limit. Although there may be exceptions, exhaust valves larger than about 90-95% of the diameter of the intake seem to produce very little extra fuel economy gain.

The simplest rule to follow here is: if power is your prime requirement, follow the normal 0.75:1 ratio; if economy is your prime requirement, install the largest exhaust valve consistent with the mechanical integrity of the head. (The location of the water jacket may limit how big the valve can be or removing metal from some areas to fit a large valve may lead to cracking problems.)

A good example of what can be done with the exhaust valve is the Chevy 186 head casting mentioned earlier. These heads are often fitted with a 1.94-inch intake valve and are usually equipped with a 1.5-inch exhaust valve. Convincing tests with this head have proven that leaving the intake stock but increasing the valve diameter to 1.6 inches helps power and economy.

COMBUSTION CHAMBERS

When selecting components for an economy/power engine, you may occasionally have to decide whether to use heads with open or closed combustion chambers. Basically, open combustion chambers were developed for two reasons. In the early- and mid-Sixties open combustion chambers were used on some engines in an

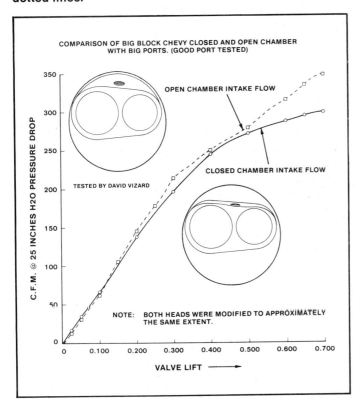

COMPARISON OF BIG BLOCK CHEVY CLOSED AND OPEN CHAMBER
WITH BIG PORTS. (GOOD PORT TESTED)

OPEN CHAMBER INTAKE FLOW

CLOSED CHAMBER INTAKE FLOW

TESTED BY DAVID VIZARD

C.F.M. @ 25 INCHES H2O PRESSURE DROP

NOTE: BOTH HEADS WERE MODIFIED TO APPROXIMATELY
THE SAME EXTENT.

VALVE LIFT

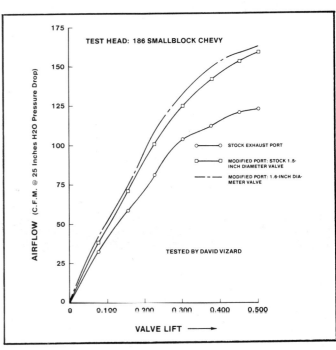

TEST HEAD: 186 SMALLBLOCK CHEVY

AIRFLOW (C.F.M. @ 25 Inches H2O Pressure Drop)

○──○ STOCK EXHAUST PORT

□──□ MODIFIED PORT: STOCK 1.5-
INCH DIAMETER VALVE

––– MODIFIED PORT: 1.6-INCH DIA-
METER VALVE

TESTED BY DAVID VIZARD

VALVE LIFT

Enlarging the exhaust valve from 1.5 to 1.6 inches, as shown here, can increase flow when the port is also suitably reworked. This can aid both power and economy.

This is the "closed-chamber," big block, Chevrolet head. Because of the compact configuration, this chamber works very well on engines employing cams with less than 0.550-inch lift.

This is a slightly different version of the closed-chamber, big block head. The area just above the spark plug is cut away to cause the mixture to swirl toward the plug as the piston approaches tdc.

CHAMBER MODIFICATIONS TO HELP FLOW OF INTAKE AND EXHAUST ON HEADS WITH CLOSED CHAMBERS WHICH SHROUD THE VALVES.

EDGE OF BORE

SECTION X-X

SECTION Y-Y

Relieving the areas that shroud the intake valve of a closed-chamber head can aid mid- and high-lift flow. However, without the aid of a flow bench it is impossible to determine how much relieving is necessary. Too much relief can cause cracking problems, compression loss and even flow loss. It is also essential not to cut back past the point where the cylinder-block wall joins the chamber (unless the cylinder-block wall is also relieved and testing proves this will increase power). The best policy is to be conservative, cut back no more than is shown here.

This 351 Ford head has an open combustion chamber, designed to meet emissions standards. Two side effects result. There is virtually no valve shrouding, a positive benefit. However, the chamber is so large that a long flame-front path is required. This makes the chamber prone to detonation problems.

effort to minimize valve shrouding. Later, as emission legislation tightened, it was found that open chambers tended to produce less emissions. This emission-type open chamber is usually recognizable by the fact that it has little or no quench area.

Even though the open chamber has been used on many performance-type engines, for normal street performance and economy, a closed-type chamber (one with valves generally parallel to the centerline of the cylinder and with a relatively large quench area) is entirely adequate. Admittedly a closed chamber can cause more high-lift valve shrouding, but if the chamber is carefully recontoured to eliminate shrouding (and sometimes it doesn't need very much grinding to do so), there will not be a problem, at least in the range of valve lift we would recommend on the street. Open-chamber heads that are used for racing tend to give minimum shrouding throughout a wide range of lift, often all the way to .700-inch, but a slightly modified closed chamber can usually produce comparable flow up to .550-inch. And, for street use it is not likely you will be using a cam with more lift than this (see camshaft chapter).

On the other hand, assuming we can obtain suitable flow from a closed-chamber head, it has some important advantages. This design has a compact combustion chamber and it allows a relatively high compression ratio (up to 9:1 or slightly more) in a street engine without the use of a high dome on the piston. High-domed pistons do not help flame travel and can often hinder combustion propagation, but they are used in racing engines because the loss of combustion efficiency is offset by the increased power created by extremely high

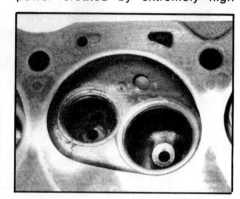

This 460 Ford head is a good compromise between open and closed design. The spark-plug side of the chamber wall slopes at an angle to minimize valve shrouding, yet there is sufficient quench area on the opposite side of the chamber to give good turbulence and quick burning.

compression (often in excess of 12.5:1 in some racing engines).

In a street-type combustion chamber efficiency is imperative and the very high compression used in a racing engine is not possible because of low-quality gasoline. *When fuel efficiency is the most important concern, a compact chamber with a flat-top or even a dished piston, is more effective than a large, open chamber with a big piston dome in it.*

COMPRESSION RATIO

The thermal efficiency and, subsequently, the fuel economy of an internal combustion engine is directly linked to the compression ratio. The higher the compression ratio is, the more fuel efficient it will be. This is one of the reasons diesel engines operate so efficiently. A typical diesel engine has a ratio of between 18: and 22:1. Also, a diesel engine is never throttled. In other words, it always has at least atmospheric pressure in the manifold, just like a spark-ignition engine at wide-open throttle. The power output

of a diesel engine is regulated by the amount of diesel fuel injected into the cylinder. This means that even at low power settings, the diesel engine is compressing a well-packed cylinder of air. When a spark-ignition engine is throttled, the effective compression ratio is reduced and, as a result, the efficiency with which the engine converts fuel into useful mechanical energy is also reduced.

High ratios are conducive not only to extra economy but also extra power. In the compression ratio graph we show how much extra full-throttle power is available as the ratio is raised. You will note that in the higher ranges, as the ratio goes up, there is less

Here we have two identical chambers fitted with valves of different sizes. Note the large valve comes much closer to the combustion-chamber wall, creating valve shrouding and flow restriction at this point. In the example here, the shrouding is so severe that the large valve will flow less than the smaller valve.

This chart indicates the power and torque increase given by a higher compression ratio. Locate the existing ratio along the right-hand edge of the chart. Select the new ratio along the left-hand edge. The number in the square where the two columns intersect is the percentage increase to be expected. For example, if the original ratio is 9.0:1 and we are thinking of raising the ratio to 12.0:1, how much power will be gained? To determine this, follow the 9.0:1 column up from the right side of the chart (indicated by arrow A) and follow the 12.0:1 column up from the left (indicated by arrow B). The answer in this case is 4.5%. (This chart is based on a street engine with a relatively short cam duration, the gain will be slightly more if the cam duration is longer.) Part-throttle economy will also increase if the compression is raised. The mileage gains (percentage) will be about double the indicated power increase.

Removing about .80-inch of material from the chamber wall, as shown here, is often worth a substantial increase in airflow in the mid and upper valve-lift ranges. However, this will also increase chamber volume and reduce compression.

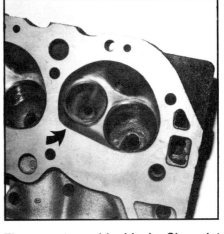

The open-type, big block, Chevrolet combustion chamber needs very little work to produce an efficient shape. The full extent of what reasonably can be done is shown here. The chamber has been cut back (arrow) to relieve exhaust shrouding.

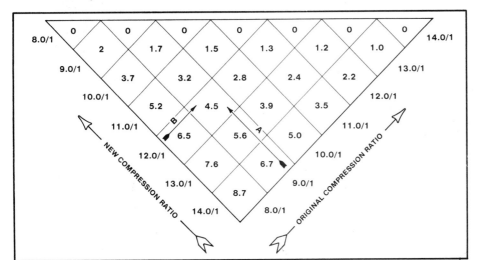

The intake flow of the closed-chamber, big block Chevrolet head can be improved by cutting .90-.125-inch from the area indicated to reduce shrouding of the intake valve. This should not produce an unacceptable loss of compression in a street engine.

corresponding power gain. This means that going up from 8:1 to 9:1 nets a far greater increase than going from 11:1 to 12:1.

The gains shown are very typical for engines using relatively short duration cams. As cam timing is increased (a cam with more duration is used) the gains become even greater than those shown in the chart. This is because the chart is based on mechanical compression ratios, i.e., compression ratios as measured by computation from determined volumes, and not on dynamic ratios.

In the real world, the effective filling of the cylinder is reduced by fluid/gas dynamics. At high engine speeds, as the piston reaches the end of the intake stroke and comes up on the compression stroke, the valve is still open. With a long-duration cam the valve may, in fact, be open for quite some time as the piston moves upward. During this time some of the mixture can be pushed back past the intake valve, into the intake port. As a consequence, instead of having a theoretical 500cc volume of induced mixture in each cylinder, there may only be 400cc. And, when the piston moves up on compression, it "squeezes" less mixture volume. The result is less "dynamic" compression. If a cam with a long intake duration is used, a higher mechanical compression ratio is helpful to compensate for the dynamic losses.

This is a two-edged sword. There is a limit to how much duration can be reasonably used. At high engine speeds, long duration and high compression work fine, but most street driving is at relatively low speeds. This is where long duration hurts. It's again a matter of mechanical and physical limitations. If you grind a cam with long duration, of necessity the overlap period will also be relatively long. At high speeds the overlap period consumes a "shorter" amount of time during each cycle and everything is fine. But, at low speeds the relative overlap time is longer, and during this time when both the intake and the exhaust valves are open, induction mixture can enter the chamber, blow right across and out the exhaust along with the waste gases escaping in the exhaust stroke. Result: terrible economy.

So there is an upper limit to compression ratio and cam timing but a street engine normally operates in more modest speed ranges. Of greater significance than the increase in power and mileage at full throttle is the potential increase in economy at part

throttle. By raising the ratio from 8:1 to 11 or 11.5:1, it is possible to increase mileage by 20% and, in some instances, even more.

High compression, of course, requires high-octane fuels, and it's an unfortunate fact of life these days that fuel octane available at the service station pump is constantly going down. This may seem to be a move in the wrong direction, in view of the fact that high compression gives increased economy. However, from an overall fuel consumption standpoint, it has been established that more miles can be derived from a barrel of crude oil if that barrel is distilled into 87-octane fuel. It requires more crude oil to distill 95-octane fuel than it takes to distill an equivalent amount of 87-octane fuel. However, here again, we're caught in a balancing act. If the fuel octane is dropped much below 87, the compression ratio of the average engine would have to be dropped so low that overall engine efficiency would be decreased dramatically, and the average fuel consumption per barrel would increase.

More compression means more power and economy, but because the current octane rating of pump gasoline is so low it is not advisable to use high-compression pistons in a street engine unless you have made other provisions to prevent detonation, e.g., water injection. If you want to use a forged-type, high-compression piston it is usually possible to machine the dome lower to reduce compression.

From our point of view, there are many ways around the problem of the incompatibility of low-octane fuel with high compression. (Some of these solutions are discussed in chapters 12 and 15). If you are building an engine from scratch and are willing to spend some time and effort to engineer a coordinated performance and economy package, you can gain tremendous benefits from higher compression. In some cases ratios as high as 11:1 have been used successfully with 87-octane fuel, but this requires a careful coordination of camshaft

design and a dedicated water-injection system.

If you opt for a completely engineered high-economy and high-performance engine built from scratch, one of the easiest ways to raise compression is with traditional high-compression pistons. However, it should be stated here and now that pistons with a very high dome should be avoided. If the desired ratio cannot be achieved by a modest increase in the piston dome height, the cylinder heads can be milled as necessary to reduce the combustion chamber volume.

If you just intend to rework a set of heads to go on an already existing short block assembly, the cost of milling the heads to increase the ratio represents one of the cheapest means of adding mileage and power. But, you must realize that you can't just pump the ratio to the moon without considering all of the other engine systems.

THERMAL COATINGS

The idea of burning fuel in the presence of air inside the combustion space of an engine is to develop heat to expand that air and force the piston down the bore. If heat is conducted away from the combustion process, potential power is effectively lost. The ideal situation exists when all of the heat goes into expanding the air, and none is lost through the combustion chamber, piston, cylinder wall, or anything else. Under these conditions, our engine would have maximum thermal efficiency. As a practical matter, it's not possible to obtain total thermal efficiency; but the better it is, the better our economy and performance will be.

In this respect, cast-iron heads are better than aluminum heads. Aluminum has higher thermal conductivity, therefore, there will be greater heat loss to the water jacket if the head is

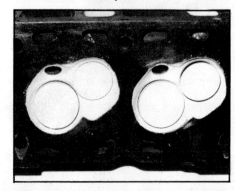

The chamber of this head has been welded and coated with a ceramic, thermal-barrier coating. This results in more power and less heat-rejection to the coolant and oil.

aluminum. For economy purposes, cast-iron heads will be better, and if we can even reduce heat loss further, it will be even more to our advantage.

A recent development in the auto industry is the use of special, high-temperature, insulation coatings. These coatings, with as little thickness as .015-inch, can cause a dramatic reduction in thermal conductivity. Currently they are still in an experimental state but it seems possible that thermal-insulation coating could become common in the future.

The amount of gain from thermal-barrier coating depends on the material from which the head is made (there is less gain with iron heads because of the low conductivity of iron) but recent tests with racing engines show that gains with aluminum heads are measurable. Depending upon the design of the head and the size of the chamber, it would seem that power gains in the region of 3% are relatively common. Likewise, gains in fuel economy at full throttle are also in the region of 3%, but it is surmised that such gains would be greater under part-throttle conditions.

Presently, because these coatings are relatively costly, they are used largely on racing engines. For a street engine it's still not entirely practical, but if a suitable coating would become widely available it could provide increased economy and performance at, hopefully, a reasonable price.

We should also point out that a thermal barrier of some sort can be beneficial to the valves. First of all, it isn't commonly realized that the intake charge picks up a great deal of heat as it moves past the hot intake valve. Most valve-related heat problems are associated with the exhaust valve (the hot combustion residue is constantly heating the relatively small exhaust valve as the exhaust stroke clears the chamber), but the intake valve also creates a heat problem because it communicates heat directly to the intake charge. By coating the front face of the intake valve, the temperature on the back side of the intake valve is dramatically reduced.

A thermal coating can, obviously, also be helpful for the exhaust valve. One of the factors that dictates the width of the exhaust seat is the amount of heat the exhaust valve picks up during operation. Most of this heat is conducted into the head when the valve is resting on the seat. If exhaust seats are too narrow, the exhaust valve simply fails to dissipate sufficient heat to keep it healthy. The result is that the exhaust valve "burns out." By coating the front face of the exhaust valve, much of the heat of combustion is prevented from reaching the valve and there is less heat to dissipate through the seat. If the backside of the exhaust valve is coated (with the exception of the seat and the area that goes into the valveguide), the heat picked up by the valve is reduced even further. This allows valve seats with a narrower profile to be used and generally leads to more exhaust flow.

COMBUSTION CHAMBER FINISH

If coating the combustion chamber is out of the question, the next best

If you are determined to polish your cylinder heads to a glossy finish, the combustion chamber is one area where it will do some good. Polishing cuts down the surface area of the combustion chamber and reduces heat loss to the water jacket.

The smallblock Chevy combustion chamber has been through many phases of development, and many subtle improvements have been implemented over the years. Prior to the introduction of the late, low-compression emissions-type head, the chamber shown here was considered one of the best for economy and power This chamber is a conventional quench-type chamber and note that the edges of the valve (indicated by the seat locations) are not excessively shrouded by the side walls. Some chamber shapes from other performance-oriented smallblock heads may have more pure performance potential when used with a high-compression piston that has a tall popup, but none significantly produce a better balance between low-rpm torque and high-rpm power (within limits). For most performance-with-economy applications this chamber would not have to be significantly modified to produce excellent all-around results.

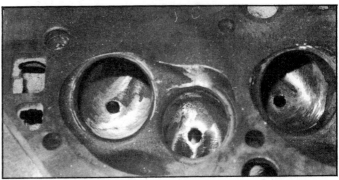

These ports and chambers may not look flashy, but remember, it's shape that counts. Despite the rough surface finish, subsequent dyno testing proved the modifications to be very effective.

This Brownfield, aluminum, small-block, Chevy head is a highly respected and expensive racing cylinder head, but note that the manufacturer has not bothered with a superfluous surface finish. The port is smooth, not polished, but careful attention has been paid to producing the best port and chamber shape.

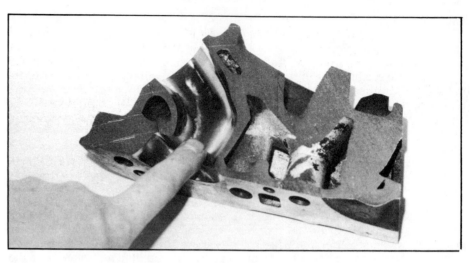

This is a cross-section of the most efficient smallblock Chevy exhaust port the author has tested (to date). The critical areas for max flow are the side of the port, adjacent to the cylinder wall (indicated), and all along the short-side (floor) radius, from the seat to the manifold face.

thing is to polish the chamber surface. This also causes a reduction in the heat loss because it reduces the surface area of the chamber. It also reduces the tendency of the chamber to collect deposits that might cause detonation. In this day of low-grade fuel, this alone is an important factor.

GRINDING YOUR OWN HEADS

Buying professionally modified cylinder heads is an expensive deal and, no doubt, you've noted that we have often made reference to do-it-yourself modifications. By now you're wondering how difficult the job is. If you have average mechanical skill, a high-speed hand grinder, like the popular Do-More grinder, and a few grinding stones, or better yet some carbide cutters, reworking your own heads is

an entirely feasible weekend project.

You're certainly not going to blow Bill Jenkins or Junior Johnson into the weeds, but you can make worthwhile gains in airflow just by cleaning and smoothing the ports to the stock form. Our illustrations also show what areas are critical to flow and how to shape these areas to gain benefits without getting into a monster metal removal program. Porting is at best a very difficult job that requires a lot of study and testing, so don't try to dramatically change the port contours. The only rule to really remember is that shape counts, not polish. Don't worry about the fact that the grindstone you are using produces a fairly coarse finish. Just make sure that you produce the right shape.

As an aside, we would like to mention another possibility to consider if you are looking for absolutely

maximum street power and your budget is limited. (Remember, the primary purpose of this book is economy and our definition of economy includes saving every dollar you can.) If you have a smallblock Chevy and don't mind grinding your own heads, you might consider the "pre-machined" heads available from Airflow Resarch.

These are high-performance 292 Chevy castings with ports that have been rough machined on an automatic milling machine. This saves you the preliminary hard work of removing vast quantities of metal but this doesn't mean the heads are ready to go on an engine. The machined surface is a good guide to show what the final contours should be, and with about one hour of finish grinding with a carbide cutter, you can finish a pair of intake and exhaust ports and one combustion chamber. This means with

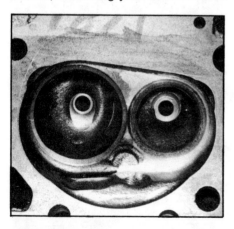

This "pre-machined" smallblock Chevy head (casting #340292) is available from Airflow Research (see Appendix). These heads are machined on a computer-controlled mill to allow the production of rough-finished, moderately-priced high-performance heads.

After approximately one hour of additional work with a carbide cutter and a high-speed air tool, the pre-machined Airflow Research rough port is easily transformed into a high-flow port. Flow bench figures show impressive results, especially considering the minimal amount of work involved.

This is another view of the Airflow Research pre-machined heads. The port on the left is as-delivered, pre-machined, the port on the right has been hand finished and is ready to run.

This cutaway of a Chevy #340292 off-road head casting shows the handiwork of a top-quality head porter at his best. (This casting number is not the same as the Chevy part number, many specific versions of this casting are available under different part numbers and they are commonly called "turbo" heads.)

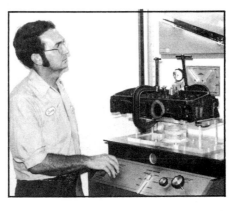

Denny Wyckoff of Motor Machine & Supply in Tucson, Arizona, (and lecturer on high-performance engines and related subjects at Pima College) has done extensive flow-bench testing on Ford 429-460 heads. Subsequent road testing has confirmed that much can be gained from simple modifications to these heads.

smallblock head, but at part-throttle they are likely to be slightly less economical. This would, however, vary according to how well the carb prepared the mixture. If good atomization is achieved, these heads can be as efficient as any other Chevy head, with or without head crossover. If the carb is excessively rich, the combination of large fuel droplets, no manifold heat and big ports can cause these heads to be gas guzzlers. On the other side of the coin, these heads have about the best stock port contours of any small-block head and, as far as pure power goes, they are worth a bunch.

EXPECTED RESULTS

So far we have looked at many aspects of head design and preparation. Just to keep all these many factors in perspective, a summary of what has been discussed may prove worthwhile.

We can say that the potential gain in power is far greater than any potential loss in economy. This, of course, assumes the heads are sensibly prepared and the pitfalls of excessively large ports, etc., are avoided. On the other hand, if cylinder heads are prepared exclusively for economy, we are only talking about small gains but the amount of gain depends on how good or bad the original head was and just how good the final prep work is.

Generally, if the head is of a normal pushrod-operated, overhead-valve configuration and provides fairly average flow in stock condition, a well-coordinated rework is likely to give fuel economy gains of about 5%. If this head was capable of good performance in stock form, the same rework could also give a performance gain of about 5-7%. On the other hand, a cylinder head that had been reworked to give maximum power for a street machine could give up to 15% more power, and in some cases even more than this. However, this strong bias toward performance will probably decrease fuel economy by as much as 2-3%, though it could be more if the modifications are not carefully considered.

On a cylinder head designed specifically to give power and economy equal consideration, we find that the potential loss in economy due to reworking the intake port is often offset by the increased flow efficiency of a well worked out exhaust port. For instance, the C&G Porting econo-power head is capable of giving a substantial increase in power, plus a gain in fuel economy.

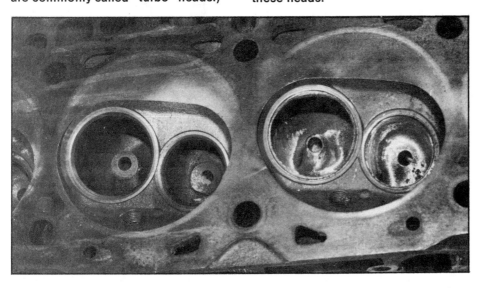

The intake port of this MM&S-reworked 460 Ford head is modified from the guide-boss area to the seat. From the boss out to the intake-manifold flange the port is deliberately left rough. In this particular instance the modifications accounted for about a 5% increase in intake flow.

The exhaust of the MM&S head is reworked in a much more extensive fashion. Thorough reshaping of the entire port is required to maximize flow. All work is done on a flow bench and along with the flow increase, both power and extra economy were improved.

about eight hours of work you can have a set of heads that flow about as much as a $600 custom porting job. Of course, the pre-machined heads will cost more than a set of stock heads, but you can still save about 2/3 of the price of a completely finished set of custom heads.

While we are on the subject of 292 Chevy heads (often called turbo heads), it should be pointed out that they were designed strictly for competition applications and can present some problems in street engines. They do not have an exhaust heat crossover passage. As a result, you will have to warm the engine longer before normal operation and you will have to adjust the choke to stay engaged longer. During full-throttle conditions they are about as fuel efficient as any other

CHAPTER  6 HEADERS

- HEADERS EXPLAINED
- MAKING THE RIGHT CHOICE
- A.R. HEADER MAGIC

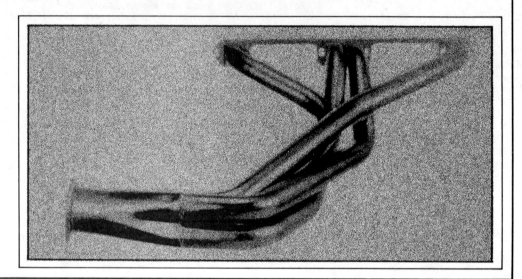

HEADERS

Virtually any properly designed tube header is better than the stock cast-iron exhaust manifold found on most engines. The reason is simple: a tube header allows the engine to more easily exhaust, or "breathe out," spent combustion gases. If the exhaust is restrictive, the piston has to use energy to expel the exhaust. Pushing the exhaust out in such a manner uses energy that was developed on the power stroke. This not only costs power but also mileage.

Just how much improvement a header provides depends on the rpm range and the throttle opening of the engine. If the engine is operating at very low crank speeds, a cast-iron manifold does a fairly adequate job, but in the mid-range and especially in the higher rpm ranges, a tube header is much more efficient.

A cast-iron manifold is not efficient at any but the lowest speeds because of the basic way it is designed. Nearly all stock manifolds have extremely short runners that join into a small common chamber. This design is simple, compact, durable and inexpensive to produce, but it is not dynamically efficient. Exhaust gases expelled from

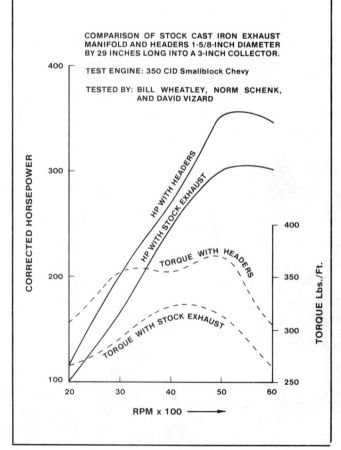

COMPARISON OF STOCK CAST IRON EXHAUST MANIFOLD AND HEADERS 1-5/8-INCH DIAMETER BY 29 INCHES LONG INTO A 3-INCH COLLECTOR.

TEST ENGINE: 350 CID Smallblock Chevy

TESTED BY: BILL WHEATLEY, NORM SCHENK, AND DAVID VIZARD

CORRECTED HORSEPOWER

HP WITH HEADERS

HP WITH STOCK EXHAUST

TORQUE WITH HEADERS

TORQUE WITH STOCK EXHAUST

TORQUE Lbs./Ft.

RPM x 100 ⟶

This graph shows the effect of adding conventional tube headers to an engine. The effect will vary, depending upon specific conditions and modifications. For instance, the engine used in this test was a "strong" street 350 Chevy, which responded particularly well. A stock, two-barrel, engine with less breathing potential may only gain 10-15hp.

54

Headers are one of the very best power investments. These dyno headers produced a gain of 50hp on this streetable 350-inch smallblock Chevy.

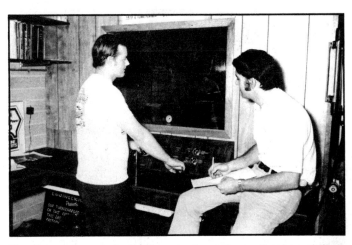

Dynamometers only produce test numbers. It takes skilled engineers to interpret these numbers. Bill Wheatley and Norm Schenck of Internal Combustion Engineering have spent many years doing research for various speed-equipment companies, and they believe that understanding what happens inside a header is one of the most complex areas of modern performance-engine design.

each cylinder enter the common chamber where they create pressure pulses and dynamic turbulence. By effectively isolating and extending the length of the individual exhaust ports in the heads, a tube-type exhaust header controls this pressure and turbulence, and uses the energy in the exhaust gases to assist engine efficiency.

WHY HEADERS?

An exhaust header is but one part of the "respiratory tract" of an engine. It must, therefore, work in conjuction with the other components that are involved in engine breathing. The command center of all engine "breath control" is the camshaft and the effect of an exhaust header is directly tied to the cam.

Even if you are not an expert on cam technology, you may be aware that cam design is based on the Otto four-stroke cycle. (Almost all modern automotive piston-combustion engine operation is based on Otto's development in 1876 of a working four-stroke

piston engine.) In the classical Otto four-stroke cycle of operation it is assumed that the intake valve opens when the piston is at top dead center (tdc). This represents the beginning of the intake stroke. When the piston reaches bottom dead center (bdc) the intake valve closes and the intake stroke ends. At this point, both valves are closed and the compression stroke starts as the piston moves upward. At the end of the compression stroke the mixture is ignited. The burning mixture expands, creating pressure in the cylinder and pushes the piston down on the power stroke. When the piston reaches the bottom of the power stroke, the exhaust valve opens, and as the piston moves upward again, the exhaust gases are expelled during the exhaust stroke. When the exhaust valve closes and the piston reaches tdc, the intake valve then opens and the series of events repeats.

In this simplistic example, the valves open and close at top- and bottom-dead center. However, as the speed of the crank (rpm) and the speed

of the piston increase, the control of gas flow in and out of the engine becomes more difficult. When the intake valve opens, it takes a brief moment before the mixture of air and fuel in the manifold begins moving into the cylinder. As engine speed builds, this delay becomes a problem. There are more piston strokes per minute and there is less relative time for each stroke to occur. If there is any delay in the induction entry, considerably less mixture is delivered to the cylinder. And, with less intake mixture to burn, less power is produced.

Engine designers quickly learned that they could "cheat" with the valve timing. By opening the intake valve a little before the piston actually comes to tdc and closing it a little after bdc, there is more time for the mixture to enter the cylinder, and there is a notable increase in power output. They can similarly extend the exhaust timing: opening the exhaust valve a little before bdc, to help start moving the exhaust gas out of the cylinder; and closing it a little after tdc, to give the gas some extra time to depart at

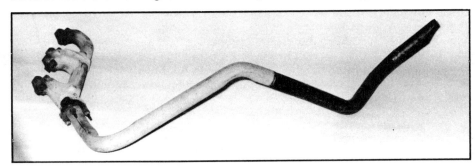

At a preset exhaust-valve lift, each exhaust port of a smallblock Chevy head flowed 69.8cfm (at 25 inches pressure drop). When the stock cast-iron manifold was installed, the flow through the port and manifold dropped to 55cfm. But, changing to...

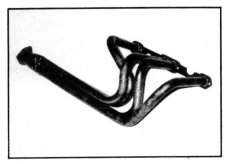

...tube-type headers raised the flow to 60cfm with 1.5-inch diameter headers, 65cfm with a 1.625-inch header and 67cfm with a 1.75-inch header.

the end of the stroke.

Extending the valve timing is helpful but it is a delicate balancing act. Holding the valve open at the end of the intake stroke is possible because, even though the crankshaft rotates through several degrees at the bottom of the stroke, the piston does not move up or down in the cylinder very much. At the same time, the incoming mixture has gained a lot of inertia, and every little bit longer the valve is open lets considerably more mixture enter the cylinder.

This is especially helpful at very high engine speeds, but you can overdo it. If the intake is held open too long, the pressure of compression will build up and push intake mixture backward, into the manifold. The resulting back-pressure pulse causes many problems in the induction.

A similar circumstance is created during the exhaust opening. The exhaust valve is opened before the piston reaches bdc to let the "blow-down" effect boost exhaust initiation. Just before the valve opens, the pressure created in the cylinder by combustion is still high (though it is a lot less than the peak pressure, which occurs when the piston is much closer to the top of the cylinder). When the valve leaves the seat early, this residual pressure causes the exhaust gases to "burst" past the valve into the low-pressure area inside the exhaust

When tube headers are installed in place of conventional cast-iron headers, the carb calibration may be affected. Unless a very significant breathing improvement has been made, the carb change will be small. However, AR-type headers will effect carb calibration and if best performance and mileage is to be achieved, the carb must be recalibrated.

port and exhaust manifold. This gets the exhaust moving out of the cylinder quickly and as the piston moves up the bore, there is less exhaust for it to mechanically push out of the cylinder.

However, there is again a limit. If the valve opens too early, the blow-down effect may clip some of the expanding pressure that could be used to provide power.

By carefully extending the valve events we achieve better intake efficiency at the end of the intake stroke and better exhaust efficiency at the beginning of the exhaust stroke, but it's at the other ends of the intake and exhaust cycles that things really get complicated. If the valve events are delayed, there is a period of time during the changeover from exhaust to intake when both the exhaust and the intake valve are open. This period is called overlap.

A short overlap period, such as is found on short-duration cams designed to operate at very low engine speeds, is not a problem. However, as we try to gain more power, we must push the rpm range upward (power is always a function of engine speed), and the cam must, accordingly, have increased valve-open duration and increased overlap. But, the penalty that is paid for increased overlap is decreased low-rpm torque.

When the cam timing gets very long, as in racing cams, the engine may not even operate at wide-open throttle below 4000 rpm. There is so much overlap between the end of the exhaust cycle and the beginning of the intake cycle that the exhaust gases can become confused. At low rpm the piston is trying to push the residual combustion gases out of the cylinder, and if there is resistance or back-pressure in the exhaust and the intake is opened early, this gas looks for someplace else to go. Since there is a relatively lower pressure area behind the intake valve, it may just decide to escape into the intake manifold, instead of heading out the exhaust port. This occurrence causes more than a little trouble. It impedes the flow of incoming mixture, dilutes the intake mixture and, if the intake manifold has short runners and an open plenum, it can create disruptive turbulence throughout the manifold.

At high rpm a very early intake opening and a lot of overlap can cause another kind of trouble. If the exhaust system is working well, an opposite effect may occur. There may be so much flow energy created out the exhaust that when the intake opens, the initial bit of mixture is "yanked" into

the cylinder and flows right across the chamber and out the exhaust port. This wastes fuel (guess what it does to economy) and may even create heat problems as it ignites and burns in the exhaust system.

This all sounds rather complicated but, in actual fact, things are not that bad. For economy and power on the street, we need to select a cam with a very reasonable amount of duration and overlap. This enhances the mid-range performance and eliminates nearly all of the strange dynamics associated with a long-duration, high-overlap cam. And, to get to the subject at hand, we need to select headers that will coordinate with this cam.

Tube headers do more than just separate the outgoing exhaust pulses. There is a physical property of gas dynamics that gives us an additional benefit. When the exhaust valve opens and the escaping gases "burst" into the tube, a high-speed wave or pulse of pressure is created. This pulse moves down the pipe toward the collector. As it leaves the end of the pipe and enters the low-pressure area inside of the collector, it "pops" or expands suddenly, and immediately a low-pressure pulse is created at this end of the tube. This reverse pulse travels back up the tube toward the exhaust valve.

These pulses resonate back and forth in the tube at speeds of several hundred feet per minute, and if the pipe is longer or shorter, the pulses reach the ends at different frequencies. By calculating the speed of the pulses and the length of the pipe it is possible to match the frequency of the pulses to the speed of the engine. In this way we can time the low-pressure reverse pulse to arrive at the back of the exhaust valve just as the valve opens. As you may guess, with a low pressure behind the valve as it opens, the exhaust gases are given an additional boost out of the cylinder. This is called "resonant tuning," and is an important part of header design.

As good as it sounds, there is a catch. The length of the tuned pipe, in header design it is called the primary pipe, is cut to a predetermined length and cannot be varied as engine speeds increase or decrease. Therefore, the resonant tuning occurs only within a narrow engine speed range. In other words, if the primary pipe is relatively short, the resonant effect occurs in the upper speed ranges; if it is relatively long, the effect occurs in the lower speed ranges.

This is an extremely simplified description of header design, but we'll forego a deeper discussion and get to

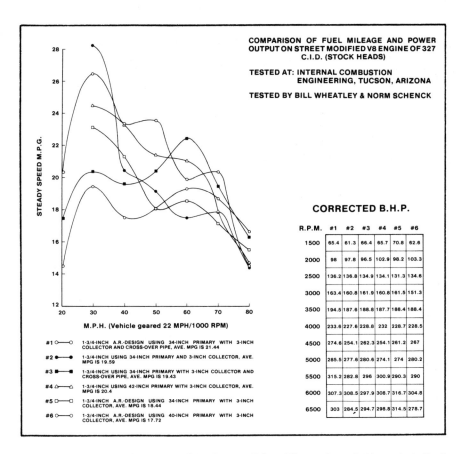

COMPARISON OF FUEL MILEAGE AND POWER OUTPUT ON STREET MODIFIED V8 ENGINE OF 327 C.I.D. (STOCK HEADS)

TESTED AT: INTERNAL COMBUSTION ENGINEERING, TUCSON, ARIZONA

TESTED BY BILL WHEATLEY & NORM SCHENCK

#1 ○—○ 1-3/4-INCH A.R.-DESIGN USING 34-INCH PRIMARY WITH 3-INCH COLLECTOR AND CROSS-OVER PIPE. AVE. MPG IS 21.44

#2 ●—● 1-3/4-INCH USING 34-INCH PRIMARY AND 3-INCH COLLECTOR. AVE. MPG IS 19.59

#3 ■—■ 1-3/4-INCH USING 34-INCH PRIMARY WITH 3-INCH COLLECTOR AND CROSS-OVER PIPE. AVE. MPG IS 19.43

#4 △—△ 1-3/4-INCH USING 42-INCH PRIMARY WITH 3-INCH COLLECTOR. AVE. MPG IS 20.4

#5 □—□ 1-3/4-INCH A.R.-DESIGN USING 34-INCH PRIMARY WITH 3-INCH COLLECTOR. AVE. MPG IS 18.44

#6 ○—○ 1-3/4-INCH A.R.-DESIGN USING 40-INCH PRIMARY WITH 3-INCH COLLECTOR. AVE. MPG IS 17.72

CORRECTED B.H.P.

R.P.M.	#1	#2	#3	#4	#5	#6
1500	65.4	61.3	66.4	65.7	70.8	62.6
2000	98	97.8	96.5	102.9	98.2	103.3
2500	136.2	136.8	134.9	134.1	131.3	134.6
3000	163.4	160.8	161.9	160.8	161.5	151.3
3500	194.5	187.6	188.8	187.7	188.4	188.4
4000	233.6	227.6	228.8	232	228.7	228.5
4500	274.6	254.1	262.3	254.1	261.2	267
5000	285.5	277.6	280.6	274.1	274	280.2
5500	315.2	282.8	296	300.9	290.3	290
6000	307.3	308.5	297.9	308.7	316.7	304.8
6500	303	284.5	294.7	298.8	314.5	278.7

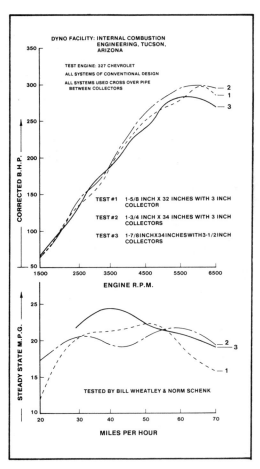

DYNO FACILITY: INTERNAL COMBUSTION ENGINEERING, TUCSON, ARIZONA

TEST ENGINE: 327 CHEVROLET
ALL SYSTEMS OF CONVENTIONAL DESIGN
ALL SYSTEMS USED CROSS OVER PIPE BETWEEN COLLECTORS

TEST #1 1-5/8 INCH X 32 INCHES WITH 3 INCH COLLECTOR

TEST #2 1-3/4 INCH X 34 INCHES WITH 3 INCH COLLECTORS

TEST #3 1-7/8 INCH X 34 INCHES WITH 3-1/2 INCH COLLECTORS

TESTED BY BILL WHEATLEY & NORM SCHENK

This displays some important header qualities. The main point to note is that A.R. headers and a crossover pipe produce the best power curve and mileage. An A.R. header *without* the crossover produced the worst mileage. A comparison of conventional headers with and without a crossover pipe (tests #2 and #3) produced very similar average mileage figures, but either produced less power than the A.R. with crossover. The engine used for these tests had stock heads. In such a case, the A.R. headers do not produce dramatic low-rpm gains. Another factor of interest is that A.R. header primary pipes do not have to be as long as conventional headers.

some practical information. *For high-rpm efficiency the header should have a large-diameter, relatively short primary with a large-diameter collector. For low-rpm efficiency it should have small-diameter, relatively long primary pipes with a small-diameter collector.*

It is always dangerous to make sweeping generalizations, but to get some baseline numbers we will give some distinct, but very general, recommendations for economy with power. These are, of course, based on the assumption that you have a suitable economy cam (see camshaft chapter). If you have an engine displacing 300-350 cubic inches and a cam that provides an imposed engine-speed limit of about 5000 rpm, select a header with 1.75-inch diameter, 30- to 36-inch long primaries. For smaller engines select a header with 1 5/8-inch diameter primaries, also 30-36 inches long. For a larger engine look for a design with a primary diameter of 1-7/8 inches, again with a 30- to 36-inch length.

We assume that you will be using these headers with a conventional exhaust system and, therefore, the size of the collector becomes somewhat immaterial. (There is a secondary resonant effect at the open end of the collector, but if the end of the collector feeds into a closed exhaust pipe, as would be the case on a street-driven vehicle, this effect is suppressed.) However, the rest of the system will be important and must be coordinated with the headers (see exhaust system chapter for recommendations).

SOME NUMBERS

How headers will affect the power and economy is going to vary substantially from one engine to the next. As far as power is concerned, it can be stated quite categorically that the more advanced the engine specifications are (several well coordinated components and modifications have been used to gain maximum efficiency), the more power the headers will give. If you have an engine that has a short-duration cam, a set of restric-

As demonstrated here, what is best for power isn't necessarily also best for steady-speed mileage. The 1-7/8-inch headers generally produced better mileage but the 1-3/4-inch headers produced the best power. This may seem contrary to the popular belief that small headers produce better economy. But as usual, there is more to the story than initially meets the eye. Notice the mileage curve for the 1-7/8-inch headers doesn't begin until 30mph. During testing on the dyno the engine would not hold a steady load (in high gear) below this speed, indicating the engine had lost low-speed "flexibility." This would require the driver to downshift at a higher wheel speed (increasing engine speed and reducing low-speed economy). Therefore, during normal around-town traffic conditions a smaller header would probably produce better low-speed economy.

This sectioned portion of an anti-reversion header shows the unique shape of the internal cone. The cone is designed to reduce unwanted reversion waves in the primary tubes.

57

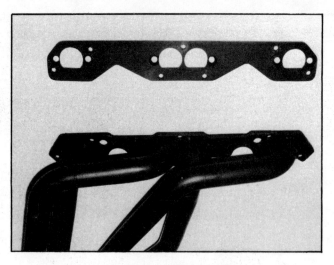

It is difficult to fit large-diameter header pipes to the smallblock Chevy because of the relatively narrow spacing between the header-mounting bolts. An adapter plate is commonly used to cure this problem on high-rpm racing engines. However, street applications generally do not require such large headers.

tive heads and an anemic two-barrel carb, a set of headers will only give a minimal gain in power, though they will still help economy. On the other hand, if the engine has a good street cam, a set of reworked heads, and a well-calibrated four-barrel manifold and carb combination, a set of headers will add a substantial amount of power.

If we use a typical 300-350 cubic inch street motor as an example, the amount of gain could be between 5 and 50 horsepower. The lower limit would be the least to be expected from a totally stock engine with no other modifications. The upper limit would be a practical limit for a street engine that had been extensively modified to take full advantage of efficient intake and exhaust breathing.

A.R. HEADERS

Recently there has been a new development in header design that could boost both street performance and economy. Until the introduction of this new type of header, known as an A.R. header, the best type of header for good low-end torque and street economy generally had small-diameter primary pipes. Unfortunately, though a small primary pipe maintains high

exhaust gas velocity and provides good low- and mid-range torque, it could become a flow restriction in the upper rpm ranges. So, if you wanted good power, you opted for larger pipes to provide high-rpm flow, but this sacrificed the low-rpm torque and economy. You could go for one or the other, but you couldn't get both low-rpm and high-rpm efficiency. The A.R. header, on the other hand, may be able to give some of both worlds.

The concept of the A.R. header (A.R. stands for anti-reversion; reversion is another term for secondary pressure pulses) is to build a header that utilizes relatively large pipes to produce top-end power. The design of the header is such as to stop reverse flow through the engine at low rpm and give the benefits of a small pipe at low rpm. Our illustration shows the key to the A.R. header. This is an anti-reversion cone at the manifold face. This cone appears to be flow and pressure-wave selective. In other words, it allows forward flow in an unrestricted manner. It does not allow reverse flow so easily. The other aspect is that it tends to allow negative pressure waves to travel right through to the valve and combustion chamber.

Negative pressure waves help power; positive pressure waves, which tend to reduce power, appear to be severely dampened at the cone.

Although less sensitive to pipe size, an A.R. header still needs to be selected on a basis of where you want to put the power. However, the penalty paid for choosing power instead of economy is far less than it is with a conventional type of header. The effect an A.R. header has on the power curve, by comparison with a conventional header, is to pull up the low-end power if, for reversion reasons, the power in this part of the rpm range is being adversely affected. Things that adversely affect low-end power are the selection of a cam with too much timing, an intake manifold that is designed to operate at a higher rpm than you had intended, etc. To a large degree, the A.R. header will compensate for this.

Another very important fact is that the A.R. header functions as well, if not better, at part-throttle operation. For the performance and economy engine this is very important. It means that the A.R. header is really working when you are driving at normal city, street and highway speeds. Almost without exception, back-to-back tests of conventional headers and A.R. headers have shown that the A.R. header is superior in every respect, that is, it provides better low-end power, better top-end power, more miles-per-gallon and better throttle response.

The extra power gained by the use of an A.R. header occurs largely in the lower rpm ranges, as the power curves in our illustrations show. This is ideal for our street power with economy engine. Moreover, if you look at the brake-specific fuel consumption, also shown in the illustration, you will see that an A.R.-equipped engine produces more power on less fuel. One of the aspects of an A.R. header is that it "cleans up" the carburetion and, as a result, the carb must be recalibrated if a change is made from a conventional header to an A.R. header. If you are using a single four-barrel Holley on your engine, typically the jet sizes will need to be reduced two or three steps, and sometimes as much as four sizes less than what had previously been used, to get the mixture approximately correct.

A final aspect to consider, as far as power is concerned, is that an A.R.-type header may allow you to select a pipe diameter one or two sizes larger than would be the case if you were using a conventional header. This means you can strike a better com-

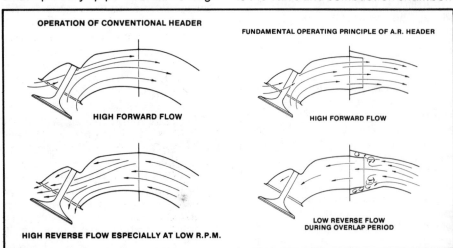

OPERATION OF CONVENTIONAL HEADER

HIGH FORWARD FLOW

HIGH REVERSE FLOW ESPECIALLY AT LOW R.P.M.

FUNDAMENTAL OPERATING PRINCIPLE OF A.R. HEADER

HIGH FORWARD FLOW

LOW REVERSE FLOW DURING OVERLAP PERIOD

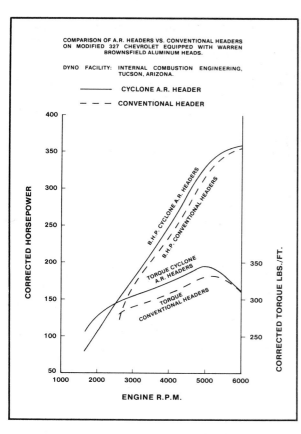

COMPARISON OF A.R. HEADERS VS. CONVENTIONAL HEADERS
ON MODIFIED 327 CHEVROLET EQUIPPED WITH WARREN
BROWNSFIELD ALUMINUM HEADS.

DYNO FACILITY: INTERNAL COMBUSTION ENGINEERING,
TUCSON, ARIZONA.

—————— CYCLONE A.R. HEADER
- - - - - - CONVENTIONAL HEADER

A.R.-type headers work well with highly-developed engines. Certain factors are important: a crossover pipe is essential and the carburetor calibration must be checked. According to the power curves here, this test engine produced more power on less fuel after the A.R. headers were installed. It also produced usable power as low as 2000rpm, whereas with conventional headers, the engine signed off at 2800rpm.

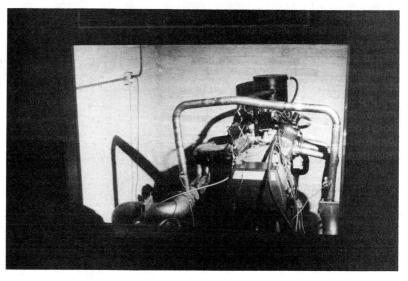

This photo of a dyno test cell (taken through a shatterproof Lexan window) clearly shows an exhaust crossover pipe connecting the header collectors. *With AR-type headers a crossover pipe is essential for correct functioning!*

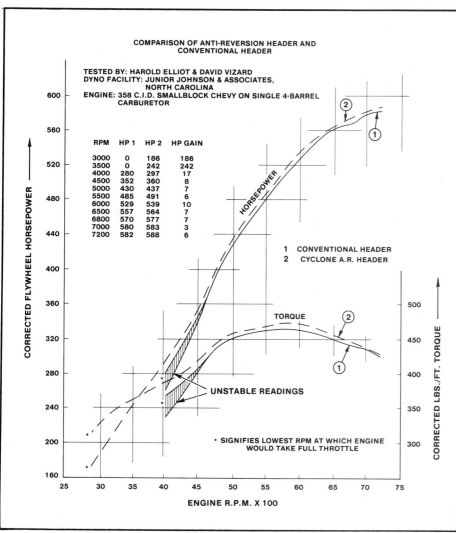

COMPARISON OF ANTI-REVERSION HEADER AND
CONVENTIONAL HEADER

TESTED BY: HAROLD ELLIOT & DAVID VIZARD
DYNO FACILITY: JUNIOR JOHNSON & ASSOCIATES,
NORTH CAROLINA
ENGINE: 358 C.I.D. SMALLBLOCK CHEVY ON SINGLE 4-BARREL
CARBURETOR

RPM	HP 1	HP 2	HP GAIN
3000	0	186	186
3500	0	242	242
4000	280	297	17
4500	352	360	8
5000	430	437	7
5500	485	491	6
6000	529	539	10
6500	557	564	7
6800	570	577	7
7000	580	583	3
7200	582	588	6

1 CONVENTIONAL HEADER
2 CYCLONE A.R. HEADER

UNSTABLE READINGS

* SIGNIFIES LOWEST RPM AT WHICH ENGINE
WOULD TAKE FULL THROTTLE

promise between economy and power. Depending on the size and original state of tune of your engine, the larger header may increase high-rpm power by 5-10 horsepower or more, and this extra power can usually be had with no apparent loss in mileage at part throttle.

A.R. MILEAGE

We have talked about the power that headers, and A.R. headers in particular, can produce. Now comes the question of economy. Again, our illustrations show typical fuel economy gains on the dynamometer. These economy gains were measured at typical road-load power settings. One thing was very evident when changing from a conventional header to an A.R. header: the amount of vacuum developed to produce a given horsepower at a given rpm increased. This indicates that the engine was further out of the throttle to develop the same horsepower.

Out on the road, these gains show up in pretty much the same way. A SEMA-controlled (Specialty Equipment Manufacturers Association) test on a Chevrolet Malibu with a 305 engine showed mileage gains from 17 to 21 miles per gallon with no other change. No doubt, had the carb been rejetted (this was not allowed due to the test regulations), the car would have produced even better mileage.

59

CHAPTER 7

EXHAUST SYSTEMS

- ● **MEASURING BACK PRESSURE**
- ● **CATALYTIC CONVERTERS**
- ● **MUFFLER PERFORMANCE**
- ● **HOW TO BUILD A SYSTEM**
- ● **USING CROSSOVER PIPES**

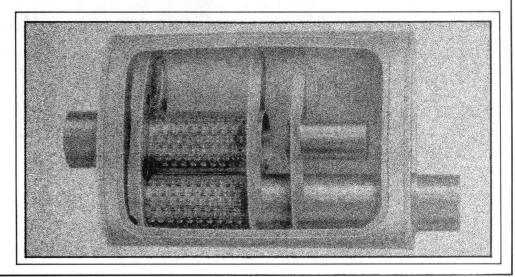

EXHAUST SYSTEMS

Whenever the conversation turns to performance exhaust systems, it will inevitably center around mufflers. There is a good reason for this. The muffler is the single most important aspect of the exhaust system, and it can make or break the performance and economy of any engine.

BACK PRESSURE

It has become a common belief that an engine needs some exhaust back pressure for best results. Such statements are usually made by someone who is more adept at turning a fancy phrase than a fancy wrench. *The truth of the matter is: the least amount of exhaust back pressure possible is always the best for both power and economy.*

No doubt someone, someplace, at some time produced a power curve that "proved" superior results when back pressure was increased. However, it is difficult to believe that such a test was done under properly controlled conditions. If the carburetor and timing were optimized in both cases, it is virtually a certainty that the engine with the least back pressure

would have been better. Once in a while there is going to be a case that upon first examination appears to defy logic (there always is); but for ordinary circumstances, if you assume that minimum back pressure is what your engine needs, 999 times out of 1000 you will be right.

This is the type of "sensitive" gauge used for virtually all of the pressure measurements displayed in the graphs contained in this book. The needle sweeps twice around the scale, giving excellent resolution.

DETERMINING BACK PRESSURE

If your engine is stock and not very powerful, the back pressure developed in the exhaust system will be less

than if you have a high-performance engine with an identical system. It seems logical that since a performance engine is breathing better (otherwise it wouldn't be a performance engine) it has to force more exhaust through the system. But, before you rip the entire exhaust system off your vehicle, it's a good idea to establish whether or not it is restrictive. As is happens, there is a relatively easy way to check the efficiency of your exhaust system.

You will need a pressure gauge that will measure up to about 8 or 9psi. Ideally, the gauge should also have a large dial so it can be read easily. Although not the best because of the relatively small dial, a typical fuel-pressure gauge can be used. Our drawing shows how the gauge should be connected into the system. The back pressure is measured by accelerating the car at wide-open throttle and, at regular rpm increments, noting the pressure readings on the gauge.

Any back pressure is undesirable; however, we have to be practical in these things. It is not possible to achieve zero restriction, so we need to establish a reasonable goal. The back-pressure graph shows average pres-

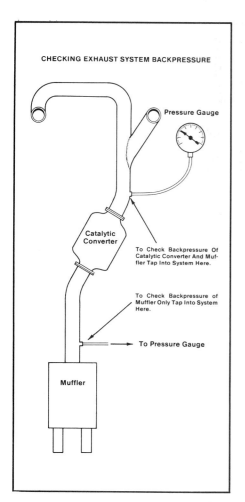

CHECKING EXHAUST SYSTEM BACKPRESSURE

Pressure Gauge

Catalytic Converter

To Check Backpressure Of Catalytic Converter And Muffler Tap Into System Here.

To Check Backpressure of Muffler Only Tap Into System Here.

To Pressure Gauge

Muffler

This example shows a typical late-model exhaust system. To check a dual system, the same technique would be applied.

sure readings that could be considered suitable for most performance and economy exhaust systems. If you are checking a stock exhaust system and your engine is also stock, note that doubling the power will increase the back pressure by a factor of four. Looking at it another way, a 40% increase in power will double the back pressure. So remember, the adverse effects of back pressure increase very rapidly in relation to engine power.

CATALYTIC CONVERTERS

One of the biggest flow restrictions in the exhaust system of any late-model vehicle is the catalytic converter. This is especially true of General Motors vehicles. Ford catalytic converters tend to flow much better than either the GM or Chrysler converters.

Catalytic converters may all perform the same function, but there is a great variation in the flow efficiency of different models.

To give an idea of the relative difference between common converters, we have included a chart comparing flow data. The major reason for the wide variation between the high and low numbers is a difference in the basic designs of the converters. The least efficient converters are generally the catalytic-pellet designs. The exhaust has to flow between the catalytic pellets and this creates a severe flow restriction. On the other hand, the Ford catalytic converter has a honeycomb core. Although it looks restrictive, it is highly efficient. The biggest problem with the Ford catalytic converter is that the entry into and exit out of the converter are restrictive. By redesigning the approach and exit of a Ford catalytic converter, as shown in the illustrations, it is possible to dramatically increase the flow. These modifications have increased flow by about 300cfm (at 10 inches of pressure difference). This is almost double the flow of the best stock converters.

The only difficulty with modifying a stock Ford converter is the high cost.

This modified catalytic converter, developed jointly by Cyril Leon and author David Vizard, produced flow figures similar to a straight length of 2.5-inch tube. The central core is made from a Ford catalytic converter, and the shaped entry allows good flow and distribution of exhaust gases through the honeycomb-core catalyst.

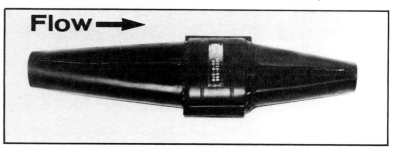

Flow →

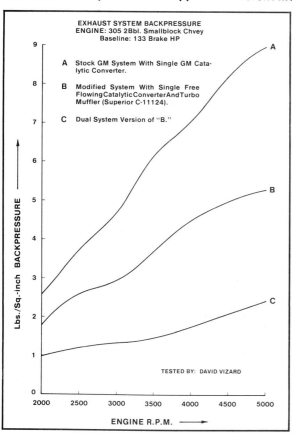

EXHAUST SYSTEM BACKPRESSURE
ENGINE: 305 2Bbl. Smallblock Chvey
Baseline: 133 Brake HP

A Stock GM System With Single GM Catalytic Converter.

B Modified System With Single Free Flowing Catalytic Converter And Turbo Muffler (Superior C-11124).

C Dual System Version of "B."

TESTED BY: DAVID VIZARD

Lbs./Sq.-inch BACKPRESSURE

ENGINE R.P.M.

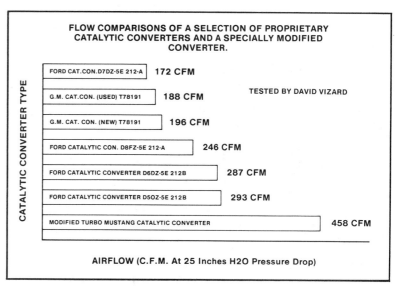

FLOW COMPARISONS OF A SELECTION OF PROPRIETARY CATALYTIC CONVERTERS AND A SPECIALLY MODIFIED CONVERTER.

TESTED BY DAVID VIZARD

CATALYTIC CONVERTER TYPE	
FORD CAT.CON. D7DZ-5E 212-A	172 CFM
G.M. CAT.CON. (USED) T78191	188 CFM
G.M. CAT. CON. (NEW) T78191	196 CFM
FORD CATALYTIC CON. D8FZ-5E 212-A	246 CFM
FORD CATALYTIC CONVERTER D6DZ-5E 212B	287 CFM
FORD CATALYTIC CONVERTER D5OZ-5E 212B	293 CFM
MODIFIED TURBO MUSTANG CATALYTIC CONVERTER	458 CFM

AIRFLOW (C.F.M. At 25 Inches H2O Pressure Drop)

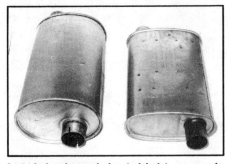

At left is the original, highly regarded, Chevrolet muffler for the turbocharged Corvair. At right is a copy, also called a "turbo muffler." Some of these copies are good, some are not. See below for an evaluation of several so-called turbo mufflers.

Currently a Ford converter costs about $200. However, we would like to mention that at least one supplier, Cyril Leon of Leon's Tune-Up & Muffler (see address in Appendix), produces and sells a modified version of the Ford catalytic converter. This high-flow converter costs less, at least as of this writing, than a stock Ford converter.

MUFFLER PERFORMANCE

When any possible restriction

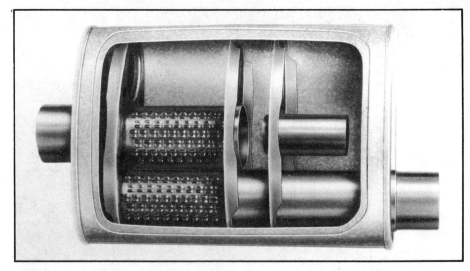

This is a cutaway of the Supreme Super C 111224 silencer. This was within 10% of the most efficient mufflers tested by the author. Max flow means max power potential (photo courtesy of Arvin Automotive).

created by the catalytic converter has been reduced to a minimum, the next obstacle to overcome is the muffler. The function of any muffler is to reduce noise, not choke the engine to death.

This is an interesting flow comparison of most popular "turbo" mufflers. The overall flow leaders are the Cyclone "Sonic" and the Walker "Dyno Max," each within 3% of the highest flow measured. Both of these mufflers are widely available in speed shops and automotive parts outlets.

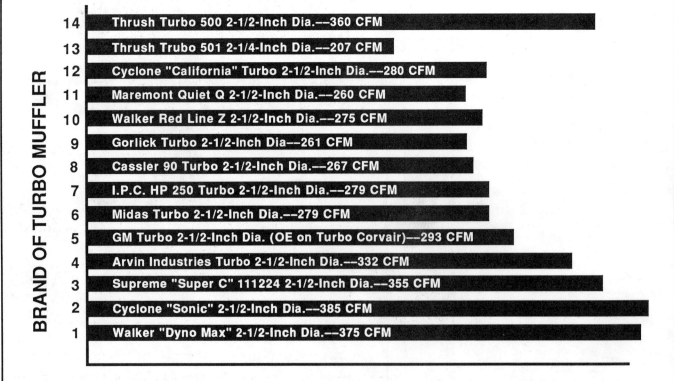

TURBO MUFFLER COMPARISON TEST
Tested by David Vizard

BRAND OF TURBO MUFFLER

- 14 Thrush Turbo 500 2-1/2-Inch Dia.—360 CFM
- 13 Thrush Trubo 501 2-1/4-Inch Dia.—207 CFM
- 12 Cyclone "California" Turbo 2-1/2-Inch Dia.—280 CFM
- 11 Maremont Quiet Q 2-1/2-Inch Dia.—260 CFM
- 10 Walker Red Line Z 2-1/2-Inch Dia.—275 CFM
- 9 Gorlick Turbo 2-1/2-Inch Dia—261 CFM
- 8 Cassler 90 Turbo 2-1/2-Inch Dia.—267 CFM
- 7 I.P.C. HP 250 Turbo 2-1/2-Inch Dia.—279 CFM
- 6 Midas Turbo 2-1/2-Inch Dia.—279 CFM
- 5 GM Turbo 2-1/2-Inch Dia. (OE on Turbo Corvair)—293 CFM
- 4 Arvin Industries Turbo 2-1/2-Inch Dia.—332 CFM
- 3 Supreme "Super C" 111224 2-1/2-Inch Dia.—355 CFM
- 2 Cyclone "Sonic" 2-1/2-Inch Dia.—385 CFM
- 1 Walker "Dyno Max" 2-1/2-Inch Dia.—375 CFM

AIRFLOW (C.F.M. @ 25 Inches of H_2O Pressure Drop)

some bad ones. No doubt the most important attribute of a glasspack is that it will make your engine "sound better," but unless you choose the right glasspack, you could easily throw away power and economy.

Fortunately, it is not difficult to tell, even without resorting to the use of a flow bench, whether a glasspack flows well. The first check is to hold the glasspack up to a light and look through the inlet. If you can see completely through to the outlet, chances are good that you have one of the better ones. Second, look at the louvres punched in the core tube. When they raise inward, into the airstream, the muffler probably produces fairly average flow. If the louvres are punched outward, away from the core tube, you can bet your socks it's a high-flow unit. Now comes the snag, a

Glass-pack mufflers are available in various lengths and diameters. These Supreme Muffler Company "Orange Peelers" are 2.25-inches in diameter. If the core louvres are punched inward and the muffler is longer, it will provide quieter operation, but the penalty is greater flow restriction.

Flow testing mufflers, especially glass-packs, is a quick and often enlightening process. However, a flow bench, as shown here, is needed.

Unfortunately, not all mufflers have been designed with an equal eye to both of these requirements.

In the past decade the so-called "turbo muffler" has become very popular for performance applications. The original muffler of this type was designed for the turbocharged Corvair engine. It was developed by the Chevrolet engineers specifically to reduce exhaust back pressure for this unique turbo application, but it gained a widespread reputation among hot-rodders. In later years some manufacturers have used the turbo muffler image to promote the sale of mufflers that have little, if any, relation to the original design.

Not all of these pretenders deserve the performance image they get from the name. Some pseudo-turbo mufflers are worse than stock mufflers. Fortunately, airflow testing provides a definite measure of muffler efficiency. If you refer to the chart listing the results of tests conducted on several turbo-type mufflers, you can see which are most effective.

GLASSPACKS

If ever there was a subject surrounded by suspicious advertising, it's glasspack mufflers. The very term "glasspack" carries the image of performance but, in fact, many glasspacks are less efficient than conventional mufflers. There are some good glass-packs on the market and there are

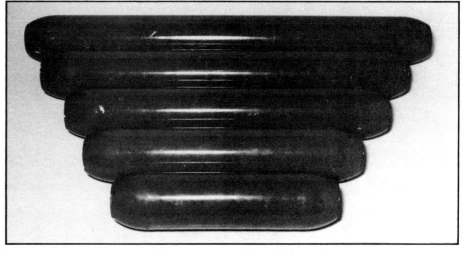

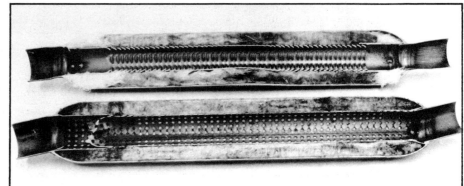

Although they all look alike from the outside, there are often major differences in the way glasspack mufflers are designed and built. The muffler at top has internal louvers that are punched inward where they protrude into the exhaust flow. This provides quieter operation but it reduces the maximum flow of the muffler. The lower muffler simply has holes punched through the core tube. This provides more flow, but it also increases the noise level.

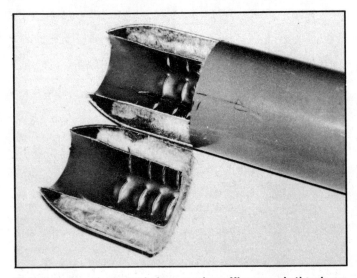

This cutaway of a typical glass-pack muffler reveals the shape of the core louvres and the way fiberglass material is packed around the core tube.

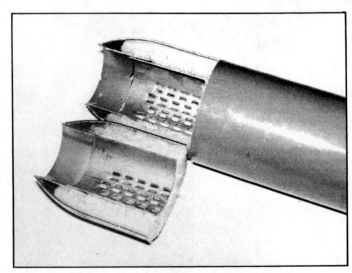

When the louvres are punched outward from the core tube, better flow results. The only drawback is that the noise level increases.

glasspack that has core louvres punched outward will make more noise, and you may have to use two or three such mufflers in each exhaust pipe to get an acceptable noise level. However, even two or three high-flow glasspacks will flow better than one with core louvres punched inward.

Before moving on, we should consider further those glasspacks that have core louvres punched inward. Exhaust flowing normally through the core will strike the upraised lip of each louvre, very much like moving backward along the teeth of a saw. But, flowing the other way, the exhaust will not be disrupted as much by each lip. This, to follow our analogy, is like moving down sawteeth in the forward direction. The difference between the two, forward and reverse flow, can be dramatic. The accompanying flow chart shows this difference clearly.

This effect can be used to our benefit. The inlet of most glasspack mufflers is clearly marked, and flow into the inlet tube moves against the sawtooth effect. This hinders the overall flow efficiency. Turning the muffler around will improve power and economy, but the noise level will go up slightly.

BUILDING A SYSTEM

For the purposes of the following discussion we will say that the exhaust system starts at the end of the header flange. Exhaust gases have to be channeled from the header, through the muffler, to the rear of the vehicle through this interconnecting system of tubes. More often than not, this seemingly simple task is accomplished with little regard for flow efficiency.

When this Trivane muffler was cut open, it proved to be quite complex. However, flow-bench testing showed that this complex construction did not necessarily improve flow. It had the lowest efficiency of any muffler checked.

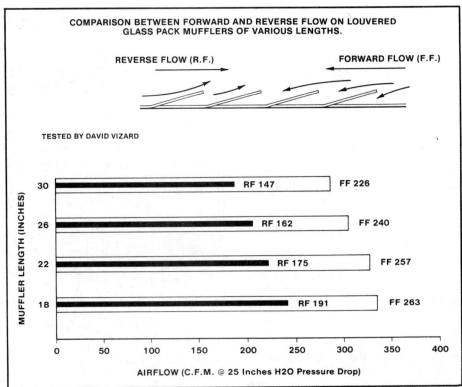

COMPARISON BETWEEN FORWARD AND REVERSE FLOW ON LOUVERED GLASS PACK MUFFLERS OF VARIOUS LENGTHS.

REVERSE FLOW (R.F.)   FORWARD FLOW (F.F.)

TESTED BY DAVID VIZARD

MUFFLER LENGTH (INCHES)

30	RF 147	FF 226
26	RF 162	FF 240
22	RF 175	FF 257
18	RF 191	FF 263

AIRFLOW (C.F.M. @ 25 Inches H2O Pressure Drop)

Any V8 engine must be equipped with a dual exhaust system. This is purely a matter of efficiency and volume. At high engine speeds the average V8 engine inducts and exhausts a large volume of air. If all of this volume is funneled through a single muffler, one of two things will be true. There will be a severe restriction and a lot of back pressure or the muffler must be the size of a 55-gallon drum. *The choice is simple: for performance and economy you must use a dual exhaust system.* Of course, if the engine in question is an inline 4- or 6-cylinder configuration, a single system is acceptable, but it must still conform to the efficiency criteria outlined here.

The pipe leading from the header to the muffler should, if possible, be about the same diameter as the collector. If the pipe is slightly smaller it will not cause much of a problem. At this point it is not the exhaust pipe (often this section of exhaust tubing is called "the header pipe") that presents the prime restriction. As the test results show, the muffler is usually the major restriction. A 2-inch pipe can flow in excess of 260cfm (at 10 inches of pressure drop), whereas it takes a very good muffler with a 2.5-inch diameter intake to flow 225cfm. Just as the weakest link determines the

Virtually every muffler manufacturer makes a "turbo muffler." Even experts like Cyril Leon, of Leon's Tune-Up & Muffler, have to rely on years of experience and continuous testing to determine which brands are best for both power and economy.

A single "turbo-type" muffler is ideally suited to small-displacement, four-ylinder engines. However, most V8 engines require at least two, or even four, free-flowing mufflers.

strength of a chain, the most restrictive part of an exhaust system dictates the effectiveness of the total system.

Although a pipe may flow well when it is straight, any bend along its length causes the flow to decrease. Sometimes it is necessary to put several bends in an exhaust system to convey the exhaust from the headers to the rear of the car. Under these circumstances it is best to use pipe with as large a diameter as is practicable. *A header pipe that is at least as large as the inlet to the muffler is preferred, but in the interest of flow and practical fabrication, it may be necessary to use a smaller pipe and increase the pipe diameter just prior to the muffler inlet.*

As an example: a 2.25-inch pipe may be convenient from the header to the muffler, but a muffler with a 2.25-inch inlet and core will flow less than one with a 2.5-inch inlet and core. It would, therefore, be better to use the larger muffler and use a short adapter section ahead of the muffler to increase the header pipe size from 2.25 inches to 2.5 inches. *What is not acceptable is to do the opposite, reduce the size of the header pipe to fit a small-bore muffler.*

CROSSOVER PIPES

Extensive dynamometer and road testing has shown that a simple crossover pipe interconnecting the two sides of a dual exhaust system, just behind the collectors and ahead of the mufflers, can increase engine power. This is true of both street machines and race cars, however, the reason this enhances power differs in both instances. In an open-exhaust race vehicle the crossover pipe transfers exhaust pulse waves from one side of the system to the other. If you could watch flow in the crossover pipe, you would see that the air or exhaust only moved a few inches, first one way and then the other. With a street system, the crossover pipe performs an additional function. Apart from transferring any favorable shock waves that may be present, the crossover allows each side of the engine to share the combined muffler flow capacity.

To gain the advantages of shared-muffler flow capacity it is necessary to use the crossover pipe in a slightly different manner. The exhaust from each side of the engine is channelled through both mufflers. Thus, instead of each bank of cylinders being limited to a muffler with a total capacity of approximately 200cfm (an average number), the capacity could be doubled, to 400cfm, if the exhaust could be

discharged through both mufflers. This is, though, a simplification of what actually happens. When eight cylinders are coupled together, the exhaust pulses overlap and 100% gain in apparent flow capability is not realized. However, gains of 25% are not out of the question.

We have illustrated several different types of crossover systems. The straight crossover pipe is acceptable when the muffler flow capacity is exceptionally high, but a double crossover system is better if the mufflers are restrictive. In simplest terms, the nearer the exhaust system is to a completely open exhaust pipe, the better the conventional crossover pipe will work.

The only positive way to determine if the exhaust system is too restrictive, is to use a pressure gauge in the manner described above. If this test shows more than 5 psi back pressure at any place in the normal rpm range, the system is not flowing sufficiently to produce maximum power and economy.

GANGED MUFFLERS

Under certain circumstances it may not be possible to get the exhaust system back pressure down to an acceptable level with a single muffler in each of the exhaust pipes. Especially with high-powered, large-displacement engines it may be necessary to use ganged mufflers connected in parallel.

In such a case the exhaust from each bank of cylinders is fed through two mufflers (see illustration), and a total of four mufflers are required if the engine is a V8. If the Y-adapter that

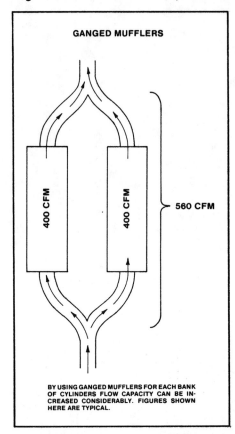

GANGED MUFFLERS

400 CFM

400 CFM

560 CFM

BY USING GANGED MUFFLERS FOR EACH BANK OF CYLINDERS FLOW CAPACITY CAN BE INCREASED CONSIDERABLY. FIGURES SHOWN HERE ARE TYPICAL.

splits the exhaust between each ganged pair is made with a thought to good flow, the effective flow of the two mufflers can be almost double that of a single one.

POTENTIAL GAINS

If the complete exhaust system has been redesigned to gain minimal back pressure, what performance and economy gains can be expected? This is a difficult question to answer accurately. The back pressure created by the original system will vary from vehicle to vehicle and from engine to engine, and the efficiency of the modified system will differ depending upon how thoughtfully and carefully the modifications have been performed.

The overall effect of such things are difficult to predict, but to show what can be done with a good system we

The most suitable type of crossover depends largely on the flow capability of the mufflers employed. If mufflers are restrictive, the double crossover (as shown in A) is the best system, as it allows the flow capacity of both mufflers to be shared by both cylinder banks. The disadvantage of this system is that is usually presents installation problems and expense. System B is a compromise of system A. It allows only minimal flow sharing but does do a good job transferring shock waves. System C is the most effective and simplest, but only functions properly when free-flowing mufflers of ample capacity are used.

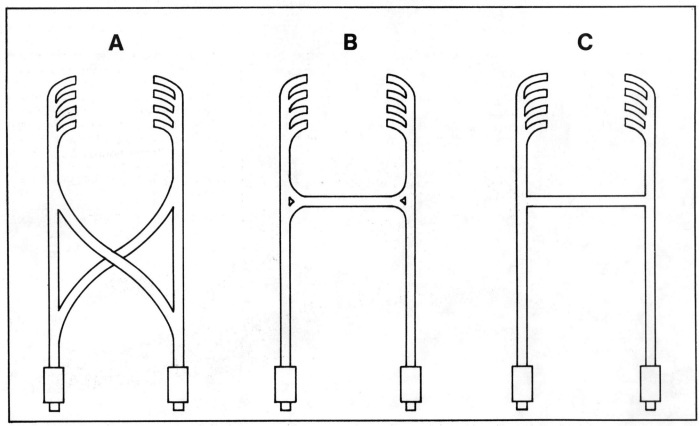

A   B   C

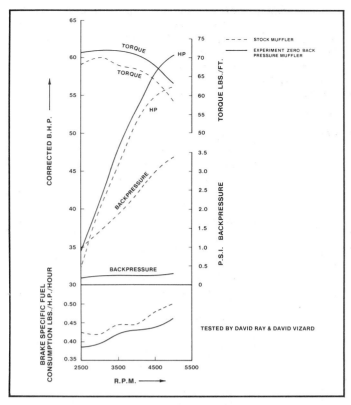

Graph labels: TORQUE, HP, BACKPRESSURE. Legend: --- STOCK MUFFLER, —— EXPERIMENT ZERO BACK PRESSURE MUFFLER. Axes: CORRECTED B.H.P., TORQUE LBS./FT., P.S.I. BACKPRESSURE, BRAKE SPECIFIC FUEL CONSUMPTION LBS./H.P./HOUR, R.P.M.

TESTED BY DAVID RAY & DAVID VIZARD

These graphs show what happens to power and fuel consumption when exhaust backpressure is reduced. In each case, a full range of mixture settings and ignition timing were tried and those settings giving the minimum fuel consumption were used for the test. Even with engine settings optimized for minimum fuel consumption, power was markedly increased. Part-throttle mileage gains varied between 4 and 8%, depending upon throttle opening.

COMPARISON OF POWER OUTPUT WITH STOCK CATALYTIC CONVERTER & MUFFLER AND WITH MODIFIED CATALYTIC CONVERTER & HIGH-FLOW MUFFLER.

SINGLE PIPE EXHAUST SYSTEM
ENGINE: 305 CHEVROLET 2-BARREL
DYNO FACILITY: AUTO RECALIBRATION, TUCSON, ARIZONA

TESTED BY BILL NELSON & DAVID VIZARD

Graph: CORRECTED REAR WHEEL HORSEPOWER vs ENGINE R.P.M. X 100. Curves labeled MODIFIED and STOCK.

have included an example. The illustration is an experimental four-cylinder engine, on which the muffler was changed from a stock design (typical of that used on many vehicles) to a very advanced muffler that had almost zero back pressure. In fact, the modified system developed as little back pressure as a straight, open pipe. With the reduction in back pressure, an 8% increase in power was obtained throughout the rev range. Along with this 8% increase in power there was a minimum 3% gain in economy. Actually, the economy increase varied from 3-8%, and in most of the rpm range it was around 6%.

A practical application of the topics we have discussed can also be seen in the V8-engine example. In this graph we illustrate the difference in rear-wheel power when a high-flow, single-exhaust system is installed on a V8-powered vehicle. In this case the stock system was replaced with a modified

Individually, these parts do not seem impressive or important, however, the exhaust system can be a gold mine of power and economy. By selecting free-flowing components the average hot-rodder can produce better results than nearly any factory system.

Ford catalytic converter and a Supreme Super 'C' turbo muffler.

Testing over a three-month period prior to and after the modification showed that the reduced back pressure produced a net gain of 1-1/2 mpg. Bearing in mind that this is still a single-exhaust system, the gains are quite worthwhile. If the exhaust system had been changed to a dual system with similar low back pressure readings, the power gains would have improved and the mileage figures would have been slightly better than those recorded with the single-exhaust system.

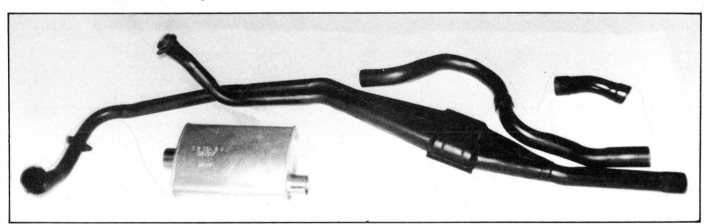

- CAMS EXPLAINED!
- SELECTING THE RIGHT CAM
- CAM TIMING FOR ECONOMY
- A LONG-LIFE VALVETRAIN

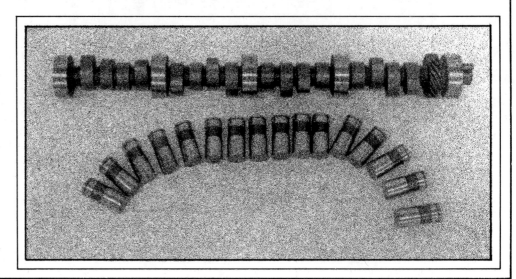

CAMSHAFT

In previous chapters we have touched upon the importance of the camshaft. No other component has such wide-ranging influence over so many engine elements, and no component has such a dramatic influence on the overall engine character. Stop for a minute to consider: the camshaft design affects the functioning of the carburetor, the intake manifold, the exhaust system, the compression ratio, the valvetrain and numerous other less-obvious factors. It affects engine performance and economy in countless ways. To put it simply, the design of the cam and the coordination of the valvetrain is the most important part of the performance-with-economy puzzle, and *selecting the wrong cam for a street performance engine is, without exception, a major catastrophe!*

SELECTING A CAM

When selecting a camshaft for performance, the two main considerations are: the desired power range of the engine and how long the cam must physically endure. If we add to these two considerations the need for econ-

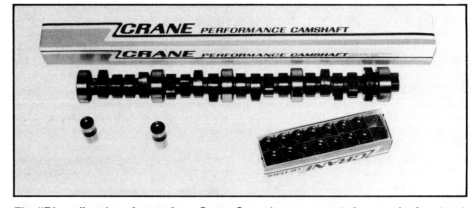

The "Blazer" series of cams from Crane Cams have proven to be popular for street engines. These designs give a wide power band and good top-end power without incurring any mileage penalties.

omy, a definite picture of cam design requirements takes shape.

If you consider power and economy and cam design, you have to make a choice. On one hand, you can select a cam that will, under the worst conditions, help power without adversely affecting economy. On the other hand, you can choose a design that will help economy without losing any power over a typical stock cam.

From a practical standpoint, if the engine already has a moderate cam designed for street use and with a broad power curve that starts right at

idle, it will be difficult to dramatically improve economy. Nevertheless, we also find that it would be possible to improve power without losing a significant amount of economy. But, it would also be easy to lose mileage if the cam design was altered improperly. In other words, if we install a series of increasingly radical—but well-designed — performance/economy cams in a typical street-type test engine, we would generally find at each successive cam change that power increases faster than economy is lost.

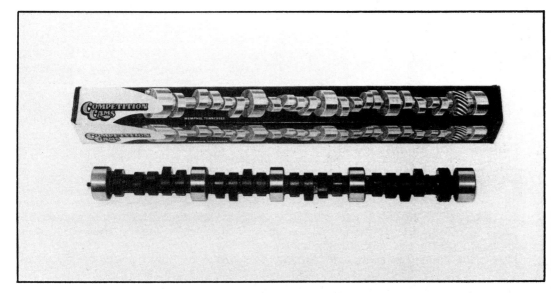

The author tested street engines equipped with a Competition Cams, 278 H8 cam and found this grind to be quite effective. It produced good power from 1500 to 6500rpm.

To put some numbers on this, it may be possible (depending on other engine variables) to change from a dead stock cam to a fairly radical street cam and pick up as much as 12% power but only lose 3% economy. In the following section we hope to give enough information to help you select a cam that will do exactly this.

LIFT & DURATION

Broadly speaking, two principal features of cam design govern the characteristics imparted to the engine

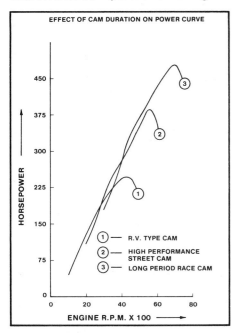

This is a comparison of the typical power curves developed by short-, medium- and long-duration cams. When duration is shorter, low-rpm power increases. A cam that develops good power in the 1200-3500rpm range is desirable for economy. Performance street cams are suitable in most cases but they usually provide less fuel efficiency than pure "economy" cams.

power curve: they are valve lift and valve-open duration. Increasing lift and duration above that given by a stock cam results in more power. It also shifts the power curve upward in the rev range. However, when you increase lift and duration past a reasonable limit, the engine will not be able to operate at low speeds. And, if the engine won't run at low speed, it is virtually useless as an economy engine. The question is: is it high valve lift or is it the extended valve-open duration imparted to the valves that makes the engine unsuitable for low-rpm operation.

Essentially, we can say that the more timing (duration) a cam has, the less suited it is to economy applications. Long timing figures are not conducive to good part-throttle operation and economical low-rpm fuel-consumption figures. Some long-duration cams may produce reasonable fuel-efficiency numbers in relatively high rpm ranges (for which they are designed) but, unfortunately, we cannot drive on the street in such a manner. *Put simply: long-duration cams are out.*

What about lift? *Increasing valve lift can be an asset because it produces more power with almost no loss in fuel economy.* So the answer is simple, design a cam with short valve-open duration and very high lift. However, mechanical realities are never that simple. Some nasty mechanical side effects are created when we try to build a short-duration cam with high valve lift.

Obviously, if there is less duration provided by the cam profile, there is also less time available to move the valve from the seat to full lift and back. Eventually it becomes impossible to mechanically actuate the valve through this cycle in the available time

provided by the duration of the lobe profile.

Generally speaking, we can say that cams with more than 0.500-inch lift are reaching the realm of impracticality for street engines. Combining more lift than this with a duration that would be suitable for low- and mid-range performance causes valve opening and closing rates that exaggerate the rate of wear on the cam lobes, valve springs, valvestems and guides in the cylinder head. Although such a cam may work when the engine is new, you could well find that you will have to rebuild the cylinder head and install a new valvetrain much earlier than would have been the case if a reasonable cam was used. Remember, you can buy a lot of fuel and go a long way for the dollars spent replacing a valvetrain.

Summarizing at this point, although a street performance engine can benefit from as much valve lift as possible, in the extreme this generates an impractical reliability situation; so a compromise must be struck. As far as duration is concerned, the shorter the timing is, the better for economy, especially at part throttle. Unfortunately, the shorter the valve timing is, the less power the engine will make.

Fortunately, there are many specialty cams available with timing figures that are quite similar to stock but with greater-than-stock valve lift. As long as the additional lift is not beyond reason, these cams are suitable for most street applications and can provide additional performance, but the loss in economy is minimal because the timing figures are substantially the same as an average stock cam.

However, since the fuel crisis of 1973, the auto industry has been

The cam must always be properly phased (timed) with the crankshaft. Manufacturing tolerances in the cam-drive system may cause this phasing to vary when a new cam is installed. Cam manufacturers provide a timing specification, and it must be checked after a new cam is in place. A degree wheel and a dial indicator are about the only special pieces of equipment required.

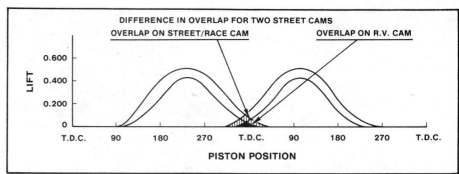

flooded with so-called "super-economy" devices. The camshaft industry has not escaped this phenomenon. Many "new" and "special" economy profiles have been heavily promoted in recent months. These cam designs, in the main, work adequately, but usually they provide only a small gain in mileage, and the penalty is often a dramatic loss in power. As such, they have no place in most performance engines.

Before we move to the next point, we need to mention the relationship between cam design and cylinder head performance. Since it is apparent that long valve-open duration hurts economy and ultra-high valve lift leads to foreshortened valvetrain life, there are limits to what can be achieved with cam design, and cylinder head flow performance becomes an important part of the overall picture.

For instance, if an intake port can be modified to give the same gross airflow at .300-inch of valve lift as was possible with an unmodified port at .450-inch lift, the same performance can be acquired with ported heads and a low-lift cam as with unported heads and a high-lift cam. *This means a high-flow cylinder head will have the same effect on performance and economy as a high-lift cam, but without the attendant*

extra stresses in the valvetrain.

OVERLAP

Cam overlap is the period of crankshaft rotation (in degrees) during the changeover from the end of exhaust stroke to the beginning of the intake stroke when both valves are open (see detailed discussion in the chapter on exhaust headers). Basically, anything more than a small amount of overlap reduces economy. From this point of view, cams with long duration are generally unsuited for street economy and performance.

The amount of overlap a cam has is governed by two factors. The first and most obvious of these is the amount of valve-open duration that each lobe has. The second factor is the lobe centerline angle or "lobe displacement" of the cam.

Adding duration to a cam, as we have already said, allows the valvetrain to operate at higher engine speeds and still produce power. The penalty paid for this is reduced low-end power. *However, under certain circumstances some of the low-end power can be retrieved by altering the*

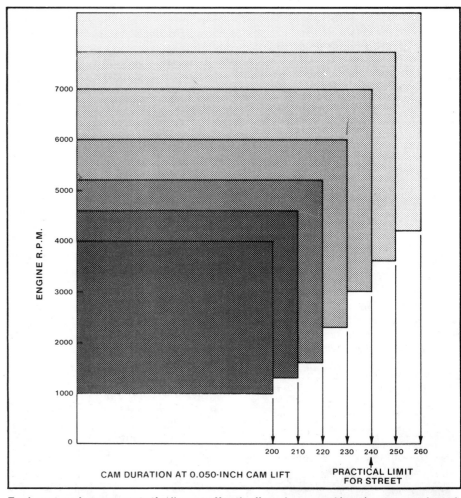

Each rectangle represents the "most effective" engine speed (rpm) range produced by the cam timing (duration) shown on the bottom scale. This graph is representative of a 350cid engine. If the engine is bigger, the usable range will be lower. If the engine is smaller, the working range will be higher on the scale. If the engine has a relatively larger displacement (long stroke), the shift in the usable rpm range will be more dramatic as cam timing (duration) is increased or decreased.

lobe centers and, thus, reducing the overlap period.

When power is the prime consideration, a typical performance cam will have a phase angle of about 105-110°. This is a relatively small center angle and causes the overlap period to be relatively long. However, if the lobe design is unchanged (therefore, the duration of each lobe remains the same) and the lobe center is increased to 112 or 114° (or more), overlap is reduced, but the valve-open duration remains the same. This will generally broaden the rpm range of the engine, but the power output at any given rpm is usually reduced somewhat.

However, we can tie this back to a previous discussion and find some benefits from a properly selected "combination." In the discussion of A.R.-type headers we mentioned that they have less effect with cams that have wider lobe centerlines than with cams that have tighter centerlines. Therefore, if you plan to use A.R. headers, select a cam with lobe centerlines closer together than would normally be the case. If you talk to your favorite cam grinder, he may be able to grind a cam with conventional lobe profiles but with the centers closed up to about 108°, or so, to complement the A.R. headers. This should give you the power range you would normally have with wide lobe centers, but increase specific power because of the tighter lobe centers.

If you study the cam chart, you should be able to determine approximately what is generally needed to suit your requirements. If you relate these figures to various cam manufacturers' specification sheets, in most cases you should be able to find a cam suitable for your specific application.

And a final word, if you have an automatic transmission, as opposed to a manual transmission vehicle, be very wary of going too far on cam timing. A cam with too much duration may severely limit low-end power, to the point that insufficient torque is available at low rpm to accelerate the car smoothly from a standing start. If you have a torque converter that stalls at 1350 rpm, you need a cam that makes good torque at 1350 rpm.

You may, at this point, be tempted to use a racing-type torque converter to increase stall speed, but at low speeds these designs are very inefficient from the fuel consumption point of view and should be absolutely avoided for street use. In fact, if you have an auto-trans vehicle, you should be looking at the reverse situation: trying to find a

After installing a high-lift cam, it is always a good idea to check the piston-to-valve clearance. This is most easily done by laying a clay strip across the top of the #1 piston, then installing the head and valvetrain to the short block. When the crank assembly is rotated, the valves will leave impressions in the clay. These impressions can be measured to determine the operating clearance between the valve head and the piston dome. When a hydraulic cam is used, the check should be performed with solid lifters temporarily installed (at zero lash) to the cylinder being tested. This prevents the lifters from compressing during the test.

torque converter that will stall at a lower speed and reduce slippage between the engine and the driving wheels.

VALVETRAIN

Selecting the right cam isn't the end of the story, to be effective, any camshaft must work with a well-coordinated valvetrain. The cam directs the action, but the valvetrain is responsible for actually getting the valves to open and close in an orderly fashion. As such, the valvetrain components affect performance and economy only to the extent that if they don't work in concert with the cam, the overall efficiency of the engine will suffer. Individually, they don't seem important, but taken together, they perform a critical function.

LIFTERS & PUSHRODS

One of the first questions most hot rodders consider is whether to use a mechanical- or a hydraulic-lifter cam. The answer is surprisingly simple: a hydraulic street cam eliminates all of the problems associated with valve-lash adjustment and provides quiet and virtually trouble-free operation. It is hard to justify any other type of lifter and cam design, especially in view of the fact that it sacrifices nothing as far as power and economy are concerned.

Many of the cams you are likely to use will require nothing more exotic than stock-type hydraulic lifters. This, fortunately, provides reliability and relatively low cost. Of course, new lifters must be used when a new cam is installed (to prevent initial break-in problems), but the overall cost and reliability of modern hydraulic lifters is very appealing.

As far as pushrods are concerned, in almost all cases, a straight, stock-type pushrod will be sufficient. (Only when considering exceptionally high operating speeds, speeds that are usually outside of the practical extremes of a realistic performance and economy engine, do we need look at supposedly stiffer-than-stock pushrods.) When using a stock pushrod, the prime consideration is that it produce correct rocker geometry. If the rocker geometry is improper, steps must be taken to rectify it.

(In most cases the easist way to check geometry is with the engine and valvetrain put together in a pre-assembly mockup. Turn the crankshaft by hand and observe that the operating tip of the number-one intake rockerarm. As it moves up and down with the valve it also sweeps back-and-forth across the end of the valvestem. If the geometry is correct, when the rocker has opened the valve to approximately one-half of total lift, the operating tip of the rockerarm should

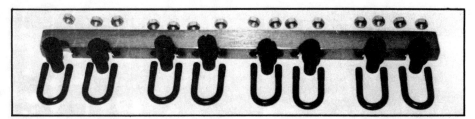

Some extremely radical street cams (especially for the smallblock Chevy) generate enough flexure in the upper part of the valvetrain to warrant a stud girdle. Such cams are not generally recommended for practical street economy because they also create high valveguide wear, but if you must use such a high-rate cam, consider using a stud girdle to support the upper valvetrain. A double-beam, racing-type girdle will probably not be necessary, but a good compromise is this Moroso stud girdle that uses a single bar and U-bolts.

be approximately at the mid-point of the valvestem end. The same should be true of the exhaust rocker.)

With ball-type rockers, such as those on the smallblock Chevy, increased lift tends to go hand-in-hand with a reduced base-circle diameter (the base circle is the portion of the cam against which the base of the lifter rides when it is not up on the lobe). But, cams that have a practical valve lift for street use (.500-inch or less) generally do not have a drastically reduced base-circle diameter. As a result, the rocker geometry tends to be very close to stock. However, when any non-stock cam is installed, the geometry should be checked.

If, for some reason, a large amount of material is milled or machined from the block and/or the head deck surfaces, the rocker geometry must be checked before final engine assembly. More than likely, the pushrods will have to be shortened a similar amount to compensate for the change in operating geometry. However, if only very small amounts have been taken from either the block or the head to

insure flat, parallel decks, the change in geometry will be of no great consequence.

Finally, if valves with longer-than-stock valvestems are installed, longer pushrods should also be used. If the rocker geometry is not correct, high valveguide, valve tip and rocker pad wear may result.

ROLLER ROCKERS

At first thought, using racing-type, roller-tipped rockerarms on an economy engine seems to be a case of gilding the lily. However, the use of a roller rocker brings about numerous less-than-obvious side benefits.

Because the operating tip of a roller rocker rolls across the end of the valve, the side loading on the valve is dramatically reduced, therefore, valvestem and valveguide life is increased. This means that higher lifts can be used without incurring the tremendous wear penalty associated with using high valve lifts with stock-type rockers.

Perhaps the biggest and most overlooked benefit of roller rockers is the

availablility of certain models that have higher-than-stock rocker ratios. On most stock rockers the fulcrum point is not in the exact middle of the rocker. It is normally offset toward the pushrod end. As a result of the lever action of the arm, whatever movement is transmitted by the pushrod to the rockerarm, produces a multiplied (increased) movement at the valve end. The relative comparison between the length of the rockerarm from the fulcrum to the pushrod cup and the length between the fulcrum and the valve-actuating tip is called the rocker ratio.

For example, if the ratio of these two lengths is 1:1.5, the rocker end will move 1.5 times the distance the pushrod end moves. Therefore, to find the actual lift of the valve away from the seat, the distance the lifter and pushrod are displaced upward by the cam lobe (lobe height) must be multiplied by the rocker ratio. A typical example is the smallblock Chevy, which has a stock rocker ratio of 1.5. If the lobe raises the lifter .300-inch, the valve lift will be .450-inch (.300-inch x 1.5 = .450-inch).

If this ratio is increased, the lift at the valve will likewise, be increased, even though the same cam profile is used. Consider our smallblock example. If we replaced the rockers in our Chevy with similar ones having a ratio of 1:1.6, with no other change the lift at the valve is increased to .480-inch (.300-inch lobe lift x 1.6 = .480-inch). This is a neat way to increase valve lift without installing a new cam or significantly changing the duration.

However, there are limits to how much you can increase the ratio

The use of roller rockers can significantly reduce valveguide wear on many engines. Even though aluminum rockers have a limited life on high-rpm racing engines, with lower valve spring pressures and rpm limits (required by reasonable street cams), they will last almost indefinitely.

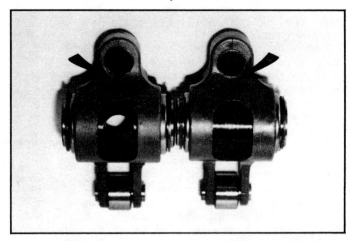

Sometimes it is helpful to alter the rockerarm ratio on a street engine. If the engine responds to increased valve lift, installing high-ratio rockers will provide more lift without changing the cam. Note the different positions of the pushrod cups on the 1.5:1 rocker (right) and the 1.6:1 rocker. Placing the cup closer to the fulcrum on the 1.6 rocker (arrow), increases the ratio (rockerarm leverage) between the pushrod and the valve movement.

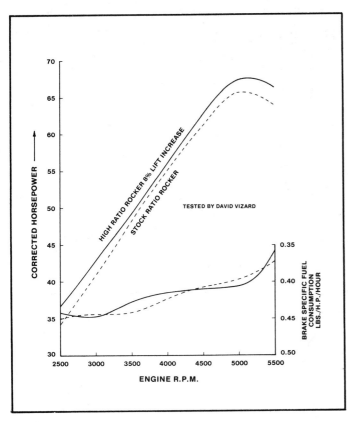

This graph demonstrates the effect of increased valve lift. On this experimental engine the percentage of power increase was far greater than the percentage increase in full-throttle fuel consumption. Part-throttle, road-load mileage was reduced by an average of 1.1%. This indicates that high-lift cams help power with a minimal decrease in economy. And note, longer-duration cams also help power, but they create more loss of economy.

These Crower stainless steel rockers (and the similar Norris rockers) represent some of the best roller bearing-mounted rockers available. They are very strong and, for street applications, virtually indestructible.

without incurring adverse side effects. We won't lengthen this explanation unnecessarily but, in general, it is possible to increase the ratio from 1.5 to 1.6 without much problem. Racing smallblock Chevys have been operated quite successfully with ratios as high as 1.75, but for practical street use, this should be considered an extreme case.

The graph presented here shows the effect of installing high-lift rockers on an experimental four-cylinder engine with very short cam timing. As can be seen, the power increased throughout the rpm range and the difference in brake-specific fuel consumption was very minimal. Our second graph shows what can be achieved in the way of extra power on an engine having a cam with typical duration figures for a practical street engine. The additional lift did not show any power gain below 3500rpm. From this point upward, the added lift proved beneficial in terms of breathing, and as a result, more power was developed.

Should you decide to use high-lift rockers, be prepared to experience a decrease in the valve-crash (valve float) speed. To maintain the same valve-crash speed when going from 1.5 to 1.6 rockers, you will typically need springs 10-12% stronger.

Another problem you may be confronted with and one that you should take care to avoid at all costs, is coil binding. If high-lift rockers, a high-lift cam or non-stock springs have been

COMPARISON OF STOCK RATIO & HIGH RATIO ROCKERS
TEST ENGINE: 350 C.I.D. CHEVROLET

TESTED BY BILL WHEATLEY & NORM SCHENCK

HIGH RATIO ROCKER 1.6/1
STOCK ROCKER RATIO 1.5/1

In some cases the practicality of swapping rockerarms may depend on the availability of high-ratio rockers for the specific engine in question. It is easy and relatively safe to increase the ratio of a smallblock Chevy from 1.5 to 1.6:1, and as shown here, the performance increase can be notable.

installed in the engine, it is imperative that the valvetrain be assembled to check for coil bind at full valve lift. This is best accomplished during the pre-assembly procedures and must never be overlooked (failure to do so may cause more damage than you can imagine).

If coil bind problems are indicated,

you have to find a suitable solution. You may opt to machine the spring seats deeper into the head or change to a dished-type valve retainer to achieve a longer installed-spring height. If it is not practical to increase the installed height, check with a reputable cam manufacturer to see if he can provide a suitable spring made from smaller diameter wire. Perhaps he will have a spring with suitable seat pressure that also allows greater-than-stock valve lift.

As a final thought, most specialty rockers are made from aluminum and are designed to have minimum weight. In the past, many rodders have questioned the durability of these rockers in long-term street operation. Aluminum rockers are subject to high-stress fatigue problems, but generally this won't occur until spring pressures and engine speeds become pretty unreasonable. If they are matched with a reasonable street cam and springs, there should be little cause for worry. In engines that are seldom operated above 6000rpm there is no reason to suppose that a typical aluminum rocker would not provide at least 50,000 miles of trouble-free service.

The benefits of high-ratio rockers are small but, when you want maximum performance without sacrificing economy, they should be considered as an alternative or as a useful complement to a high-lift camshaft. Every little bit helps!

CHAPTER 9 IGNITION SYSTEMS

- ● STOCK VS TRICK
- ● MULTI-STRIKE UNITS
- ● TIMING CONSIDERATIONS
- ● WHY USE ADVANCE?

IGNITION SYSTEMS

Some of the boldest advertising claims in the performance industry are made by manufacturers of ignition systems. It would be unfair to say that all of these claims are false, but it wouldn't be out of line to say that many of them should be carefully evaluated by the prospective buyer. A good ignition system is a necessity for both performance and economy. There are limits, though, to what any conventional or, for that matter, what any nonconventional ignition can achieve. If the performance enthusiast has a clear idea of how the ignition system works and what it can and cannot reasonably be expected to do, he will not be tempted to waste money on unneeded frills.

Within reasonable street-engine rpm limits a well-tuned, conventional, breaker-point ignition system won't be too far off the best that's possible from the standpoint of both power and economy. This may sound like a general condemnation of all nonconventional and specialty ignition systems. In fact, it isn't meant to be that. The problem is that over the years so many misconceptions have developed that the true picture is somewhat obscured. *Any ignition system, no matter what type or brand-name, has two functions: to generate the means of igniting the mixture, and to ignite the mixture at precisely the right instant in relation to the rpm/load conditions of the engine and the density of the charge in the cylinders.*

Taking first things first, let's look at the different ways and means of generating a spark and analyze the effect each method has on a high-performance, economy engine.

CONVENTIONAL VERSUS ELECTRONIC IGNITIONS

The term "conventional ignition" is usually applied to one that uses a contact switch to initiate an electrical discharge from a high-voltage transformer (induction coil). The switch is commonly called a "contact breaker," or "breaker points" or sometimes just "the points." It switches primary voltage (12-volts) on and off to the coil. The primary voltage is stepped up to 10,000 volts (or more) by the coil. This high voltage is then channeled in proper firing-order sequence through the distributor rotor and cap, through the spark plug wires and to the spark plugs. As this high voltage arcs across the gap between the spark plug electrodes, combustion ignition is created in the cylinder. This basic method of operation is simple and has been used effectively to create combustion ignition in gasoline engines for more than 50 years.

An "electronic ignition" system operates in much the same manner, except the primary voltage is "electronically switched" by a transistorized circuit, rather than the conventional breaker switch. The transistor switching circuit is normally housed in a separate "black box" and receives a switching signal from the distributor. This signal is usually some sort of low-grade energy "pulse" created by a light-sensing switch, a proximity switch, a magnetic-field sensor or some similar device that replaces the conventional breaker points. In one form or another, these pulse signals are synchronized in time with the camshaft/crankshaft by the rotating distributor shaft, exactly like the conventional breaker switch is controlled by the distributor shaft.

When the contact breaker system is working as it should, it will deliver the goods. If a comparison is made between a good electronic ignition system and a good contact-breaker

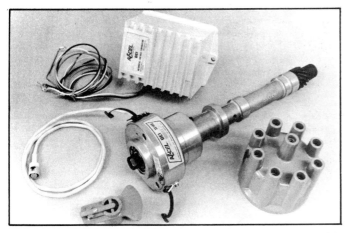

Nonconventional, "breakerless" ignition systems provide long-term performance and economy benefits. They eliminate primary voltage decline and dwell variations caused by breaker-point oxidation in conventional systems.

A conventional breaker-point ignition system can provide excellent performance as long as the points are replaced regularly. Specialty electronic "conversions" can also be used to reduce breaker-point wear.

system, the differences are very small. However, most comparisons are made under less-than-fair conditions. The conventional system is usually replaced after several miles of operation, just as it has deteriorated to a sorry condition. As a result, the electronic ignition appears to give a big boost in both mileage and performance. Under these conditions, an electronic ignition system will always seem to be much better.

The biggest disadvantage with a contact-breaker ignition system is that the level of performance drops off relatively rapidly. The contact surfaces of the breaker switch gradually deteriorate with use and the switch must be replaced regularly to keep the system in perfect working condition. On the other hand, when everything is in order, the typical electronic switching system will operate at peak capacity nearly indefinitely. But, this is not to say they are perfect. If a problem develops in the transistorized circuitry, an electronic system signs off permanently. In other words, it's either working perfectly or it's not working at all.

Even though a well-tuned conventional system provides adequate ignition, there is significant advantage to some electronic ignitions. A conventional system only applies 12 volts to the primary windings of the coil (in fact, most systems apply less than 12 volts to the coil after the engine has started), but many electronic systems can put more than 12 volts into the coil, and because the electronic switching occurs more quickly, they can often apply the voltage to the coil for a longer period of time. This produces a hotter and "fatter" secondary voltage (spark) to ignite the mixture. Very often the average hot rodder fails to utilize this extra spark energy and, as a result, the

full potential of an electronic ignition system is not realized.

If a high-voltage breakerless electronic ignition system is used, certain changes should be made to gain the maximum benefit from such a system. First, due to the greater secondary-voltage capability, an electronic ignition system will often allow the engine to be fitted with spark plugs one or two heat ranges colder than stock. This normally leads to a small increase in power, although this will not be true in every case.

Second, because of the higher secondary voltage, the spark plug gap can safely be increased, thus generating a bigger spark to ignite the mixture. This, in turn, usually means a

quicker propagation of the flame front and, consequently, the ignition timing can be slightly retarded without a loss in performance. If the ignition is not retarded when the flame propagation times are reduced, the result can be a small reduction in power. Usually, just a small amount of retardation is all that is needed. This, of course, assumes that the ignition advance was optimized prior to converting to the electronic system.

The real-world gains are, in almost all cases, very small. The graphic comparison of a controlled test is shown here to demonstrate this point. Each ignition system was adjusted and optimized to give maximum fuel economy.

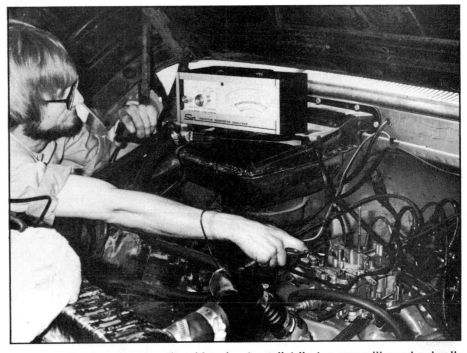

If your engine has a conventional breaker-type distributor, you will need a dwell meter to set and readjust the point dwell at regular intervals (the more often, the better). Here, a Sun engine analyzer from a home tuneup kit is being used to set the dwell on a smallblock Chevy distributor.

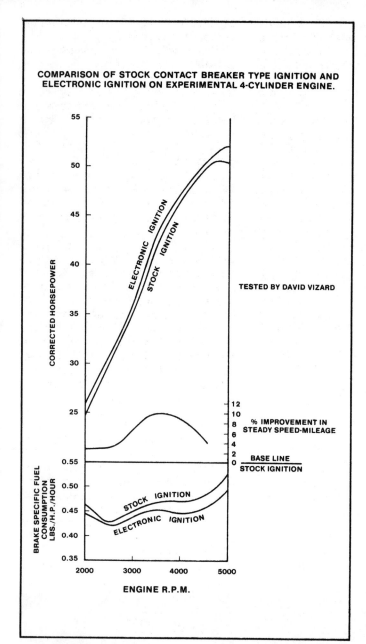

COMPARISON OF STOCK CONTACT BREAKER TYPE IGNITION AND ELECTRONIC IGNITION ON EXPERIMENTAL 4-CYLINDER ENGINE.

TESTED BY DAVID VIZARD

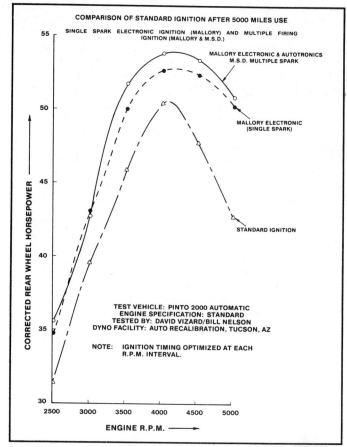

COMPARISON OF STANDARD IGNITION AFTER 5000 MILES USE
SINGLE SPARK ELECTRONIC IGNITION (MALLORY) AND MULTIPLE FIRING IGNITION (MALLORY & M.S.D.)

MALLORY ELECTRONIC & AUTOTRONICS M.S.D. MULTIPLE SPARK

MALLORY ELECTRONIC (SINGLE SPARK)

STANDARD IGNITION

TEST VEHICLE: PINTO 2000 AUTOMATIC
ENGINE SPECIFICATION: STANDARD
TESTED BY: DAVID VIZARD/BILL NELSON
DYNO FACILITY: AUTO RECALIBRATION, TUCSON, AZ

NOTE: IGNITION TIMING OPTIMIZED AT EACH R.P.M. INTERVAL.

However, the untold part of the story is not shown on the graph. After 10,000 miles the electronic ignition system was still functioning in top form. Over the same period the performance of the conventional system had dropped off considerably. Spark intensity was down, due to pitting of the points, and the ignition timing had changed due to wear of the cam-follower block of the contact points and the subsequent deterioration of the dwell angle.

The big advantage, then, with an electronic system is the virtual elimination of distributor maintenance. *Because it doesn't require maintenance, an electronic system inevitably improves economy on nearly every engine. It prevents gradual decline in ignition efficiency, saving fuel, and eliminates the recurring cost of replacing the points and condensor at* *regular intervals.*

MULTI-FIRING IGNITIONS

In recent years the development of multi-firing ignitions has produced some interesting effects not previously possible with conventional ignitions. Instead of producing a single spark during the firing cycle, a multi-fire ignition delivers a chain of sparks. Depending on the design of the system, the number of sparks at idle can vary from 6-24, but the frequency drops off as engine speed increases. The multi-firing ignition systems are probably the next best thing to multiple spark plugs.

The principle advantage of multiple ignition sparks is that the initial phase of combustion is faster. The flame is started from several points, rather than one, and the flame front spreads evenly throughout the chamber. Just

The MSD-7A pumps out enough energy to really fry your wieners! This is a sample: enough secondary voltage to bridge a 2-inch gap. Such extraordinary energy may provide cross-firing and leakage problems inside the distributor cap and plug wires, but when properly controlled, it gets the job done.

how much this will improve the power and economy of an engine depends on the flame characterisitics of the combustion chamber. Some cylinder heads have chamber designs that produce adequate turbulence for good flame propagation. The performance of engines with this type head will, therefore, benefit little from multifiring ignition. On the other hand, cylinder heads with open-type combustion chambers characteristically produce slow flame fronts and engines equipped with such heads almost always benefit considerably from these ignitions.

Power gains will vary in every case, but typically the improvement may range from none at all, on an engine like the smallblock Chevy that has compact chambers, to as much as 3% on an engine with open, emission-type chambers. This gain is in addition to that given by a good electronic ignition that had previously been optimized.

Also, a multi-firing ignition system usually requires less timing advance to get optimum results. When most engines are converted to a multi-firing system the total advance can be reduced by 2-4° without affecting performance. Here again, like other performance parameters, the total advance should be maximized through testing on a dynamometer. This is the only way to get the best setting for a non-stock application and maximize performance and economy.

Another aspect of multi-firing ignition operation worth considering is the possible fuel savings during cold starts. Personal testing by the author with a carefully calibrated carb and a multi-firing ignition system has shown that it may be possible in some applications to eliminate the carb choke. This particular test vehicle had a multi-fire ignition and a two-barrel Holley with manual choke. On days when the temperature was a little above freezing, it was found that two stabs on the throttle would inject enough fuel from the accelerator pump to start the engine without the choke, but it wouldn't quite maintain a smooth idle.

It usually took two or three starts before the engine would achieve a constant idle. Then the car could be driven away without the choke. If the choke was used, it was found only necessary to use the choke for about the first 50 feet.

Since this test was performed on only one vehicle, it would be difficult to surmise that all cars would respond in a similar manner. However, similar experience has been reported by other multi-spark users, and it seems certain that if a multi-spark ignition doesn't eliminate the need for a choke in more temperate climates, it will at least reduce the amount of time the choke must be engaged. The multi-spark operation greatly improves both the cold- and warm-idle quality of most engines because misfiring is virtually eliminated. If the first spark doesn't light the mixture, one of the successive ones will. (This quality has also been verified by many racers who use multi-spark ignitions on engines with very long cam timing and relatively unstable idling characteristics.)

ELECTRONIC IGNITIONS—OTHER CONSIDERATIONS

If you have changed from a conventional to an electronic ignition system, apart from electrical modifications that need to be made, there are several changes you can make to other engine settings to get the best from your electronic ignition. None of these changes will make a startling difference, but taken together, they

can add up to significant performance and economy gains.

First of all, it is often possible to use a leaner mixture with an electronic ignition system and, subsequently, if the carburetor is adjusted to provide a lean mixture, it may be necessary to readjust the ignition timing. It is also possible that an electronic ignition can change the advance characteristics provided by the distributor. The exact nature of this change is determined by the characterisitics of the electronic circuitry in the system and the design of the breakerless triggering device in the distributor.

Some electronic systems have a tendency to retard the total ignition advance at high rpm. This "built-in" retard was fairly common with early electronic systems, but modern high-quality systems will not retard the spark more than 1-2° and some of the very best will not affect the advance at all. However, if the system is of lesser quality, it may have a very significant affect on performance and economy. Although by no means common, the author has installed and tested electronic ignition systems that, with no other mechanical change, drop the total advance back as much as 12°, as compared to the same distributor with conventional breaker-point activation.

Sometimes this high-speed retard may be desirable (often turbocharged engines benefit from ignition retard at high engine speeds) but generally it will be detrimental to both performance and economy if the advance

If you are looking for the ultimate ignition, this may be it. The Autotronic Controls MSD-7A is a multiple-spark amplifier designed strictly for racing applications, but it can be used with most conventional or breakerless distributors.

The Autotronic Controls MSD-6C amplifier is designed to work with the standard Chrysler breakerless ignition system. It is a "plug-in" replacement for the stock electronic box and converts the system to multi-spark operation. This particular unit is designed for street use.

curve has already been optimized. After an electronic system is installed, the ignition should be checked on a distributor machine or, better yet, the engine and chassis combination should be thoroughly tested on a chassis dynamometer. Unfortunately, if this phenomenon occurs, it is difficult to correct, and often the only cure is to get rid of the system and find a better one.

If a super high-energy ignition system is used, the spark plug wires should be checked to make certain they have sufficient insulation qualities to avoid crossfiring. If the spark plug gap has been increased to take full advantage of the high energy, be especially aware of problems with the plug wires. When wide gaps are used, the resistance in each secondary lead is increased. The high spark energy generated by the coil will have difficulty jumping the wide gap at the plug, and it will seek a route to ground that has less resistance. Any small crack or imperfection in the plug wires or the distributor cap will provide a suitable escape route for this energy, and the result is misfire.

As far as plug gaps are concerned, tests have shown that there is little point in increasing the gap beyond .050-inch. Beyond this point the measurable improvements in combustion quality decrease considerably and the voltage required to jump larger gaps is extremely high. Very few practical electronic systems can reliably develop the enormous energy needed for daily operation at such levels, but the real problem lies in successfully

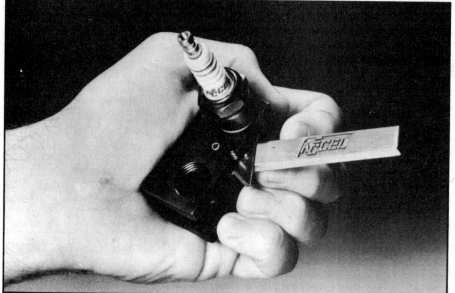

If a high-energy ignition is used there may be gains on some engines by increasing the spark plug gap. Testing has shown that opening the gap to .050-inch may improve both performance and economy. However, more gap than this gives little additional benefit. When wide gaps are used, an accurate tool must be used to insure precise settings and the gap must be checked and reset regularly.

Calibrating the ignition centrifugal advance requires knowledge and experience. The normal procedure is to perform an extensive series of power tests to determine the optimum advance at various engine speeds. However, if the engine is not an oddball combination, experts like Kevin Rotty of Automotive Recalibration can often rely on past experience to preset a suitable advance curve.

delivering this ultra-high voltage to the plugs. Extraordinary insulation measures are needed to prevent crossfire and misfire malfunctioning. And, since the gains are small in relation to the problems, the situation becomes totally impractical.

WHY IGNITION ADVANCE?

Apart from distributing the high-voltage developed by the coil to the spark plugs, the distributor has another important function: the mechanisms it contains must determine the best time to deliver the voltage to each plug. For maximum performance and

When a high-energy ignition is used to increase performance, a set of high-quality, large-diameter, silicone-jacketed spark plugs wires must also be installed to insure proper delivery of exceptionally high secondary voltage to the plugs.

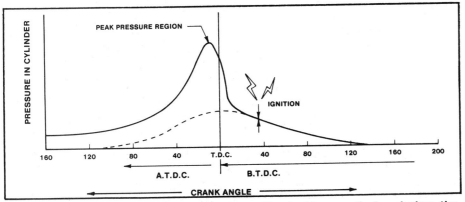

This graph approximates the pressure profile inside a cylinder during the compression, ignition and power strokes. When ignition occurs at about 36-38° btdc in a low-compression cylinder, the pressure is slow to rise because the inducted mixture has not been adequately compressed into a highly "explosive" mixture, and combustion is localized in a small area. Note though, that the pressure rise doesn't deviate from that created in a cylinder with higher compression until the piston is relatively close to tdc. By this time the initial combustion nucleus has expanded considerably, and a flame front bursts across the cylinder very suddenly. This is indicated by the rapid rise in pressure just before tdc. This spike of pressure occurs before the piston is ready to move down on the power stroke and robs power from the engine. *Providing too much ignition advance on a low-compression engine can cause the peak pressure rise to occur too early in the changeover from compression to power. The result is less power or, even worse, engine-destroying detonation!*

economy the point of ignition, often called the ignition timing, must be carefully controlled.

Under any set of operating conditions there is a precise, optimal point when the mixture should be ignited to obtain maximum work output from the charge of fuel and air. If the mixture is fired too soon, the combustion pressure in the cylinder will rise too early. This pressure will try to push the piston downward before the rod and the crank throw reach the optimum point in the crank rotation to gain the most work from the combustion. If this premature ignition is small, the result is simply a loss in efficiency and power, but if it is very large, the cylinder pressure and temperature can become quite high and create what is known as detonation. In the extreme,

this condition can actually pound holes in the tops of the pistons, destroy the rings and generally ruin the engine.

On the other hand, if the ignition timing is too late in the cycle, the mixture will not burn completely and expand at the best rate to deliver the highest possible amount of work to the piston, rod and crank assembly. This wastes energy that should be used to produce power and economy.

It could be said that the best system would ignite the entire mixture at the ideal time and all of the combustion energy and pressure available in the mixture would be used to push the piston down the bore. However, in actual practice it takes time for the relative volume of mixture spread throughout the chamber to ignite. For

the first few milli-seconds after combustion begins, a small amount of mixture burns and the pressure rise is extremely small. But, as the flame spreads through the mixture, the rate of pressure rise goes up very rapidly. The object of ignition advance is to start the combustion process just early enough so that the maximum pressure rise occurs when the piston is in the exact position in its downward travel on the power stroke to receive the maximum effect of the combustion processes.

This picture is complicated by several factors. First, as engine speed (crank rpm) increases there is less time during each cycle of operation for the ignition process to be completed. The speed with which combustion occurs will also change somewhat as rpm varies, but engine speed increases much faster than combustion speed. Second, the density of the mixture in the cylinder will also vary as engine speed changes and as the operating efficiencies and interaction of various components like the carburetor, manifold and camshaft change. And, as the density of the mixture changes, the speed of combustion and the time when the pressure rise occurs will vary accordingly. Third, the speed with which the pressure rise can push the piston downward will change according to the load on the engine. If there is a lot of resistance against the rotational motion of the crank (high load), the piston cannot move downward quickly (remember the engine is hooked directly to the drivetrain of the car). The pressure spike will try to push the piston down, but the high crank load will not allow the piston to move as quickly as the pressure rises. The only way to prevent these two forces from banging against each other is to initiate combustion earlier.

We have presented a graphic view of a typical pressure variation during combustion. Note that there is a very prominent spike when maximum pressure rise is created. For best power and economy this pressure spike should always occur at the optimal time in the power stroke. The object of spark timing is to somehow monitor all of these eventualities and create the spark in the cylinder at the exact right time to gain this best possible efficiency.

Before moving on we should mention that one of the most common mistakes made by hot rodders is to assume that the engine should have a lot of ignition advance. This is simply not true. If the combustion process inside the chamber can be effectively

For maximum part-throttle (cruise) economy the distributor must be fitted with a working vacuum-advance system. Numerous Delco-Remy vacuum cannisters are available, each starting the vacuum advance at a different vacuum reading and/or providing a different amount of vacuum spark advance.

The centrifugal weights and counterbalance springs of a GM Delco-Remy distributor are easily changed or modified to suit specific engine requirements. The size of the weights and strength of the springs determine the "rate" of advance (how fast the ignition advances in relation to engine speed).

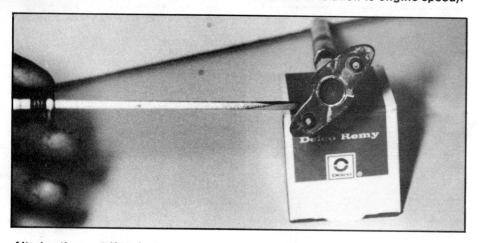

Altering the centrifugal-advance curve of a Delco-Remy distributor is simple, but it requires a little work. Sometimes the centrifugal-weight cams on top of the centershaft must be reshaped. These cams interact with the centrifugal weights to control the "shape" of the advance curve.

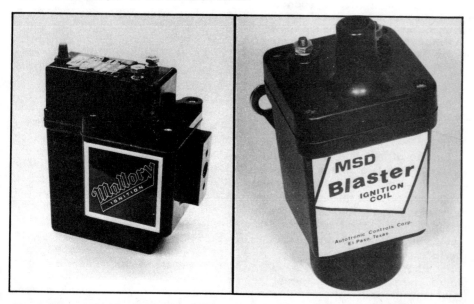

The ignition coil is one of the items most often overlooked in the search for performance and/or economy. The coil is a simple electrical transformer that steps up the 12-volt primary current to the very high secondary voltage needed to fire the spark plugs. Special aftermarket coils may be used to increase the step-up ratio, but no matter what brand is used, it is essential that the ignition coil always be in perfect condition.

completed with greater efficiency, the engine will require less ignition advance. In fact, an efficient engine needs less advance to achieve maximum power and economy. When considering ignition advance, always keep in mind that some is good, more is worse and too much will ruin the engine!

SPARK ADVANCE

The distributor governs the amount of ignition advance in two ways. First is the centrifugal advance mechanism. This advances the ignition timing in relation to engine speed. As engine speed goes up, the centrifugal advance increases the amount of spark advance. This offsets the reduced time available for combustion as engine speed increases. However, as engine speed continues to climb there is also more turbulence created in the inducted mixture. This causes the mixture to be "mixed" better and burn more quickly. As a result, the rate of rpm-related advance is not directly proportional to engine speed. Typically, as engine speed increases in the lower rpm ranges, the centrifugal mechanism provides a lot of spark advance, but as the engine speed continues to build in the higher rpm ranges, the amount of advance provided is relatively smaller. If engine speed and "best" centrifugal advance are plotted on a graph, the result is usually a curve with a significantly reduced rate of advance above 3000-3500rpm.

The other major factor affecting the ignition advance is the mixture density. When the engine is at idle the carburetor throttle blades are nearly closed and the breathing ability of the engine is artificially inhibited. This creates what we call "high manifold vacuum" and a low-density mixture volume in the combustion chambers. This means each cylinder is only filled to a fraction of capacity. Consequently, when the mixture is compressed, the pressure at the end of the compression stroke is lower than would have been the case if the engine was at full throttle and a high-density mixture was produced in each cylinder. In other words, such action has artificially reduced the effective compression ratio by virtue of throttling the engine. Because the charge density in the cylinder is less, the combustion rate is slower. As a result, more time is needed to burn the mixture and, therefore, more ignition advance is required.

The second way spark advance is controlled is through the vacuum-advance mechanism in the distributor. This mechanism monitors the pressure (vacuum, if you will) conditions in the manifold and increases or decreases the spark advance accordingly. It is simplest to consider this as the engine-load ignition control. *As far as economy is concerned, vacuum-advance control is the single most important ignition factor affecting part-throttle economy. If economy is in any way a consideration, under no circumstances should any engine be operated without a distributor that has a functional and thoroughly-tested vacuum-advance mechanism.*

When any major engine modification is made, the vacuum-advance requirements will invariably be altered. The chart included here shows how typical modifications affect the advance characteristics. To insure top performance and continued economy the vacuum-advance curve must be optimized for each specific engine and chassis (load) combination.

If the combined effect of vacuum and centrifugal advance are considered, the situation quickly gets complicated. The only way to guarantee that the ignition advance is optimal at all engine speeds and operating conditions is to have it thoroughly tested on a chassis dynamometer. A talented operator can accurately plot rpm and power requirements and establish the optimum ignition advance dictated by the actual operating conditions. These plots should be made from data acquired at part throttle and at full throttle to determine both centrifugal- and vacuum-advance characteristics. After the dyno operator has established what advance characteristics are needed, a distributor machine can be used to test and alter the advance mechanisms in the distributor until the desired results are achieved.

Adjusting the centrifugal advance is a relatively straightforward procedure. It usually entails swapping centrifugal weights and counterbalance springs until the desired curve is achieved.

The vacuum advance can be a little more difficult. On many Ford distributors an adjustable vacuum control is provided. In this case some simple adjustments with an Allen wrench will usually bring the vacuum advance to the desired point. On the other hand, General Motors and Chrysler distributors do not have adjustable vacuum-advance controls. The controls are replaceable, but this means you will have to sort through the numerous available vacuum-advance cans to find one that will give the desired results. A better solution might be to install an adjustable vacuum-advance unit, such as that being produced by Crane Cams. This utilizes an adjustable mechanism, similar to the Ford unit, and can be dialed in to give the desired results.

IGNITION REQUIREMENTS CHART

ITEM	EFFECT ON TOTAL ADVANCE	EFFECT ON CENTRIFUGAL ADVANCE	EFFECT ON VACUUM ADVANCE
Low octane fuel	Retard from ideal because detonation limits advance.	Rate of advance slows down and total advance should be less.	At high vacuum fuel octane makes little difference. As vacuum drops, less advance can be used due to detonation limits.
Raise CR	Needs Less TOTAL timing.	Advance rate stays about the same or slightly slower.	Vacuum advance stays about the same.
High energy ignition	Needs less TOTAL timing.	Advance rate stays about the same or slightly slower.	Vacuum advance stays about the same.
High lift, stock duration cam	Needs slightly less total timing.	Advance curve needs slowing down from 2500.	Stays about the same.
Longer period than stock cam	Needs slightly more total timing.	Needs quicker advance up to approx. 2500-3000 RPM.	May need about the same total advance but may need to come in quicker.
Reworked heads	Needs less total.	Stays about the same.	Stays about the same.
Headers and high flow exhaust systems	Usually needs less total but if initial charge temp. drops, due to good scavenging, may need more total advance.	Advance curve may need to go faster or slower depending upon scavenging characteristics.	Usually need a little more vacuum advance.
Turbochargers	Needs less total.	Usually needs quicker centrifugal curve.	Approx. the same total vacuum but should have pressure retard.
High flow intake manifold and carbs	Needs less total.	Slightly slower from 2500 on up.	Could require more or less depending on manifold characteristics at part throttle.
Water injection	Needs more total.	Remains unchanged.	Remains unchanged.

CHAPTER 10 BLUEPRINTING

- ● COMPONENT SELECTION
- ● MATCHING COMPONENTS
- ● PISTON COATINGS
- ● CON RODS & CLEARANCES
- ● VALVE PREPARATION

BLUEPRINTING FOR ECONOMY & POWER

If you are building an engine from scratch to produce both performance and economy there are numerous blueprinting techniques you should use to increase the efficiency of the engine. These are not fancy tricks as much as they are ordinary blueprinting techniques followed by most engine builders. The important thing to remember is to aim for a realistic power goal. It is possible to have respectable street performance and very acceptable economy but, as we have said right from the beginning, you can't have it all. If you're smart, you'll shoot for a reasonable power goal and use the techniques described here to squeeze as much mechanical efficiency as possible from the engine. If you plan carefully, spend your money wisely and aim for a realistic goal, you will be proud of the results every time you turn the ignition key.

DECIDING DISPLACEMENT

When building an engine from scratch, you may be able to select the stroke length of the crank and the bore size of the block from among several available options. In this way you can vary the displacement of the engine to suit your needs. The smallblock Chevrolet engine is a prime example. Over the past 25 years this popular engine has been available in factory-stock displacements ranging from 262 to 400 cubic inches. And, by swapping the various cranks and blocks, it is possible to gain a displacement nearly anywhere in this range.

The question then becomes, what is best for performance and economy. This is not as easy a decision as it would at first appear, because we have two totally contradicting situations. If you are looking for maximum economy, the engine displacement should be kept as small as practicable. If you want maximum performance, there's an old racing adage that says there's no substitute for cubic inches. In other words, the bigger the engine is, the more power it will produce. When you consider both factors, the problem becomes, where to draw the line. The choice often boils down to selecting between a heavily modified, small-displacement engine that will produce less low-rpm torque but deliver good power at a relatively high engine speed, or an engine with greater displacement and fitted with perform-ance equipment designed to develop max torque at a low engine speed. To a certain extent, this decision is often based on cost and convenience factors rather than technical and efficiency considerations. But, by any measure it is an uncertain decision, and some general guidelines may help you make a suitable selection.

If we consider the selection of displacement from a technical standpoint, the choice should be based on two primary factors: how much power is desired and in what rpm range the engine is expected to produce usable torque and power. Both of these factors are limited by a great number of technical factors. For instance, it's not possible to just say "I want 500 horsepower," and then proceed to build the engine. The selection of a practical power level is almost always limited by mechanical constraints, like reasonable engine life expectancy, operating conditions and stress limitations.

The point in the rpm range where peak torque is developed and the point where max horsepower is produced will, in the same way, be dictated by a different set of technical criteria. For example, if the car is relatively heavy, is fitted with an automatic transmission and has a relatively high differential gear, the engine must be able to produce a lot of low-rpm torque (and will, therefore, have less high-rpm power). If it does not, you'll probably be able to measure low-speed and standing-start acceleration with a sun dial. On the other hand, if the vehicle is light, has a manual transmission with a very low first gear ratio and a relatively low final drive ratio, it is possible to use a smaller displacement and design the engine to produce horsepower at a relatively higher engine speed.

This may be confusing, but let's put some numbers into the picture. If we are building an engine for a relatively light vehicle and want strong and reliable street performance, we should get good results, both from the point of view of performance and economy, with a specific power output between 0.8 and 1 hp/inch. Considerable experience has shown that this output level is realistic for a modified street engine. And, for our purposes, you may assume that a higher specific output (power per inch of engine displacement) would require a rather radical engine configuration and would limit the economy potential of the engine.

From this specific power goal we can determine a suitable displacement in relation to power. Here is an example: let us assume we want 360hp from a smallblock V8 engine. (This is not an unreasonable expectation.) And we want to be conservative (realistic!), so we select a specific output in the middle of the range just quoted, and figure on about 0.9hp/inch. We then divide 0.9 into 360 and get a displacement of 400 inches.

Of course, there is some leeway here. Such a power figure could also be extracted from a 350-inch engine, but the specific power would be above 1 hp/inch. This would make it necessary to use a more radical cam, and would make the engine less efficient in the lower rpm ranges most often used on the street. Also, it would affect low-speed performance, especially if the car was heavy or had an automatic transmission and/or a high rearend ratio. It takes pure low-rpm torque to accelerate a heavy or highly geared (2.50-3.30:1) vehicle. In such cases, a large-displacement engine, in conjunction with a short cam, will give far better performance results than a small engine.

From a fuel-efficiency standpoint, a smaller engine operated at a higher engine speed will produce about the same fuel efficiency, at the same power output, as a larger engine operated at a lower engine speed. Let's look at a random numerical example (these figures are selected just to show the relative effect and should not be taken as a factual example): for comfortable freeway cruising it might be possible to gear a 300-inch engine so the vehicle runs 21mph per 1000rpm (in high gear). If the 300-inch engine was replaced with a 400-incher that produced the same absolute power (and, therefore, developed less specific power), and we wanted to get approximately the same acceleration performance, it would be possible to raise the gear ratio. After the change we might find (depending upon the actual gear ratio selected) that the larger engine produced 30mph per 1000rpm and, subsequently, to cruise at the same speed the engine rpm would be lower. *If both engines produced about the same overall power, during cruise conditions they would probably produce similar fuel economy.*

Note however, that if we do not change the gear ratio when the larger engine is used, the cruise rpm will remain the same in both cases. The larger engine should then use more fuel at cruise and it should produce lower overall economy. But, the acceleration performance would be considerably improved, obviously, at a sacrifice of economy.

Moreover, a real difference can be found if car weight is brought into the picture. If we can reduce weight, the same performance can be retained with a smaller engine and a higher gear ratio. As a result, fuel economy will increase. For instance, an 1800lb car with a 150-inch engine is going to be a lot more fuel efficient, yet have the same approximate performance as a 3600lb car with 300-inch engine. (In fact, this generalization does not account for mechanical and aerodynamic losses, but for our purposes it illustrates the general concept.) *It is carrying simplicity to extreme, but we can say the best possible combination for performance and economy would be a light car, a small engine, a broad torque curve and a low gear ratio. But, as in all things, what is theoretically possible is always limited by real-life practicalities.*

Once the displacement decision has been made and the basic engine components selected, the final results will still depend largely on the quality of the preparation and assembly work.

Engine building is an art as much as it is a science. Good workmanship during assembly is essential for power and economy. Novice engine builders are well-advised to plan carefully and seek professional help for the more difficult tasks.

Block preparation is important and the most important consideration is the bore finish. When possible, a honing plate should be mounted on the deck during the final finish. The honing plate simulates the distortion created when the cylinder head is bolted to the block. This technique gives a "truer" bore shape, but this type of prep is usually more expensive. If you are looking for maximum performance and economy, however, the extra money will be well invested.

CYLINDER BLOCK PREP

The most important aspect of block prep is the finish of the cylinder bores. There are two primary factors to consider: size and finish. *Generally speaking, small piston-to-bore clearances are better, so long as they are consistent with avoiding piston seizure.*

Sealed Power Corporation produces piston rings with a smaller-than-normal end gap. This allows the engine builder to custom fit each ring to gain the minimum acceptable gap when the ring is installed in the bore. There must be enough clearance to prevent the ring ends from butting together when the engine reaches operating temperature, but a tighter fit will prevent combustion pressure from escaping past the ring. Unless you are experienced, don't set the gap too small; follow the manufacturers instructions carefully.

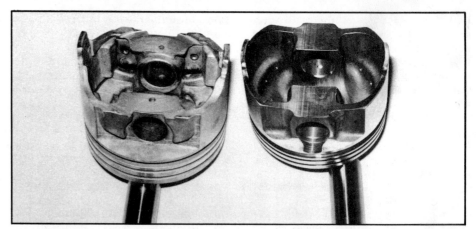

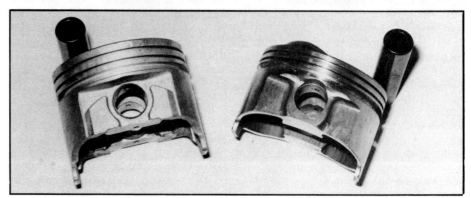

However, the finish size must be judged in relation to the pistons. The amount of clearance required to retain the correct clearance when the engine reaches operating temperature will vary, depending upon the design and construction of the piston, and will be discussed in detail in the piston section.

The other factor to consider is the finish. On many high-performance and racing engines it has become customary to put a very fine finish on the bore. In these cases the final prep is completed with meticulous care. The bores are honed on an automatic honing machine such as a Sunnen CK-10 Cylinder King, the block is fitted with a deck plate to simulate the cylinder-head mounting stresses and the operator is thoroughly proficient.

If you are preparing your block under these stringent conditions, a relatively fine finish can be used, although it is still preferable to not have quite as fine a finish as used on most racing engines. A 400-grit stone is commonly recommended for the final hone of a street engine. The hone pressure is adjusted to give a surface finish (RMS) between 8-16 micro-inches (as specified by the Sunnen manual). If moly rings are used, it's best to use less hone pressure and develop a finer finish, around 8 micro-inches. When using the wider, cast-iron rings, more pressure should be used to give a finish around 16 micro-inches. If the

For racing-type applications, forged pistons are considered essential to withstand the abuse of constant, high-rpm operation at or near the detonation limit. For street engines, an impact-extruded (cast) piston has enough strength and is considerably cheaper. Cast pistons (left) also allow tighter wall clearance and, consequently, increased oil control and ring life.

finish is too fine with cast-iron rings, it will take a long time for them to break-in. If the honing procedure is not able to follow an accurate bore center (for instance, if the finish is done by hand), a coarser finish should also be used to assist break-in.

If chrome rings are used, an even coarser finish is necessary. The finish required by the chrome can vary widely, depending on whether the rings in question have a surface treatment to assist break-in. You should check the recommendations given by the manufacturer and consult with your machine shop to make certain they know what kind of rings you will be using and what special prep, if any, will be required.

PISTONS & RINGS

For high-performance applications it's normal to select forged pistons and ignore the so-called cast-type piston. However, in engines designed to produce average or moderately high power output, cast pistons are better than forged pistons. Cast pistons have better ring-groove life, and they have marginally less heat conductivity, so more heat is kept in the chambers. They are designed to allow a closer fit in the bore, thus giving better control of the piston rings. And, best of all, they are a lot cheaper than forged pistons. (This is the sort of economy we can all understand.)

If you intend to build a normally-aspirated engine that will produce peak power around 4500-5000rpm, cast pistons should be considered. If high engine speeds and relatively high power are expected (specific output above approximately 0.8hp/inch), a forged-type piston becomes desirable. Nonetheless, when shopping for forged pistons, remember that close piston-to-wall fit is still desirable.

Many of the specialty pistons available are made of high-expansion alloys. They may be perfectly acceptable under racing conditions, but they are not as suitable for street-driven applications. Pistons that fit loosely in the bore when the engine is cold are definitely not going to help economy or factors like oil contamination, emissions, etc. The ultimate consideration, whether a cast or forged piston is used, is to select a design with low expansion characterisitics, so the fit between bore and piston can be closely controlled under all operating conditions.

The current trend with high-performance pistons is to use narrow rings. This is to prevent so-called "high-rpm ring flutter" and reduce frictional drag between the ring and bore wall. Under competition con-ditions narrow rings perform well, but they produce accelerated bore and ring face wear. Unless you are building an engine that is capable of, and repeatedly expected to produce, exceptionally high engine speeds (above 6000rpm), you will be happier with normal-width rings. *Inevitably, conventional rings and pistons are cheaper, they will last longer and the performance difference is so small that it cannot be detected without extensive dynamometer testing.*

PISTON COATINGS

If you must use custom pistons, there is at least one feature (among many) that should be checked. If the top ring is located high on the piston, near the deck, the piston-to-bore seal will be improved and performance will be better, in terms of both power and mileage. The gains may be small but they are there. However, if the ring is put too close to the top of the piston, the ring land is likely to collapse because of the higher temperatures close to the top of the piston.

It is possible to combat this by coating the piston with a thin layer of special insulating material. This coating is a ceramic compound bonded to the piston, and it effectively contains combustion heat in the chamber, rather than allowing it to transfer into the piston crown. To date, the only commercial insulation coating widely available is Heanium, a process devel-oped by Heany Industries. They have several years experience coating pistons for applications ranging from Grand-National racing engines to huge, diesel, pumping engines and just about any other sort of engine you can imagine. *Numerous dynamometer tests of all-out racing engines fitted with Heanium-coated pistons have shown that power increases between 4-8% are possible.*

Another advantage of coating the pistons is that it increases reliability. The coated piston crown is less susceptible to detonation damage. During detonation the concentrated temperature at random spots on the deck can rise to a very high level. Since the strength of aluminum drops off rapidly as temperature rises, especially above 250°F, the piston deck may fail in a matter of a few seconds if the detonation is allowed to persist. However, an insulation coating on the deck may prevent any damage for as long as 20 or 30 minutes.

After a coating is applied, localized heat does not build as rapidly, giving the engine an effective safety margin. With open-exhaust engines, detonation is usually not readily apparent and a standard piston can easily be damaged before the detonation is detected. On an engine equipped with mufflers the detonation can often be heard and the engine stopped before any damage occurs. However, even momentary detonation, accumulated over a period of months, can cause

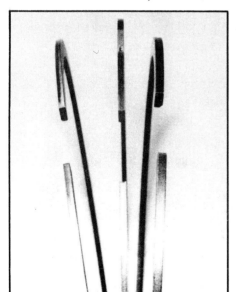

In recent years thin rings (left) have become popular in racing engines. However, for street use a wider ring (right) will provide better long term sealing and durability.

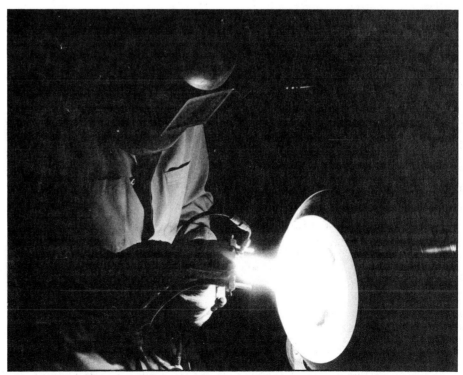

Heanium coating is applied through a high temperature plasma process. Here, a large commercial piston is being coated.

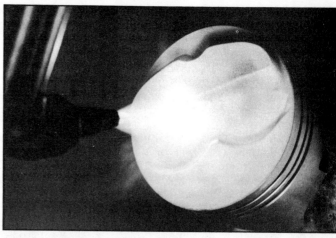

Pistons are not the only items that can benefit from ceramic, thermal-insulation coating. The turbocharger housing (left) has been coated to prevent heat loss to the atmosphere.

A thermal coating protects this piston from the flame of a oxy-butane torch. The flame would very quickly cut through an untreated piston.

damage to the ring lands and rings. *The strength of a coated piston is increased substantially by virtue of the lower operating temperature, but couple this to the fact that the top ring can be moved closer to the crown of the piston, creating better cylinder sealing, and the benefits of piston coating become quite attractive.*

CONNECTING RODS

The most important part of connecting rod preparation for a high-performance engine is to make sure they are straight. Bent and distorted connecting rods can rob an engine of substantial power and economy. It goes without saying that checking rod alignment must be on every rebuild list.

Now let's deal with all the other things you can do to stock rods to help them from the performance and economy point of view. It is a good idea to have the bearing bore checked for size. If necessary, the bore should be reconditioned to bring the diameter to prescribed limits. When the rod has

been subjected to detonation, the journal bore may be distorted. If such a rod is used without reconditioning, it can seriously foreshorten bearing life, resulting in an expensive teardown much sooner than would otherwise be the case.

If the engine is expected to operate at high engine speeds, it is best to size the rod bearing bore to the low limit of the tolerance specification. This will increase bearing-retention "crush" and reduce the chance of bearing failure. It is bearing crush that holds the bearing in the rod bore, not the bearing tangs, and the crush is created by the bearing bore squeezing the bearing insert tightly inside the inner circumference of the bore.

It is especially important that bearing retention be maximized because you will want the compression ratio to be as high as practicable (for fuel efficiency) and with the marginal octane of current fuel supplies, detonation is a constant problem. If the bearings are not tightly retained in the rods, this detonation will surely lead to a spun bearing. And, a spun bearing is

usually the first of a short series of events that lead to total engine destruction.

When you inspect the rods after teardown, if you find that the journal bores have suffered damage due to a spun bore, do not attempt to reuse the rod. If the bore has become out-of-round by more than .001-inch, it will not be possible to bring it back to a tight tolerance without angle-cutting the cap. This practice produces unwanted stresses at the corners of the rod-bolt notch. This is not desirable, especially in a performance engine, and can lead to premature rod failure.

If you find evidence of prior bearing trouble, buy a new connecting rod. Avoid buying a reconditioned rod unless you know it has been reconditioned from a good core. Otherwise, you may have a rod that suffers from the same problem as the one you are

Some engines are susceptible to bearing failure if they are subjected to long-term detonation. This tendency can be markedly reduced by sizing the crank-journal bore of the rod to the minimum size, giving maximum "crush" when the rod bearing is installed.

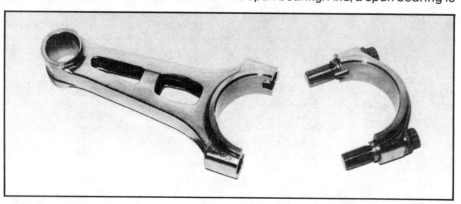

Lightweight engine components, such as this MechArt stainless-steel connecting rod, produce quick engine response and slightly better acceleration, especially in the lower gears. Of course, it is difficult to justify such exotica in a street engine, but intelligent efforts to lighten stock components can, with very little expense, achieve similar results.

If the rods have been reworked and extensive material has been removed from the balancing pads in an effort to lighten the rods, the crank assembly should be rebalanced.

Before machine work begins, the crank should be fitted into the block with the bearings to be used in the final assembly. If the crank binds when it is turned, one of three things can be wrong. Either the block is distorted (pulling the main bearing bores out of alignment with each other), the crank is crooked or the bearing clearance is too tight. To find the problem, begin by checking the crank clearance. If the clearances are correct, check main-bore alignment with a long, true straight-edge. The last thing to suspect is the crank.

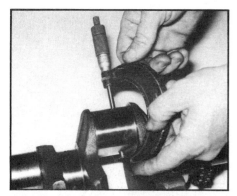

Unless the journals of a used crank are severely scored, there is little reason to regrind a crank if it is intended for a street engine. Some manufacturers have a selection of bearing sets with different inside diameters. Selecting the right set often eliminates the need to "resize" the journals. If you must have the crank reground, have the main and rod bearing surfaces sized to fit on the low side of the clearance recommended by the bearing manufacturer.

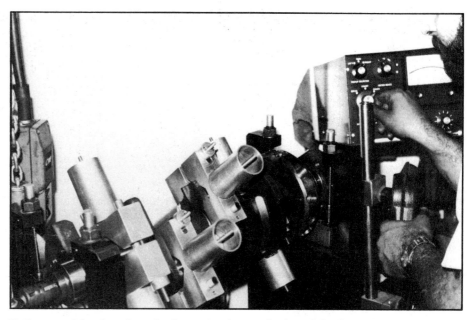

If the combined rod and piston (reciprocating) weight has changed due to lightening or component replacement, the crankshaft may also need to be rebalanced.

rejecting. If you cannot buy a recon-ditioned rod from a trustworthy source, buy a new one. It is, by far, the safest bet.

Another aspect to consider is rod weight. Most connecting rods have large balance pads at both the pin and journal ends. These balance pads can be reduced in size to lower overall rod weight, although some of the material should be left so that the rods can be balanced before final assembly. By removing the flash marks left from the forging and reducing the balance pads to more sensible proportions, the weight of the connecting rods can, in many instances, be reduced by 10-15%. This does not increase power but it does improve engine response and produce better crank acceleration.

Racing engines are often fitted with a high-pressure or high-volume oil pump, but these modifications are not intend-ed, nor required, for most street engines. A special pump may solve peculiar oiling problems but under normal conditions, when operating clearances are carefully controlled and a reasonable rpm limit is observed, excessive oil volume and/or pressure only leads to oil-control problems.

But, any economy gains created by reducing reciprocating weight would be small and difficult to measure.

After the rods have been reworked, they should be checked for surface cracks. Magnafluxing is one of the most common crack-detection sys-tems and many shops have equipment to perform these tests. If minor surface imperfections are located, they can be eliminated by polishing. If major cracks are discovered, the rod should be discarded and replaced with one that is free of major surface imperfections.

BEARING CLEARANCES

If the clearance between the crank journal and the rod bearing is too wide, bearing wear will be greatly accel-erated. If the bearing clearance is too tight, unnecessary friction will be created. This will hurt both power and economy. Generally speaking, the best bearing clearance is that specif-ied in the manufacturers' overhaul manual or, if you are using non-stock bearings, follow the instructions given by the manufacturer of the bearing inserts. This applies to both rod bear-ings and crank bearings. By using recommended clearances, the effects of small alignment errors between various components are minimized, yet clearances are not so wide as to require increased oil delivery.

A common, but unfortunate, back-yard hot-rod trick is to increase the bearing clearance and raise oil pres-sure by increasing the spring tension in the pressure-relief valve of the oil pump. It remains uncertain what gain this "trick" is expected to produce, but this should not be done unless you have a very good reason (and there are few good reasons). Abnormally high pressure increases pump drag, absorbs engine power (albeit a small amount) and creates ring problems because of the excess oil thrown onto the cylinder bore walls. Generally, engines that will not exceed 6,000rpm and that have bearings set to stock clearances should be limited to oil pressure around 40-50psi. In all cases, the oil pressure should be limited to the absolute minimum consistent with reliable operation.

CYLINDER HEAD PREPARATION

In the camshaft chapter, reference was made to the problem of increased valveguide wear created by high-lift cams. Even if the engine is equipped with a modest cam, guide wear can still be a problem. When valveguide clearance increases, at high rpm the valves may not seat squarely and provide proper cylinder sealing. This results in a loss of power. Also, worn guides will let oil pass into the combustion chamber. Subsequently this oil mixes with the intake charge, diluting the octane value of the fuel. And, present-day fuels are already bad enough without reducing the octane further. An oil-contaminated intake charge will increase detonation problems, a situation that may be especially troublesome if the engine was built with the highest useful compression ratio.

To combat such a problem when overhauling cylinder heads, it is a good idea to utilize a long-life guide. Typically, bronze guide inserts will last longer than cast-iron guides and, though they are somewhat more expensive, they are a good investment. In all cases the valvestem-to-guide clearance should be checked carefully to bring it within the low range of the acceptable clearance specification. This can be an aid to both power and economy.

Not only should the guides be in sound condition, but the oil seals must also be in top shape. Many production cylinder heads do not use a positive-sealing stem seal. If you are rebuilding this type of head, it is advisable to install the best oil seals you can get. This may require some additional machining of the guides to accept the seal, but this is a good investment.

If the valves are also worn and need to be replaced, consider using a replacement valve that has a chrome-plated stem. Such a valve will have a

The valvestem-to-guide clearance must be tight (but not so as to cause galling) and effective oil seals must be used to minimize oil leakage into the chambers, especially with current low-octane fuel. If oil passes down the guides, the fuel octane is "diluted" and the likelihood of detonation increases. Bronzewall valve-guide inserts are often used to replace worn cast-iron guides. They are also popular with racers because they can be operated with minimal guide clearance.

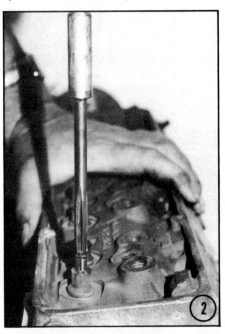

Installing bronzewall guides is fairly simple if a guide-reconditioning machine is available. The machine is aligned with the centerline of the existing guide, and the guide is reamed to a larger diameter to accept the new insert.

considerably longer service life. They cost a bit more, but ultimately they are worth it. They can be fitted to bronze guides with minimal clearance and little danger of seizure, and can be expected to operate for 100,000 miles or more.

Once the guide has been reamed, a tapered reamer is used to prepare the entry so the bronze sleeve can be pressed into place.

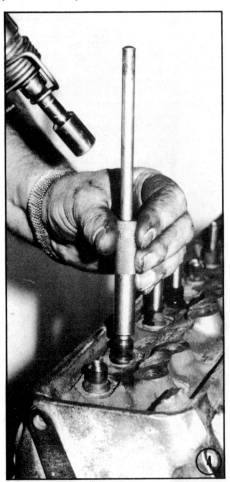

The guide insert is fitted to this special installation tool and an impact air hammer is used to drive the insert into the reamed guide.

Once the insert has been pressed in far enough, the excess length is cut off.

After a special knurling tool has been run through the guide to expand it into the base metal, the guide is reamed to size.

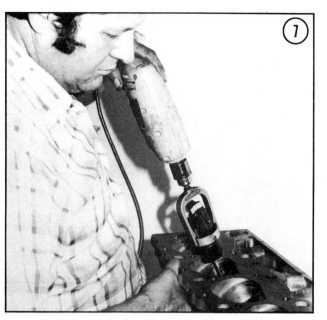

Exacting engine builders prefer to hone the inside of the guide to gain the desired clearance with the valve-stem. The most common method is to use a Sunnen valveguide hone to prepare each guide, as demonstrated here at Townsends Racing Works.

To get an exact fit, the inside diameter of the guide must be measured carefully with a snap gauge and a micrometer and this must be compared to the outside diameter of stem of the specific valve to be fitted in the guide.

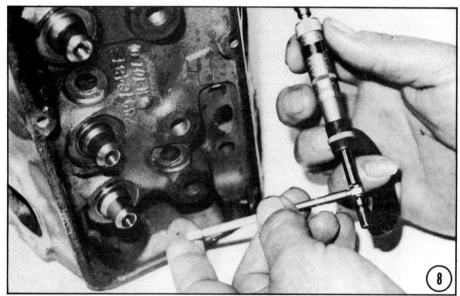

For absolute oil control, the top of the guide may have to be machined to accept "positive" oil seals. The most commonly available brand is the Perfect-Circle seal. But, several other types are available, and almost all of them work very well when properly installed.

CHAPTER 11 DRIVELINE

- REAR END & TRANS RATIOS
- USING OVERDRIVES
- SAVE GAS—GET POWER
- AERODYNAMICS

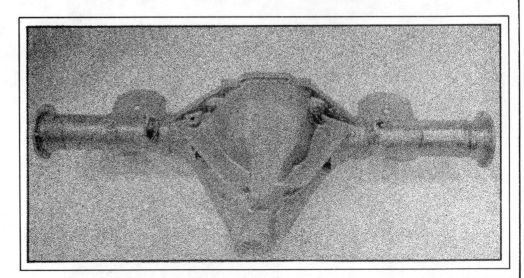

DRIVELINE

Some of the components that have the greatest effect on performance and economy are contained in the driveline. To this point we have been concentrating on building an engine that will deliver high-performance and suitable fuel efficiency for reasonably economical day-to-day driving. However, the power developed by the engine is delivered to the drive wheels through the transmission and the rearend. The gear reductions (ratios) contained in the transmission and the rearend differential gears will ultimately determine how successfully the power developed by the engine is translated into the actual movement of the vehicle. And, as our outlook on economy changes, the general configuration of the high-performance driveline will also change.

GEAR RATIOS

First, let's make certain we all are speaking the same language. Throughout this book we have often explained that nearly all engine components are designed and should, accordingly, be selected to work effectively in a certain engine speed range

Selection, coordination and installation of proper driveline components is among the most important decisions made by the backyard mechanic looking for both performance and economy. A muscle car of yesteryear, as exemplified by this clean '68 Plymouth Barracuda, can provide outstanding all-around performance when a sensible, modern driveline is installed.

(rpm). It's not possible to build an internal-combustion engine that produces torque and horsepower throughout an unlimited engine speed range. Because of the mechanical limitations inherent in the general design of such engines, they are highly

efficient only in a relatively narrow rpm range. *Therefore, the key to efficient overall operation is the coordination of all the components so they are effective in the same engine speed range.*

We have also pointed out that once the specific combination of components in an engine has been selected and assembled to work in a certain rpm range, the driveline gear ratios should be selected to complement that speed range. Specifically, if the best engine speed range is high in the rpm band, the rearend gearing should be low. And, if the combination is selected to be most efficient at low engine speeds, the gearing should be high. The question now becomes, what are high gear ratios and what are low gear ratios?

A 4.10:1 gearset is an example of what is normally called a "low ratio," and a 2.73:1 gearset is typically considered a "high ratio." This is a little confusing, but we'll try to make it as simple as possible. If the numerical ratio is large (e.g., 4.10, 4.88 or 5.13 is large relative to 1.00), the gearing has a low ratio, and vice versa, if the numerical ratio is low (e.g., 2.73, 3.07 or 3.25 is small relative to 1.00), the gearing has a high ratio.

This stems from the fact that engineers consider a 1:1 ratio (this is the ratio of the drive gear to the driven gear) to be a high ratio. In this case there is no gear reduction and there is no torque multiplication. But, if the drive gear has fewer teeth than the driven gear, the ratio is said to be reduced and the torque multiplication increases. This is the case in normal differential gearing. There are fewer teeth on the pinion gear (the drive gear), and there are more teeth on the ring gear (the driven gear). The rearend gearing is designed in this matter so that the torque of the engine can be multiplied sufficiently to accelerate the relatively heavy mass of the ordinary vehicle from a standstill up to a cruising speed.

Now that we generally know what a gear ratio is, let's see how the ratio affects engine performance. From our earlier discussions we know that engines are more economical when they operate with a higher effective compression ratio. But remember, the effective compression ratio is governed by how much the throttle is opened. If you look at the graph on page 94, you will see the effect of running a vehicle with high gears, relatively low engine speed and the throttle almost closed; as compared with a low gear ratio, higher rpm and more throttle opening.

In each case, the maximum power output is identical, but look at the steady-state (cruise) economy figures. Note that the vehicle with a higher gear ratio achieves better mileage. *A basic rule of thumb is that if you increase the overall gear ratio and, therefore, decrease the engine rpm in* *relation to vehicle speed, "theoretical" mileage will increase approximately the same amount as the percentage decrease in engine rpm.* For instance, if the gear ratio is increased and the resultant engine speed at 55mph is reduced by 10%, the overall economy will increase by approximately 10%.

However, in real life the mileage increase will not be quite this great because of the nature of stop-start driving. During cruise conditions the highly-geared vehicle will use less fuel than the one with lower gears, but these gains are offset somewhat by the increased throttle application required to accelerate the car from slow speeds (the high gear ratio makes it more difficult for the engine torque to accelerate the car).

This is all well and good as a general discussion of gear design, but what about some specifics. Choosing a gearset for your vehicle is going to be difficult. On one hand, you will probably want a low ratio because it will make the car accelerate like a rocket. (Cars built strictly for drag racing often have ratios as low as 5.57 or 6.17:1!) But, this is also going to send your gas mileage into orbit. On the other hand, you may want a high ratio, something like a 2.73 or 3.07:1, to get good gas mileage. The acceleration perform-

ance will drop off, but the engine cruise rpm will be reduced a lot and this means more mileage.

Between these two extremes there are many other choices. Your job is to find a ratio that will give the perfect compromise between acceleration performance and cruise economy. This balance can only be determined by your specific desire for performance and your willingness to pay for the gasoline to feed that desire. And, with the cost of gasoline, the smart enthusiast will always think and act conservatively.

Though it is tempting to go for a low ratio, before long you may regret the decision every time you dump another $30 in the gas tank. It makes more sense to select a higher ratio. When you get the right balance between performance and economy, you can take pride in the fact that you have built the "perfect machine" for your personal needs. Maybe you won't have the hottest thing on Main Street, but while the guy with 4.88 gears leaves his car in the garage six days a week because he can't afford the gas, you can cruise the street with a truly functional street machine. Selecting a reasonable rearend gear is a mighty big step in this direction.

The specific ratio choices available

Selection of a suitable rearend ratio is the key to a satisfactory balance between performance and economy. As economy becomes a more important consideration, it is essential that the final drive ratio be increased to improve cruise mileage.

The ever-increasing emphasis on economy has rekindled interest in manual transmissions. A four- or five-speed manual trans will provide good fuel efficiency and performance.

When the rearend ratio has been increased to improve cruise economy, it is often possible to select or modify a manual trans to lower the relative ratios of first, second and third gears. This will improve acceleration from low speeds and still allow the car to cruise at a low engine speed (rpm) in direct drive.

to you will be dictated by the type of rear axle the vehicle has and what sort of work may be required to install the gearset (sometimes the axles, the axle tubes or the differential carrier may have to replaced or altered in order to install a very high or very low gearset). The complete range varies from a high of 2.20-2.50:1 to a low of 6.5-6.7:1. We can, however, break this wide range into some general categories. Anything in the 2.0-3.0 could be considered an economical street gear. The 3.0-4.0 range encompasses what we would presently call performance street gearsets. Gears from 4.0 to 5.0 are strictly for racing or something like a street/strip machine (though anything in this range is far better suited to serious racing than street driving). And, differential gear below 5.0:1 is strictly all-out drag racing territory.

So, what is a good choice for an all-around street machine? First of all, forget what you read in magazines that talk about the good old days. The good old days are gone and they're not going to come back. We live in the 1980's. *Unless you have a time-warped mind and a bottomless wallet, don't try to run anything lower than about 3.25-3.50:1, especially if you drive the car daily.* In times past, a 3.90 or 4.10:1 gearset was considered a good street/strip gear. This is currently too much gear for a practical V8-powered vehicle. (And, as we shall soon see, it's not necessary.)

Let's look at a specific example. If we team a 3.50:1 rearend gear with a rear tire that has an overall tire diameter of about 26-27 inches and a rolling radius of about 13 inches, the engine rpm at a cruise speed of 55mph will be approximately 2400rpm. With the right induction setup and camshaft, this should provide excellent acceleration and reasonable gas mileage. If the ratio is lowered to 3.90:1, the 55mph cruise rpm goes up to 2700 rpm. This will improve acceleration performance but reduce economy by about 20% (theoretical). If we raise the ratio to 3.25:1, acceleration performance will decline but economy will go up by about 14% (theoretical).

(The figures given above were calculated from the formula: OR x MPH = 0.006 x RAD x ER; where OR = overall gear reduction, MPH = miles per hour, RAD = tire rolling radius, ER = engine rpm and 0.006 is a constant. By algebraically solving this equation it is possible to determine any one of the variables if the other variables are known. In the case above we solved the equation for RPM and substituted the known quantities: overall reduction in direct drive [3.50, 3.90 or 3.25], rolling radius [13 inches] and miles per hour [55mph].)

There are other ratios between 3.25:1 and 3.90:1 and many outside this range. You simply pay your money and take your choice. But, before you make a decision you must think about what kind of transmission is going to be used.

TRANSMISSION RATIOS

The transmission gears are used to provide additional torque multiplication. This is necessary to keep the engine in the relatively narrow efficient-rpm range while still allowing the

The Doug Nash Engineering Street Five-Speed is a surefire route to rocket-like acceleration and excellent cruise economy. This rugged specialty design is a bolt-in replacement for most factory-type four-speeds, and provides a super-low first-gear ratio and an additional fifth ratio to improve gear spread and driving flexibility.

vehicle to operate in a wheel-speed range from 0mph to 55mph (or, perhaps, more). To accelerate the vehicle in a reasonable fashion, the gear reduction in the rearend is multiplied by the gear reduction in the transmission. This very effectively increases the torque application to the rear wheels.

For example, if the first gear of the transmission has a ratio of 2.50:1, the "overall reduction" is obtained by multiplying this reduction times the rearend ratio. Suppose the trans is in a car that has a 3.50:1 rearend gear, the overall first-gear reduction is 8.75:1 (2.50 x 3.50 = 8.75). The same can be said of the rest of the gears in the transmission. Of course, in high gear the ratio is usually 1:1 (also called direct drive), so the overall reduction is simply equal to the rearend ratio (1.0 x 3.50 = 3.50).

Without much imagination we can see how this additional gear reduction considerably broadens the overall picture. Suppose we combine a high rearend ratio with a trans that has a low first-gear ratio. Example: let's assume we can build a car with a 3.0:1 rearend gear and a transmission with a 3.50:1 first-gear ratio. When the car is cruising in 1:1 high gear, the overall reduction is only 3.0:1 (1.0 x 3.0 = 3.0) and the engine speed as 55mph with a 26-inch tire will be about 2000rpm. This will give excellent economy with most V8 engines. But, when we leave the stoplight with the trans in first gear, the overall reduction is 10.5:1 (3.5 x 3.0 = 10.5). And, if you're not certain, take our word for it—even with a modest engine this is enough gear reduction to satisfy all but the serious racer.

In past years this scenario would have presented quite a problem. The automotive transmissions of yesteryear did not generally provide this much first-gear reduction. Typically, a four-speed automotive transmission would have a first-gear ratio of about 2.2 or 2.5:1. Combined with a rear gear of 3.5:1, this would give an overall reduction of 7.7 or 8.75:1. Not very impressive. With a 4.10:1 rear gear the picture brightens. The overall ratio would go up to 9.0 or 10.25:1, but as we have already seen, this would raise the cruise engine speed in direct drive to a very high level - 3000rpm at 55mph with a 26-inch tire.

But, the picture is changing. Manual transmissions with super-low first-gear ratios are becoming available. An example is the Doug Nash Engineering Street Five-Speed. This transmission was originally intended for specialized racing applications that re-

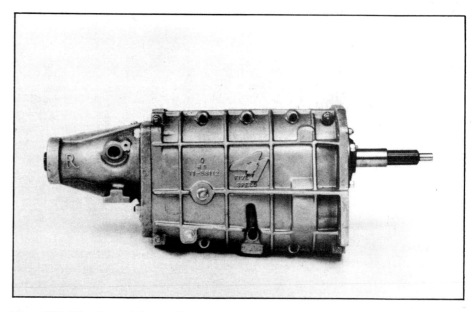

The DNE Five-Speed has a first-gear ratio of 3.27:1. Combined with the recommended rearend ratio of 3.08:1, it will provide an overall first-gear ratio of about 10:1. In effect, it provides cruise economy of 3.08 gears and acceleration comparable to a factory four-speed with 4.56 gears!

quired very low first-gear reductions, but the original concept has been altered slightly by the designers at Doug Nash Engineering to make it suitable for street use.

The DNE Five-Speed is a direct replacement for most General Motors Muncie four-speed transmissions (which normally have a first-gear ratio of 2.2:1 or 2.52:1), and it can readily be adapted to other applications. The street version has a 3.27:1 first gear and the Nash engineers recommend that it be combined with 3.07:1 rearend gear for best overall street performance and economy. This gives an outstanding overall first-gear ratio of 10.04:1. With a 26-inch tire the 55mph engine speed is an equally outstanding 2100rpm. (Compare this to a trans with a 2.20:1 first gear. To get the same overall ratio, the rearend ratio would have to be 4.56:1 and the 55mph engine rpm would be 2800rpm, resulting in a 25% drop in economy.)

As fortune would have it, this transmission is not cheap (though most people consider the high design and construction quality of this transmission to be worth the price). Nonetheless, it is an excellent example of what can be done by carefully selecting and matching a high rearend ratio with a trans that has a relatively low first-gear ratio.

OVERDRIVE TRANSMISSIONS

Another approach to building an efficient driveline for performance with economy is to use an overdrive transmission. An overdrive transmis-

The new B&M Super Drive torque converter can improve the fuel efficiency of most automatic transmissions. It can be installed in place of a stock converter and is designed to reduce the economy losses normally associated with torque converter "slippage."

sion attacks the problem differently. *With an overdrive transmission, the vehicle can be fitted with relatively low differential gears that will give good acceleration, but for cruising, the transmission can be shifted into overdrive to decrease the overall reduction and increase cruise economy.*

An overdrive decreases overall gear reduction in exactly the opposite way that a normal transmission increases reduction. An overdrive has more teeth on the drive gear than on the driven gear. The ratio is usually expressed as a percentage. For example, we might say an overdrive gives a 90% reduction. The ratio of drive teeth to driven teeth will be .90:1. The overall reduction is calculated in the same way as described above. If we have a 3.50:1 rearend gear and the trans overdrive gear has a reduction

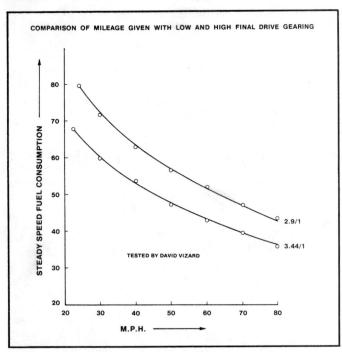

COMPARISON OF MILEAGE GIVEN WITH LOW AND HIGH FINAL DRIVE GEARING

STEADY SPEED FUEL CONSUMPTION

2.9/1

3.44/1

TESTED BY DAVID VIZARD

M.P.H. →

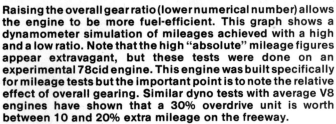

Raising the overall gear ratio (lower numerical number) allows the engine to be more fuel-efficient. This graph shows a dynamometer simulation of mileages achieved with a high and a low ratio. Note that the high "absolute" mileage figures appear extravagant, but these tests were done on an experimental 78cid engine. This engine was built specifically for mileage tests but the important point is to note the relative effect of overall gearing. Similar dyno tests with average V8 engines have shown that a 30% overdrive unit is worth between 10 and 20% extra mileage on the freeway.

These two tires show the difference between a normal- and a low-profile tire. Low-profile tires will increase the acceleration, cornering and braking ability of the car. (The increase in cornering power is usually brought about by the lowered ride height.) But, tires with a taller profile, such as the Goodyears shown here, produce more economy because they have the effect of increasing the overall gear ratio, and they usually produce a smoother ride because of greater tire flexibility.

ratio of .90:1, the overall ratio is 3.15:1 (.90 x 3.5 = 3.15).

Manual transmissions with overdrive gears were commonly available 30-40 years ago. Their popularity died away during the years when gasoline was plentiful, but current conditions have brought them back to the forefront. Some Detroit automakers are now offering automatic transmissions with an overdrive top gear. The specialty manufacturers are also getting into the act. An "overdrive" torque converter has recently been introduced for conventional automatic transmissions, and some companies are burning the midnight oil to develop a low-cost, performance-type, add-on unit that can be used as an overdrive gear with standard three- or four-speed manual transmissions.

It's still a little early in the ballgame to make a sound judgement of how durable these devices may be, but there can be little doubt of their theoretical value. *A well-designed unit will reduce engine cruise speed and the result will be better economy.*

POSSIBLE SAVINGS

When fuel was cheap, the savings offered by a super-low trans, a five-speed trans or an overdrive were not enough to make them necessary or worthwhile, but as fuel prices go up, these driveline devices become very attractive. *Their use and general availability is bound to increase dramatically in the next few years.*

In terms of mileage gains, an overdrive transmission or a super-low first-gear transmission (with a high final-drive ratio) is absolutely one of the best investments available to the performance enthusiast. There can be no doubt of their mechanical value. They offer notable potential fuel savings, while retaining excellent acceleration performance. In effect, they reduce the cruise rpm of the engine, and it's relatively simple to estimate their overall value. We mentioned this general rule earlier, and it is worth highlighting again: economy gains will be approximately proportional to the decrease in cruise engine speed. It is this simple: if the cruise speed can be decreased by 10%, the gas mileage will increase by about 10% (approximate).

The devices we have been discussing are all designed specifically to decrease engine cruise rpm. The economy gains for any of them can be calculated by determining how much they reduce cruise rpm (at least, to a certain point, e.g., it's not practical to consider cruise engine speeds much

below 2000rpm, because the engine cannot develop enough power at such low speeds to overcome rolling and wind resistance). There are also some nice side effects from this approach. When the cruise engine speed is reduced, engine wear (per mile driven) will also be reduced and the engine noise in the interior of the car will decrease.

Of course, overdrive transmissions, super-low and five-speed transmissions are all currently somewhat expensive. There are several types and brands available, but most of them cost about $600 to $1000, and you will also have to figure some installation expenses in addition to the initial cost. This is unquestionably a big cash expenditure for the sake of economy. But, when combined with a properly selected differential gear ratio, most of

Selecting a "taller" tire (one with a larger rolling radius) can improve economy. The gains are always small, nonetheless if the tire rolls further during each revolution, the obvious result is better mileage.

these devices can provide blood-stirring acceleration performance and very reasonable cruise economy. It would probably take many miles of driving to totally recover this kind of money through gas savings. However, each individual will have to make his own decision about cost versus fuel and performance.

We must mention, though, from our point of view, that any improvement in gas economy means less U.S. dollars sent to foreign countries. In a way, spending more money on an efficient transmission makes better sense than sending our U.S. dollars to OPEC countries by the shipload, in exchange for barrels of crude oil.

TIRE SIZE

If you are working with only a limited budget, a similar effect can be achieved by selecting rear tires with a larger diameter. Larger tires have a larger rolling radius and a longer circumference, and they roll further each time the wheel makes a full turn. This is, in effect, a cheap way to slightly increase the gear ratio (provided, of course, that the large-diameter tires replaces worn-out tires, otherwise the change would not be very economical). This has long been a trick used by bracket (and some professional) racers to fine-tune the overall drive ratio for maximum performance, but it is not without some snags.

First of all, ensure that the larger tires will fit within the confines of the rear fenders without any undue problems. Check this carefully before buying the tires, or be prepared to beat on the inner fender panels and possibly

undertake some minor (or major) body sculpting to accommodate the big tires. You must also face the fact that you will lose some acceleration performance. Remember, this is the equivalent of raising the differential ratio (the amount of change will vary, depending on the ratio of the new tire circumference to the old tire circumference).

In addition, rear tires that are exceptionally tall will raise the back of the car, possibly affecting the handling characteristics adversely and increasing the aerodynamic drag. All of these factors may weigh heavily against any possible gains in economy, so think carefully about the results before you make a decision you might regret. Tires are expensive and a wrong decision will sting for a long time. Nonetheless, the next time you have to buy tires, it is something worth considering.

AERODYNAMICS

At typical highway speeds, the major portion of the power developed by the engine is used to push the car through the surrounding air. Any reduction in aerodynamic drag not only helps economy but also helps performance. Unfortunately, the image of a heavily raked Funny Car streaking down the quarter-mile is about the worst approach to take as far as aerodynamics, road handling and stability are concerned. Those big tires sticking out in the wind and the rear-end jacked up a dozen inches do

nothing to help aerodynamics or performance and economy. When you have 2000 horses and six seconds to get to the end of the strip, the traction and aerodynamic considerations are entirely different than when you have 300 horsepower and all day to make it down Main Street.

Most modern tires have ample traction to launch a street vehicle without excessive wheel spin. There is little reason to increase the rear ride height of the chassis, and putting big tires on the rear and allowing them to stick out in the breeze is about like dragging a parachute around behind the car. It is much smarter to try to build a car with the least amount of drag. Lower the car as much as practicable without creating ground clearance problems and use wheels and tires that are as wide as possible but able to fit inside the stock fenders.

Fortunately, "racy-looking" add-ons like air dams and spoilers not only add to the performance image but also increase aerodynamic efficiency. Recent tests have shown that reducing airflow under the car can be especially beneficial. A front air dam that comes as close to the ground as possible will prevent air from rushing under the car. This reduces lift and drag. As a result, performance and economy will increase. The gains are very small, so it will not pay to become fanatical about this, but if you can install a front air dam without excessive cost and you like the racy look it adds to the car, feel doubly justified in the expense.

Attention to aerodynamics equals better economy. For example, if you are going to install super-wide tires, they should be completely enclosed within the fenders to reduce drag. This often requires that the fenders be extended, or "flared," as exemplified by this slick **IMSA Mustang race car.** Even with the greater frontal area, attention to aerodynamics has given this car less wind resistance than a stock Mustang!

CHAPTER 12 WATER-INJECTION

- "BURNING" WATER!
- CARB JETTING MODS
- SPARK ADVANCE FOR POWER
- BUYING THE RIGHT UNIT

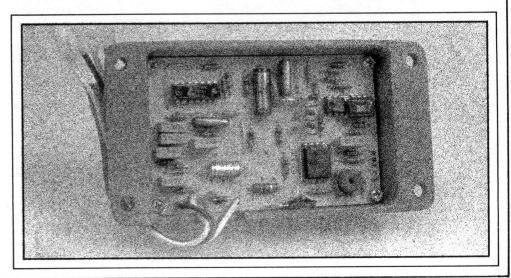

WATER INJECTION

Water injection has fascinated inventors almost since the advent of the internal-combustion engine. Invariably these devices have been accompanied by extravagant advertising and promotional claims of truly impressive stature. If any of this puffery is to be believed, water injection is the ultimate panacea for power and economy.

If you have read some of these claims, you may well ask why water injection should help power and mileage. After all, water doesn't burn! If you have asked this question, you get an "A" for logic, because adding a water-injection system to your engine and making no other changes will not help the power or the mileage one iota. In fact, a water-injection system does not help the performance of the engine in any way, but it does allow certain changes to be made that will help performance.

In other words, a water-injection system is a secondary economy device. By injecting water into the cylinders, the effective octane of the fuel is increased. The more water that is injected, the more the apparent octane of the fuel goes up (at least to a certain point). This is the result of the cooling effect created as the water is vaporized during induction and combustion. To give an example, with a properly metered water injection it is possible to successfully use fuel with a measured octane as low as 70-75 in an engine with a compression ratio as high as 17:1. Without the water, detonation would be so severe that the engine would be destroyed in seconds, but with the correct amount of atomized water added to the incoming mixture, the detonation is totally suppressed.

If you are uncertain whether you need a water-injection system, there is a very simple rule to follow. If your engine is not detonating and the ignition timing has been advanced to the maximum point for best power, it is very unlikely that a water-injection system will help the economy or power of your engine. If you don't have a detonation problem but the ignition timing has been retarded to a less-than-optimum condition to prevent detonation, water injection will definitely help. It will prevent detonation and allow the ignition to be advanced to the best overall timing for power and economy.

Although it is difficult to give an exact numerical value to the gains provided by water injection, it is possible to compare the relative power output of a water-injected engine running on low-octane fuel with the power given by a nonwater-injected engine using high-octane fuel. Under these conditions a high-compression engine burning high-octane fuel, without water-injection, gives more power as long as detonation is not encountered. However, if the compression is lowered to permit the use of low-octane fuel and water is not injected, the power is substantially reduced. But, if the compression is kept high and low-octane fuel is used along with water injection, the power level is raised. This leads to one conclusion: if water injection allows a higher compression ratio to be used, it means that the octane rating of the fuel is effectively raised. This is achieved with no other sacrifice, other than the initial cost of the water-injection apparatus.

Although water injection provides less maximum power than racing fuel, it does have a distinct advantage when you consider economy of operation. When operating under throttled conditions, an engine needs less octane to function, and detonation is usually not a problem because the engine is relatively lightly loaded. This means a

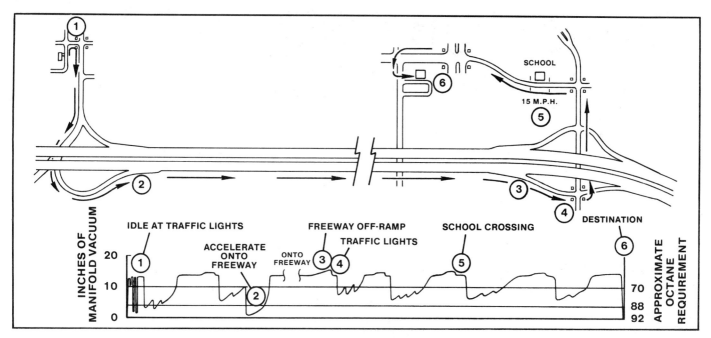

INCHES OF MANIFOLD VACUUM — APPROXIMATE OCTANE REQUIREMENT

IDLE AT TRAFFIC LIGHTS — ACCELERATE ONTO FREEWAY — ONTO FREEWAY — FREEWAY OFF-RAMP — TRAFFIC LIGHTS — SCHOOL CROSSING — DESTINATION

vehicle cruising down the road at 55mph with approximately 12-14 inches of vacuum would probably get by quite nicely on fuel of around 60-70 octane. But, when manifold vacuum drops, due to the throttle being pushed open, the cylinders become more packed with air. This is when the detonation problem occurs, and this is when water injection can be a big help. By utilizing a water-injection system to suppress open-throttle detonation, the static compression can be raised as high as 10: or 12:1. Such high ratios produce very good part-throttle mileage figures and, if you study a typical driving cycle, you will note that most driving is done under high manifold-

This is a representation of a typical suburban trip. The graph is a plot of engine vacuum along the trip. Note that for most of the trip 70-octane fuel would suffice because the manifold vacuum is high (low load) and for more than 95% of the trip 88-octane fuel would prevent detonation. The engine actually "needs" high-octane fuel only during a small portion of the driving cycle but it must be operated on relatively expensive 92-octane fuel all the time to prevent detonation. However, a water-injection system will allow this engine to run on 70-octane fuel, and during brief low-vacuum conditions, the water-injection will suppress detonation.

vacuum conditions. During such operation the engine is least efficient and, therefore, stands to gain the most by an increase in the compression ratio.

However, even with water injection the engine will lose about 5% power, compared to a high-compression engine with high-octane fuel. To a large degree, this discrepancy can be offset, but not without some additional expense. The power loss can be limited

by mixing alcohol with water in about a 1:1 ratio. Of course, you may think it's easier to mix the alcohol with the fuel. But consider this: high octane isn't needed when the intake manifold vacuum is high, because the cylinder filling is insufficient to require high octane. By injecting water and methanol only when it is needed to suppress detonation, a minimum amount of anti-detonant is consumed. As a

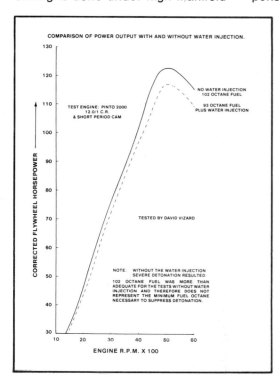

COMPARISON OF POWER OUTPUT WITH AND WITHOUT WATER INJECTION.

CORRECTED FLYWHEEL HORSEPOWER

NO WATER INJECTION 102 OCTANE FUEL

93 OCTANE FUEL PLUS WATER INJECTION

TEST ENGINE: PINTO 2000 12.0/1 C.R. & SHORT PERIOD CAM

TESTED BY DAVID VIZARD

NOTE: WITHOUT THE WATER INJECTION SEVERE DETONATION RESULTED. 102 OCTANE FUEL WAS MORE THAN ADEQUATE FOR THE TESTS WITHOUT WATER INJECTION AND THEREFORE DOES NOT REPRESENT THE MINIMUM FUEL OCTANE NECESSARY TO SUPPRESS DETONATION.

ENGINE R.P.M. X 100

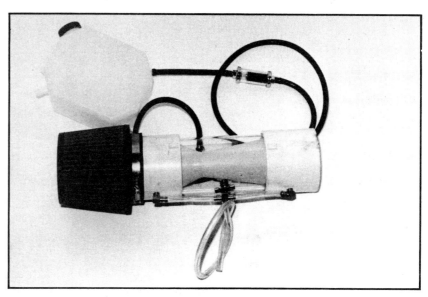

The Clifford system is not a water-injection system, in the normal sense of the word. The incoming air is "humidified" as it is drawn through the porous venturi. Generally speaking, the Clifford system is equivalent to an increase of 3-5 points of octane. However, it has limitations. It may restrict maximum airflow, reducing high-rpm power, and the flow at low rpm may be too low to humidify the air sufficiently to totally suppress detonation.

result, less alcohol is used and operating costs are reduced.

JETTING

If a water-injection system is used, especially with a water-alcohol mix, it is possible, even beneficial, to lean the carburetor main metering system a small amount. During normal operation, excess fuel is metered into the air at wide-open throttle to prevent detonation through the cooling effect of the evaporating fuel. If water is injected, the cooling action is brought about by the presence of the water, and normally the equivalent of one jet leaner will give the same power but better fuel consumption.

The method will vary, depending on the make of carburetor, but the popular Holley carburetor can easily be calibrated to accommodate a water-injection system. The part-throttle mixture can be leaned by reducing the main jet orifice size by one step, as indicated by a Holley jet chart. This will also lean full-throttle mixture, but if the full-throttle mixture is correct without water injection, it will be necessary to reduce the wot flow (wide-open throttle) by reducing the fuel admitted through the power-valve system.

When the manifold vacuum drops off at full throttle or under heavy load, the power valve opens, admitting extra fuel through the power-valve channel restrictions to the main wells. This system is designed strictly to increase wot/full-load fuel delivery. Reducing

If a water-injection system is added to an engine equipped with a Holley carb, and if the carburetor was accurately calibrated prior to the installation, the power-valve channel restriction may have to be reduced slightly to maintain the most efficient air-fuel ratio throughout the rpm range.

power-valve enrichment is not easily done, but it is possible to reduce the area of the channel restriction. However, if you are not well-versed in Holley operation and modification you would be wise to limit metering changes to just replacing the main jets (these modifications are covered in detail in the book *Holley Carburetors* available from S-A Design Publishing Co., see page 128).

If water-methanol mix is used, the methanol will contribute to the combustion process and increase power output slightly. This should also be considered when reducing the gasoline fuel delivery. With the water-methanol system it is entirely possible to develop more power from a low- or medium-compression engine and low-octane fuel than from a non-injected, high-compression engine and straight high-octane gasoline.

IGNITION TIMING

To get the maximum benefit when a water or water-alcohol injection system is installed on an engine, it is necessary to experiment with the ignition timing. The part-throttle ignition timing is not likely to be significantly different (the water injection is not working under these conditions), but the ignition timing at full-throttle/heavy load should be checked.

Depending on the type of combustion chamber, charge temperature and several other factors, it may be necessary to provide more or less ignition timing when the water injection is working. Each engine must be treated individually. Generally speaking, most engines will be able to use more ignition timing, and this will aid power and economy.

Another point to consider is that if the ignition system is giving a marginal spark without the water injection, when the water is added to the incoming mixture, a misfire problem could appear. To avoid this, make sure the ignition will deliver enough voltage at all times for a strong spark.

TURBO ENGINES

On turbo engines a water-injection system can be used to suppress

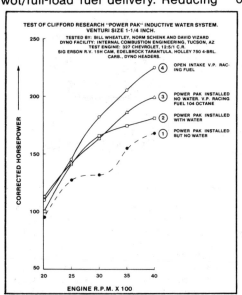

The author tested the Clifford Research Power Pak system on this 327-inch Chevrolet. The system appears to produce the equivalent of an octane increase of about 3-5 points, but the presence of the venturi in the airstream may, depending on engine size and crank speed (rpm), restrict maximum airflow at wide-open throttle. Curve #1 of the graph was generated with the Power Pak installed, but no water was used. The power curve was limited when detonation occurred and it was necessary to reduce the throttle setting to avoid engine damage. Curve #2 was produced with water in the unit. This suppressed the detonation and allowed more power to be developed, but at 2000 and 2500rpm, traces of detonation could still be identified. Power curve #3 was taken using V.P. brand racing fuel and no water in the Power Pak. (Relative humidity during tests was about 10% and, for practical purposes, the ambient air was considered to be dry.) On test #4, again using V.P. racing fuel, the Power Pak was removed, and the intake flow was unobstructed.

Water injection is very beneficial on turbocharged engines. Two different methods may be used to control the system. First, a boost-sensitive switch may be used to turn on the water. Second, when boost pressure develops in the manifold, this pressure can be fed into the water reservoir to force water through the water-injection system. No matter which type of control is used, the most common place to inject the water is into the carburetor venturis.

The Edelbrock Vara-Jection kit is a conventional-style water injector that monitors engine speed and vacuum to determine how much water and when the water should be injected. It is a complete kit with extensive mounting and electrical hardware and unusually extensive installation and operating instructions.

detonation under boost conditions. This is especially helpful with high-boost systems that must use low-octane fuel (normal pump gas). If the water is injected in proper proportion, it is feasible to use 15-17lb of boost in an engine with an 8.5:1 compression ratio. Under these conditions, the water injection will normally allow a substantially greater amount of boost to be used, thus making it possible to gain more power from the engine than would be attainable without that water.

Again, a water-alcohol or water-methanol mix is better than just straight water. The alcohol will improve the charge cooling effect, and if water-methanol is used, the methanol will contribute to combustion and, in most cases, will produce additional power.

BUYING A WATER INJECTION UNIT

When you decide to buy a system, be aware of the vast technical differences between the many various types and brands of currently available water or water-vapor injection systems. The most important characteristic to consider is that the system will be able to inject sufficient quantities of water to do an adequate job. There are some devices on the market that introduce a very small amount of water into the airstream, and it is often claimed that these systems will operate for thousands of miles on a pint of water. Such a small amount of water will have only a limited effect on the engine operation.

If the system is not able to inject

enough water, at the exact right time, it isn't going to suppress detonation. Basically, a water-injection system must be "load sensitive." As the throttle is opened and the engine works harder to accelerate the car or push it up a hill, the system should begin delivering water in a progressive fashion. As the load increases, more water should automatically be delivered.

Engine load is a function of both manifold vacuum and engine speed. An efficient system will sense both of these variables and control both the "timing" of the water delivery (when the injector is switched on or off) and the amount of water that is injected. This is very important. The system should be calibrated to inject just

enough water to suppress detonation and no more. Any excess water will only serve to reduce combustion efficiency and power.

A properly calibrated water-injection system can provide some impressive results. Of course, this will vary depending upon how well the system is designed, how well it has been calibrated to the engine and how well the engine has been tuned to gain the full efficiency of the water, but the author has had excellent results with a Spearco Injectronic II system. Using such a system he has been able to operate engines with as much as 11.5:1 compression on 88-octane pump gas without detonation problems.

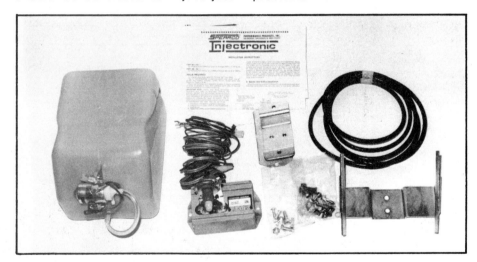

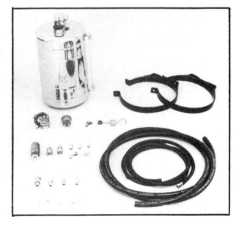

The Spearco, electronic, water-injection system is one of the most sophisticated systems available. The system monitors engine vacuum and rpm, and uses an electronic circuit to control when and how much water is injected. The author has used Spearco systems on numerous test engines and has operated engines with compression as high as 12:1, even with short-duration cams (creating high effective compression), without detonation problems.

Gale Banks Engineering offers this water-injection system designed specifically for turbocharged applications.

CHAPTER 13

NITROUS-OXIDE INJECTION

- GET POWER WITH ECONOMY
- SUPER POWER WITH TURBOS
- NITROUS SYSTEM DESIGN

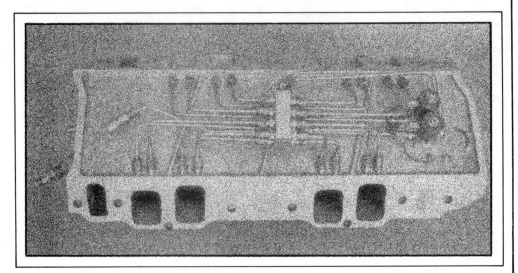

NITROUS-OXIDE INJECTION

Nitrous-oxide is a simple chemical compound that contains 36% oxygen, by weight. When it decomposes, free oxygen is released, and as every hot-rodder knows, oxygen is important. Air is drawn into the engine and mixed with fuel so that the oxygen contained in the air will support the eventual burning (combustion) of the fuel. In effect, all forms of supercharging create more power because additional oxygen (in the form of extra, or denser, air) is forced into the engine. Additional fuel is added to the enlarged charge of oxygen and when this "supercharged" fuel-oxygen burns, more power is created.

Nitrous-oxide works in much the same way. Instead of mechanically forcing more air into the engine, nitrous-oxide is injected into the inducted airstream along with an extra dose of fuel. As the nitrous-oxide breaks down, the oxygen it contains mixes with the fuel-rich intake charge. And, since the intake charge now contains an artificially enlarged amount of oxygen and fuel, the power output of the engine is increased. In simplest terms, nitrous-oxide injection can be viewed as "chemical

Horsepower in a bottle! This nitrous-oxide bottle contains 10lb of liquid nitrous oxide. When the tap is turned on, the gauge will read the vapor pressure in the bottle. The pressure varies with temperature and does not indicate how much nitrous is left in the bottle.

supercharging."

Nitrous-oxide is also beneficial because it cools the intake charge, increasing the density and oxygen content even more. When it is stored under high pressure, it is in liquid form. When the pressure is relieved, the liquid nitrous-oxide expands rapidly and converts to a gaseous state, releasing oxygen and creating a temperature drop. This expansion can create localized temperatures as low as -128°F. This temperature drop cools the surrounding air, and as our physics teachers always told us, when the temperature goes down, the density goes up. As a result, the density (and oxygen content) of the intake charge will increase considerably and, subsequently, power is increased. (This effect can loosely be correlated to the intercooling systems used on some racing turbocharged engines.)

A nitrous-oxide injection system is unusually simple. A storage tank for the pressurized nitrous-oxide is installed in a suitable location, usually the trunk of the car, and an electric fuel pump is added to the fuel system to supply the additional enrichment fuel. The enrichment fuel is pressurized by the electric pump, and the pressure inside the nitrous-oxide container

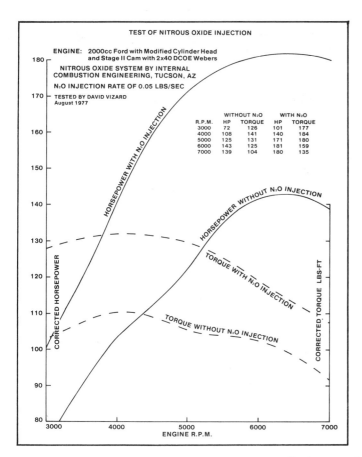

TEST OF NITROUS OXIDE INJECTION

ENGINE: 2000cc Ford with Modified Cylinder Head
and Stage II Cam with 2x40 DCOE Webers

NITROUS OXIDE SYSTEM BY INTERNAL
COMBUSTION ENGINEERING, TUCSON, AZ

N₂O INJECTION RATE OF 0.05 LBS/SEC

TESTED BY DAVID VIZARD
August 1977

R.P.M.	WITHOUT N₂O HP	WITHOUT N₂O TORQUE	WITH N₂O HP	WITH N₂O TORQUE
3000	72	126	101	177
4000	108	141	140	184
5000	125	131	171	180
6000	143	125	181	159
7000	139	104	180	135

The effect of nitrous-oxide injection on power output is clearly shown here. Note that the same amount of nitrous and enrichment fuel injected into an engine with larger displacement produces about the same level of power increase, not the same percentage power increase. *The power increase is related to the volume of nitrous-oxide and enrichment fuel added to the engine.*

(around 750psi) is sufficient to inject the nitrous-oxide into the engine manifold. The injection is normally controlled by a pair of electrically-operated solenoid valves, one for the nitrous and one for the fuel. With such a setup, the solenoid valves can both be controlled by a single manual push button or some similar electro-mechanical switch. This results in instant response, yet when the system is not in use, it does not interfere with the normal running of the engine.

This sounds almost too good to be true. Without much imagination, anyone can see that a nitrous-oxide system could be used on virtually any engine, even a super-mileage economy engine. All you need do is push the button and the nitrous-oxide will supply a massive dose of power, only when it is required. From this point of view, nitrous-oxide injection does not compromise the mechanical economy of an engine. In fact, you can build all of the economy features you want into your engine and then rely on the nitrous-oxide to give a squirt of power whenever you want, however, it's not quite that simple.

As we shall soon see, there are some problems with nitrous-oxide in-

jection, but before we look at the drawbacks, let's find out how much real-life power we can expect to gain from liquid supercharging. Some makers of commercially-available nitrous systems claim their systems can add as much as 150 horsepower to an engine. Such claims are hard to substantiate and they are, likewise, hard to refute. It would not be totally unrealistic, therefore, to say that the power gains are probably in the range of 50-150hp. And, no matter how you look at it, this is a considerable bundle of "instant power."

Some diehards may not think 100 horses is much of an increase, but the effect of nitrous-oxide is somewhat unique. When the injection is turned on, the nitrous and enrichment fuel are translated into a massive increase in

NOTE: NITROUS AND FUEL MAY BE INJECTED IN EACH INDIVIDUAL PORT RUNNER OR INTO MANIFOLD PLENUM IF APPLICABLE.

AT POINT X BOTH NITROUS AND FUEL LINES WOULD GO TO A DISTRIBUTION BLOCK TO FEED EACH CYLINDER.

This schematic shows the basic operating components of a nitrous-oxide injection system. The nitrous-oxide and the enrichment fuel can be injected into each individual manifold port or into the intake-manifold plenum. The simplest method is to use a spacer between the carb and the manifold, with the relevant plumbing installed in the spacer to inject the nitrous and enrichment fuel into the airstream as it leaves the base of the carb.

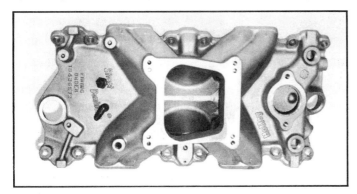

This Holley, Street Dominator manifold looks quite innocent from this angle...

...but it contains all the plumbing for a well-disguised nitrous-oxide injection system.

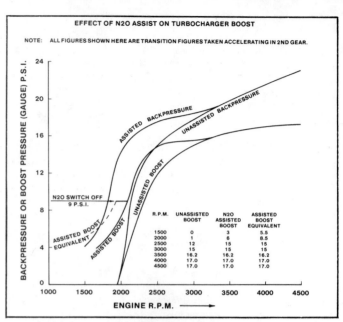

This complex carburetor-adapter/solenoid has been designed by I.C.E. to eliminate turbocharger lag. When the throttle is opened rapidly (non-boosted condition), a quick shot of nitrous is injected below the carb. This immediately increases the combustion volume and temperature and produces an immediate response from the turbocharger.

The injection of nitrous and enrichment fuel into the intake produces a large increase in the resultant exhaust volume. This exhaust will rapidly accelerate a turbocharger and produce boost pressure very quickly. Apart from this, the nitrous system is also increasing the torque output and the result is "instant throttle response."

low-speed torque, and this is what accelerates the car. In fact, it is probably better to rate nitrous-oxide systems according to the amount of torque they produce. As incredible as it may seem, a typical 100hp system may give an instant torque increase of 100lb/ft. And, the performance increase resulting from this torque will be a lot more noticeable than obtaining an actual 100hp at a much higher point in the rpm range.

Translated into simpler terms, we can say that a 100lb/ft boost has about the same effect as adding 100-200 cubic inches of displacement to your engine. On the dragstrip this torque boost will launch the car much harder, and will produce a very substantial reduction in elapsed times and a good gain in top speed.

On the face of it, this sounds like an ideal way to go, but it's not all a bed of roses. Though the concept is simple, a nitrous-oxide system does have some limitations. Just how big these problems are will depend on your attitude toward performance and economy.

The first problem is that the nitrous-oxide tanks will require periodic refilling. How often this is necessary will depend on the amount of use the system undergoes and how effective it is. If we assume the average system delivers about 100hp and is fairly efficient (this is a big factor), it will use about 1 pound of nitrous-oxide for every 10 seconds of use. The size of the storage tanks varies but most systems use a 15lb bottle, and will give

The simplest nitrous-oxide systems inject the nitrous beneath the carb, through nozzles installed in a simple spacer plate. The system shown here is by Internal Combustion Engineering. Note the large solenoid-operated valves. Some manufacturers routinely claim their systems will add 150hp to an ordinary 350-inch engine but they often use valves that can't deliver enough nitrous to produce such optimistic results. The I.C.E. kit has been tested by this writer and it lives up to their claims!

about 2-2.5 minutes of operation before a refill is required.

Getting the bottle refilled is inconvenient but not difficult. Most commerical suppliers who have bottled oxygen, acetylene, etc., also supply nitrous-oxide. It is widely used in the medical profession and should be available locally in most parts of the country. Fortunately it isn't too expensive, and the cost could be considered very reasonable, in view of the substantial performance gains it gives.

Even though nitrous-oxide looks like the perfect answer to performance with economy, and though there is some bother with refilling the storage

bottles, the real problems are more technical in nature. First of all, contrary to some beliefs, nitrous-oxide makes the engine more prone to detonation. The nitrous-system manufacturers usually get around this problem by injecting a surplus dose of enrichment fuel. This fuel is far in excess of the amount required to compensate for the oxygen released by the nitrous and acts, in effect, as an expensive internal engine coolant.

The ultimate factor that will limit the power gained from nitrous-oxide injection is the extremely high temperatures created in the combustion chambers. We must always remember that injecting nitrous-oxide is the same thing as adding a massive dose of oxygen to the intake charge. If the correct amount of enrichment fuel is not also added, the result is a super-lean mixture. The amount and proportion of nitrous and enrichment fuel must be carefully controlled or we wind up turning on a super-heated blowtorch inside the engine. The cylinder head and piston temperatures will skyrocket and, if not controlled, the automotive equivalent of a reactor meltdown occurs. If a well-designed system is carefully installed and used in moderation, this will not be a problem. However, every nitrous user must be aware that a system malfunction can literally melt the pistons in an engine in a matter of seconds, and the same results may occur if he gets power crazy and injects too much nitrous!

TURBOS & NITROUS

For many years a common complaint about turbocharging has been that the exhaust-driven turbocharger does not respond rapidly when the throttle is pushed open suddenly. This apparent lag between throttle and boost response is generally called turbo lag. Although many devices have been invented to eliminate turbo lag, in essence the best only reduce it somewhat. But, if nitrous-oxide injection is used on a turbocharged engine, it can truly eliminate turbo lag. Apart from this, it has some other advantages when used with turbocharging.

First of all, in engines that are boosted fairly high, i.e., 8lb or more, the evaporative cooling of the nitrous affects all of the already-supercharged intake charge. As a result, the density increase is more effective, and this produces more power than if the same quantity of nitrous was injected into a normally-aspirated engine. Just how much power is gained depends on the boost level, how high the intake temperature is elevated by the turbo and how efficient the nitrous system is, but on engines boosted between 8 and 25lb it is possible that the nitrous could produce 1.5 to 3 times more power than if the same quantity was injected into a normally-aspirated engine.

In addition, the effect of nitrous is almost instantaneous. As soon as the system is activated, the engine responds with a sudden surge of intake mixture, almost like activating a giant accelerator pump. This pushes the engine into boost more quickly and effectively eliminates turbo lag. With this problem eliminated it is now possible to use a turbo housing with a much larger A.R. ratio than might otherwise be selected for the engine. Some systems are designed with turbochargers that have an unusually small A.R. ratio (in overly simplified terms the A.R. ratio can be considered as the efficiency level of the turbo) to improve the low-speed boost response. In other words, the turbo is "small" so that it will "spool up" faster when the throttle is pushed open. But this is a tradeoff. If the ratio is too small, the turbo becomes a restriction in the exhaust system and chokes the engine. Even though the boost in the intake manifold may be very high, the restriction in the exhaust is also high. In this case, the engine becomes "pressurized" on both the inlet and the exhaust side, and the supercharging effect is nullified. So, although a small A.R.-ratio housing can provide very

high manifold pressure, it might not necessarily increase power.

By using nitrous-oxide to boost the low-end response, a turbo housing with a larger A.R. ratio can be selected. The housing can now be sized to give the engine the desired amount of boost in the mid and upper speed ranges, where turbochargers work most efficiently. This gives the engine excellent low-speed torque response and tremendous top-end power, and eliminates the need for a wastegate or other boost restricting devices. It also cuts down the resistance to exhaust flow during the low throttle openings normally used at highway speeds. The result is better cruise economy.

Apart from using less fuel, the nitrous-assisted turbo also uses less nitrous, as compared to its normally-aspirated counterpart. As was stated earlier, less nitrous-oxide is needed to produce the same power increase in a turbo engine. In addition, some nitrous systems designed specifically for street-driven turbo engines use a unique two-stage setup. An initial heavy shot of nitrous and enrichment fuel is used to "kick" the engine into boost, and then a lighter shot is provided to sustain the boost until the engine speed is high enough for the turbos to reach maximum efficiency. With such a system, the initial shot of nitrous may last between .5 and 1 second and the sustained delivery between 1 and 5 seconds (this will vary depending on the weight and gear ratio of the vehicle).

Typically, a nitrous-assisted turbo setup will deliver approximately 200 full-power runs down the dragstrip on a

single 15lb tank of nitrous-oxide. This makes the use of nitrous very economical. If this is added to the fuel saving gained by the bigger turbo housings, it looks like the nitrous-assisted turbo system can produce some truly impressive performance numbers without boosting the fuel consumption to equally-impressive levels.

A mid-size sporty car, such as a Firebird or a Camaro, with a single-turbo, non-wastegate 350cid small-block and nitrous-assist system should be able to consistently run 13-13.5 second quarter-mile times and produce economy ranging between 20 and 25mpg. This would, of course, vary depending on how the car was set up, but it could be achieved without the super-low gear ratio normally required to get such quick times on the dragstrip. A conventional street gear (3.08-3.50) could be used, avoiding excessive engine rpm and all of the problems associated with low gear ratios on the street.

The turbo system shown here is nitrous assisted. But, the nitrous is injected directly into the turbo housing to increase the response.

This is an overall shot of the nitrous-assisted turbo installation. The 350-inch smallblock Chevy engine shown here powers a half-ton Chevy pickup truck to 105mph trap speeds in the quarter-mile.

CHAPTER 14!

TURBOCHARGING

- TURBOS AND MILEAGE
- BUYING THE RIGHT CAM
- CARBS FOR TURBOCHARGING
- THE RIGHT EXHAUST SYSTEM

The relatively new twin-turbo system from Gale Banks Engineering is designed specifically for high-boost automotive applications. It utilizes the latest sophisticated techniques to provide outstanding wide-open-throttle performance and "reasonable" cruise economy. But make no mistake, turbocharging is not a mystical route to economy. If the driver cannot resist the power potential provided by turbocharging, overall economy will definitely decline.

TURBOCHARGING

There is nothing like starting off with a bombshell, so here goes: *contrary to popular opinion and the rumors circulated by turbo and turbokit manufacturers, turbochargers are not economy devices*. If you find that hard to swallow it's perfectly understandable. Unfortunately, too many publications have unwittingly perpetuated the turbo economy myth, and it is time to set the record straight.

Numerous road test vehicles that have been modified by the addition of a turbo have shown mileage increases. However, it seems likely that the mileage gains were due, not so much to the addition of the turbo, but to the removal of the mileage-robbing stock components. Had that same vehicle been equipped with the usual hot-rod equipment, such as modified heads, a good economy cam, headers, high-flow exhaust system, etc., the odds are 10 to 1 that it would have produced more mpg than the turbo vehicle. How can I be so sure of this? There are two substantial reasons that lead me to such conclusions. First, my own experience of designing both turbo and normally-aspirated engines for one of the Big Three automakers, and second, a simple theoretical analysis. This analysis reveals the fallacy of turbo economy over that possible from a normally-aspirated engine.

From earlier chapters it will be remembered that two of the prime economy features of an internal-combustion engine are: a high compression ratio and low exhaust back-pressure. Let's see how the turbo engine stands on these counts. First let's consider compression. If high compression is used in a turbo-charged engine, as soon as the boost comes up, the engine will simply blow itself to bits from excessive detonation. The boost pressure effectively increases the compression ratio, but how often do you drive with the engine in boost? Most economy driving is done at part throttle, and at part throttle the engine does not receive boost from the turbo system. We now have a situation where high compression, an important aspect of part-throttle economy, cannot be used, and therefore, the overall economy potential will inevitably suffer.

Now let's look at the exhaust system. On a normally-aspirated performance-economy engine the exhaust will flow freely from the engine, due to the characteristics of the headers. Compare this to the exhaust system of a turbo engine. The exhaust passage through the exhaust manifold and turbocharger turbine wheel is very tortuous. It doesn't take a flow bench to establish that the airflow through such an installation is going to be far less than the flow through an efficient set of tube headers.

However, you may say, the turbo is there so we can get boost, which will help offset the flow restriction. But once again, how often do you drive with the engine in boost, especially when you are looking for economy? The exhaust system of a turbo engine is relatively restrictive all the time, no matter if the turbo is functioning in the boost mode or not!

For some of you readers these considerations may have clouded the turbo picture and, at best, it must now seem confusing. After all, many Detroit manufacturers are now installing turbos on their "performance engines," but the situation for them is a little different than it is for the average hot rodder. Under the current circumstances the turbo may be the only saving grace for the factory high-performance car of the future. Turbocharging is plausible for manufacturers like General Motors, Ford and others because it does help the emission situation. When it's necessary to meet extensive government-dictated test standards, a turbo system can be designed specifically to meet reasonable economy and emissions standards, as well as produce surprising performance.

Another aspect to consider is that turbo technology may allow the manufacturers to maintain reasonable power levels from a smaller engine, and that smaller engine will inevitably be lighter. This means a smaller car can be used to carry the engine, and the overall car weight can be reduced considerably. This all adds up to more economy at part-throttle (no boost) cruise.

However, the average hot rodder is

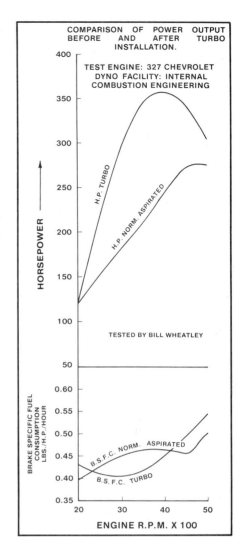

A before-and-after comparison shows how effective an efficient street turbo system can be. The power curve for the normally-aspirated engine was produced by a 327cid smallblock Chevy equipped with a Sig Erson hydraulic cam (RV15H) and an Edelbrock C3B manifold with a 600-cfm, Holley carb. Exhaust was handled by a set of Cyclone 1.625-inch, 29-inch primary headers with 3-inch collectors. The only engine modification performed when the turbo kit was installed was to change the exhaust routing to accommodate the turbocharger (i.e., the same carb, heads, cam and intake manifold were used). Note that fuel consumption was generally higher on the normally-aspirated engine. This was due to rich, maximum-power jetting in the secondary barrels of the carb. Under part-throttle conditions, the normally-aspirated engine was more economical.

This turbocharged big-block Chevrolet was built for marine use by Internal Combustion Engineering. It produced over 900hp (with intercooling) and during three years of operation it has proven to be quite reliable. Turbocharging is particularly suited to marine operation because of the relatively constant engine speeds.

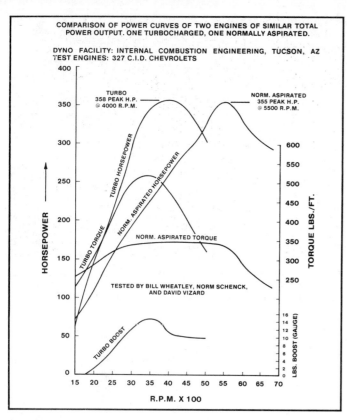

COMPARISON OF POWER CURVES OF TWO ENGINES OF SIMILAR TOTAL POWER OUTPUT. ONE TURBOCHARGED, ONE NORMALLY ASPIRATED.

DYNO FACILITY: INTERNAL COMBUSTION ENGINEERING, TUCSON, AZ
TEST ENGINES: 327 C.I.D. CHEVROLETS

TURBO 358 PEAK H.P. @ 4000 R.P.M.

NORM. ASPIRATED 355 PEAK H.P. @ 5500 R.P.M.

TURBO HORSEPOWER
NORM. ASPIRATED HORSEPOWER
TURBO TORQUE
NORM. ASPIRATED TORQUE
TURBO BOOST

TESTED BY BILL WHEATLEY, NORM SCHENCK, AND DAVID VIZARD

HORSEPOWER
TORQUE LBS./FT.
LBS. BOOST (GAUGE)
R.P.M. X 100

Turbocharging has become an increasingly popular modification for street engines and the proliferation of kits and specialty equipment is obviously going to continue. This is good news for turbo aficionados but the neophyte should study the available information and equipment carefully before attempting a do-it-yourself project.

The "peak power" figure rarely tells the whole story about an engine. Here are two engines, each of similar peak power output, but note how the power curve of each varies. The turbo engine produces maximum power at 4000rpm and a peak torque output of 520lb/ft. The normally-aspirated engine equaled this peak, but the point of peak power was 1500rpm higher in the speed range. To produce this power the n-a engine had be fitted with a camshaft that reduced the usable rpm band, i.e., low-rpm torque falls off, and the engine becomes "less flexible." Note, even though the n-a engine produced a "flatter" torque curve, the maximum torque was only 345lb/ft, and torque is what is needed to accelerate a car!

not designing a complete engine and car from scratch, and he doesn't have multi-million dollar resources to research, build and test every possible engine and chassis component. Under the conditions that Detroit manufacturers face, the turbocharger offers some interesting performance possibilities. *As a bolt-on piece of equipment for the average hot rodder, it has less-than-outstanding potential when both performance and economy are important considerations.*

Ignoring the somewhat brash advertising claims of some turbo-kit makers, let's look at what turbocharging can realistically do for the average guy who wants both performance and

economy from a homebuilt engine. We have already listed some negative points, what about the plus side? If you have never driven a car with a well-designed, high-boost turbo installation, you haven't lived. The exhilaration has to be experienced to be believed. The fact that a turbo engine can outperform a normally-aspirated engine is a proven fact.

The question you have to ask yourself is: how much power do I need? Unless your needs range into the rabid white-knuckle worlds, you could be wasting money on turbocharging. If practical considerations limit your requirements to less than one horsepower per cubic inch of engine displacement, it is questionable whether you need even consider turbocharging. If you absolutely must have performance beyond this level, you should consider a turbo system. If you try to raise the specfic power of a naturally-aspirated engine above this level it will lose a significant amount of low-rpm torque and gain many of the traits of an all-out race engine, which will not make it very practical for street performance or economy.

Another factor to consider is expense. A lot has changed in the past few years, but as things now stand it's still cheaper for the average hot rodder to get power through more cubic inches than through turbocharging. For instance, if you are looking for about 350 horsepower and you have, we'll say, a 283 cubic inch engine, you

may find it much cheaper to enlarge the displacement to 350 inches and use conventional performance techniques to increase the power, rather than go to the expense and trouble of installing a turbo system on your 283.

Another fact to consider is that many of the currently available turbo kits produce fairly modest power gains. A good street kit, designed to deliver reasonable power, should be able to produce one horsepower per cubic inch, or slightly more, and it should deliver this power at relatively low engine speeds. To produce high power levels at low rpm the engine must develop a tremendous amount of torque. The graph presented herein shows the different "power curve shape" produced by two engines that have comparable total power outputs. You will notice that the turbocharged engine produces much higher torque in the mid-range. This makes the engine feel as if it has a substantially larger displacement. Moreover, note that the normally-aspirated engine must be operated at a much higher engine speed to make the same power. If we compare the performance and economy of these two engines, under most conditions the turbo engine would, assuming no turbo lag, produce the best acceleration times by a small margin, but the normally-aspirated engine would give better mileage.

We have looked at the numbers and turbocharging still doesn't look too good for performance with economy, but we haven't come to the end of the line yet. Except for certain non-performance applications, such as RV's and the like, the turbocharger isn't a path to total performance unless it is designed to give a respectable amount of boost. About the lowest boost level you should consider for performance applications is 6-8psi. *Once boost approaches 10psi, or more, on a well-prepared engine, the all-out performance potential of turbocharging is unassailable.*

There is, however, a problem with high-output V8 turbo systems. In most cases, twin turbos are needed and this considerably increases the overall system cost. Unless you are willing to spend an additional 30-40% on the installation, stick with a single-turbo system. *But, for very high output, on the order of 2/hp per inch or more, two turbos are a must on engines with 300 inches of displacement or more.* Nonetheless, do not use a twin-turbo setup if a single turbo will do the job.

So far it looks like turbocharging has more to offer as a performance device than as an economy booster. The fact is, a turbo can provide performance gains without completely killing economy, but little mention has been made of the most often heard turbo complaint—turbo throttle lag. We can't ignore this problem. If the system is professionally and intelligently designed, throttle lag should be minimized, however, the buyer needs to be wary. There are a variety of devices on the market that purport to "eliminate" throttle lag. Such claims are often an exaggeration. Some of them don't even work in the first place, and others only marginally help the situation.

Most of these devices work on the bypass principle. When the throttle is floored, the engine draws air straight into the intake manifold, bypassing the turbo. This causes the engine speed to build more rapidly, so it will produce enough exhaust to accelerate the turbo quickly and generate enough airflow to produce boost. As soon as the engine starts to achieve boost, extra exhaust is produced and this quickly drives the turbo to the full boost point. At best, these bypass systems serve only to reduce throttle lag. By their very nature they cannot eliminate it.

Actually the term "throttle lag" is wrong. The term that should be used is "boost lag," because it is the boost that lags behind the throttle opening. The throttle opens as fast as the driver pushes the pedal to the floor. However, calling this throttle lag is somewhat

This Pontiac turbo system is an option on 301-inch, Trans-Am Firebirds. Wires and tubes virtually fill the engine compartment to overflowing, but most of it is not related to the turbo system. Beneath this mess, the turbo installation is neat and compact.

excusable on the basis that the sensation given by boost lag is that the throttle action is lagging way behind the pedal movement.

Because the boost lags behind the action of the throttle pedal, the engine performance can be described as "soft." In other words, it is impossible to get a fast engine response to a wide-open throttle action. This slow response is most noticeable with automatic-transmission vehicles in situations when you need low-end power to cross a stoplight intersection. Slamming the throttle pedal to the floor does not result in instantaneous acceleration. Instead, the resulting acceleration is more like a stock engine trying to urge the vehicle across the intersection. However, as the vehicle builds speed, the boost begins to develop and the engine finally "comes to life." By the time it reaches the other

side of the intersection, the engine is really making power.

One possible solution to this dilemma would be to use a higher compression ratio. This would not work with high-boost systems, but a higher static compression ratio would help produce low-rpm torque when the engine is not receiving boost from the turbo. Unfortunately, high compression also leads to detonation problems. But, detonation can be controlled in various ways, as discussed in other chapters. If the detonation can be eliminated, higher static compression will help, not only from the standpoint of low-rpm response but also from the standpoint of economy.

CAMS FOR TURBO APPLICATIONS

Many manufacturers are now producing cams designed specifically for

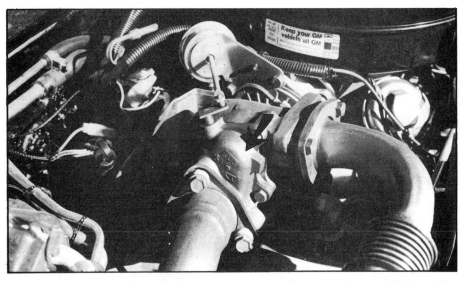

Unlike the turbochargers used in some specialty systems, most factory-installed turbos are custom-built for the application. The Pontiac turbo, for instance, has an integral wastegate in the turbo housing. This simplifies the boost-control system.

use in turbocharged engines. These are basically short-duration, high-lift cams. It is difficult to say how much they have to offer over the many similar cams designed for conventional low-rpm performance applications. Before these special turbo cams were available, many engine builders used RV (recreational vehicle) cams. All of these cams are generally designed to increase low-rpm breathing through increased lift, while retaining a very short valve-open period.

In a turbo engine a short-period cam will, by comparison with a long-duration cam designed for a naturally-aspirated performance engine, increase the low-rpm torque. This is important to offset the soft low-end response of a low-compression turbo engine. Unless you are planning a racing or semi-racing application, one of the several turbo or RV-type cam designs now widely available will work just fine. (For a racing turbo application you should consult a reputable engine builder with a lot of experience in turbocharging.) If you install a cam of this type it should aid overall economy, as well as improve low-speed response.

CARBURETION FOR TURBO-CHARGED ENGINES

Most of the turbo-kit manufacturers retain the stock carburetor in the system to help reduce cost. Some, but not all, supply a few carburetor recalibration components, but very few of these kits have adequate instructions to help the buyer analyze and solve carburetion problems that may occur on a turbocharged engine. Virtually all modern carbs are designed for normally-aspirated engines. When any of these carbs are forced to work in a nonconventional manner, that is, with a turbocharger forcing an artifically increased amount of air to flow through it, the carb systems are often forced to function outside of the normal design limits.

A good example of this is the power-valve system. In a draw-through turbo application it is possible for the engine to be in a relatively high load condition, with the engine manifold (downstream of the turbo) in a high-pressure (boost) state, while the carb manifold (upstream of the turbo) is still in a relatively high vacuum condition. (This condition is most common if a very small carb is used on the engine and the carb is fitted with a power valve that opens at relatively low manifold vacuum.) When the load increases on a conventional engine, the so-called manifold vacuum

A well-designed turbo system provides power "on demand." In other words, it makes a small engine produce power like a big engine, but only when the power is needed. This Pinto 2000 engine, built by devoted Pinto enthusiast Jim Flynn, cranked out 306hp on gas, and would be streetable except for the cam, which is a little too wild for day-to-day traffic.

Although a stock, conventional carburetor provides a good starting point, a turbo system needs a fuel-metering device that has been specifically tested and developed to operate with the system. The transition circuit and the main-metering circuit of this Internal Combustion Engineering-reworked Holley have been modified for turbo applications. It also has a boost-referenced power valve (rather than the the standard vacuum reference).

(sensed at the carb baseplate) drops off and the power valve opens, increasing the fuel delivery. But with the turbo between the carb and the engine, under certain part-throttle conditions, the engine load may increase, calling for more fuel enrichment, but the turbo may be drawing so much air through the carb bores that the throttles do not have to be opened very wide. In this case the manifold vacuum below the

carb can actually increase, and as a result, the power-valve is not activated. This creates a part-throttle lean condition and can lead to piston damage. Indeed, if the engine is operating in a loaded boost condition, there should be some mixture enrichment to hold down piston temperatures.

To prevent this situation from occurring, a carb for a turbocharged application needs to have a boost-

Since most turbo systems force the carburetor to work outside of normal operational limits, the carburetor is often a source of problems. Carefully considered modifications can usually overcome these limitations, but the job is seldom easy. This incredibly complex piece of engineering is an extensively modified Holley carb for a high-boost blow-through system. When the boost level exceeds about 10lb, fuel delivery and control becomes very difficult.

sensitive power valve, rather than a vacuum-sensitive power valve. Usually this can be accomplished easily by "externally referencing" the valve so that it monitors the vacuum conditions downstream of the turbo in the engine manifold. This provides fairly normal load-related power-valve enrichment, similar to conventional power-valve operation.

This is but one example of the carburetor problems that must be solved by the hot rodder bent on using turbo technology for everyday driving. Although almost all carbs can be modified, with varying degrees of success, for turbo applications, the Holley two- and four-barrel carbs are currently very popular and can be readily adapted to turbo requirements. However, we don't have sufficent space to cover all of the required modifications. This could be the subject of an entire book, but it should suffice to say that

EXHAUST SYSTEMS

To prevent detonation or mechanical damage to the engine it is often necessary to limit the total amount of boost delivered by a turbo system. Two of the most popular methods to achieve this are to increase the back-pressure in the exhaust system and to restrict the intake system. Either of these techniques (or both) are, in effect, methods of choking the engine, and they can only be used to a limited extent before it is necessary to resort to an external boost-control method.

There are various ways to externally limit turbo boost, but one of the most popular and most effective methods is to use a wastegate. A wastegate is an exhaust bypass device controlled by intake-manifold pressure. When manifold boost pressure reaches a predetermined level, the wastegate opens, allowing exhaust pressure to bypass the turbo. This effectively restricts the amount of boost developed by the turbo but it does not restrict the intake or exhaust breathing of the engine. As a result, although a wastegate-controlled engine may not necessarily make more power than one limited by exhaust or intake restriction, it will generally produce a more usable power curve and will usually be more fuel efficient.

For the ultimate in fuel efficiency, the part-throttle-open wastegate is a good idea. Obviously, if you are driving at part throttle and no boost, there is not much demand on the engine. Under these conditions, a part-throttle-open wastegate allows some exhaust to bypass the turbo and flow out of the engine in an unrestricted manner. This is almost like running the engine with an open exhaust system. As soon as boost is needed, opening the throttle fully will cause the wastegate to close, passing all of the exhaust through the turbo. When the boost reaches a predetermined level, the wastegate once again opens, bleeding off excess exhaust. This type of wastegate, though the most complex, is the most fuel efficient.

When the exhaust system is not used to control boost by virtue of restriction, an exhaust system for a turbocharged engine should have the minimum amount of backpressure, exactly the same as one for a non-turbocharged application. Under these conditions, mufflers with a very high flow capability should be utilized.

To gain maximum efficiency from turbocharged engines the exhaust system must be carefully designed and constructed to reduce back-pressure as much as possible. Considerable effort has been spent to fabricate the the headers on this Gale Banks racing engine. Note that the free-flowing primary tubes join into a common plenum below the turbo to dampen exhaust pulsing. Because of the high operating temperatures, the headers are made of stainless steel.

CHAPTER 15

ALCOHOL, GASOHOL AND ADDITIVES

- ● OCTANE EXPLAINED!
- ● USING RACING GAS
- ● CONVERTIBLE ALCOHOL CARB
- ● OCTANE BOOSTERS TESTED
- ● OILS AND MILEAGE

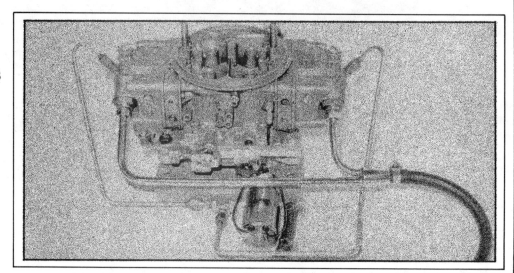

ALCOHOL AND CHEMICAL ADDITIVES

FUEL OCTANE RATINGS

The effect of compression ratio on power and economy has already been discussed at length. We confirmed the advantages of increasing compression to the maximum limit, but it's also true that high compression is impractical today because of the condition of currently available pump gasoline. *Therefore, if the benefits of high compression are to be realized, something needs to be done to compensate for the relatively low octane value of modern motor fuels.*

Before we can intelligently formulate a solution to the compression problem, we need to understand the relationship between fuel and compression. A good place to start is with fuel octane. The term octane is used widely in technical engine discussions, but what precisely is the octane value of fuel?

The octane number of any fuel is, essentially, its resistance to detonation. Originally, octane was measured in a variable-compression engine by comparing the detonation point of the fuel being tested with the detonation

Octane numbers are displayed on most gasoline pumps, but only one thing is certain, the octane of future fuels will continue to decline. It is essential, and possible, to build an efficient performance street engine to operate on low-octane fuels, but it requires careful planning.

point of a known fuel mixture (a constant value). In this case the constant is a mixture of iso-octane and heptane. Iso-octane has been arbitrarily assigned an octane number of 100. Heptane has been assigned an octane number of zero. Iso-octane is resistant to detonation; heptane is not. An 80 octane gasoline is one that will detonate at the same compression ratio as a mixture of 80% iso-octane and 20% heptane. Similarly, a 90 octane fuel is one which detonates at the same compression ratio as a mixture of 90% iso-octane and 10% heptane. 100 octane fuel has the same detonation resistance as 100% iso-octane.

Some modern fuel blends (notably, racing gasolines) have octane ratings above 100. Such octane numbers cannot be measured by this method because the reference fuel can only contain 100% iso-octane. To measure these fuels a different reference system has been devised. In these cases the octane number is related to the amount of tetra-ethyl lead that

must be added to the reference fuel in order to delay detonation to the same point as the fuel being tested.

This sounds simple, but real life is never simple, especially in this day and age. Recent legislation has dictated that fuel pumps must show the minimum octane value of the fuel being dispensed. Some pumps have a small label that says the octane value displayed is derived form the formula (R + M)/2. The "R" stands for Research octane rating and the "M" stands for Motor octane rating (these are the two separate rating methods described above). In general, the Research octane rating method tends to produce a higher octane number than the Motor rating method, but to prevent confusion (???) the oil companies have decided to average the two ratings to give a single number for standard comparisons. When comparing fuels it is important to know what rating method was used, and during the rest of our discussion, the octane figures quoted will be those derived from the R + M)/2 formula. Now that we are all talking the

same language, let's get down to the business at hand—evaluating the methods of boosting effective fuel octane, so as to utilize high compression ratios for more power and economy.

RACING GAS

About the highest octane fuel that is currently available is specially blended racing gasoline. These blends are intended for special-application use, and can be purchased in limited quantities from specialty companies. The octane value of these blends varies from about 100 octane up to 116 octane.

Generally speaking, the higher the octane of the fuel, the more expensive it is. *A point that should always be remembered is that your engine only needs a fraction more octane value than is necessary to avoid detonation. More octane does not mean more power.* If you have a 13:1 engine that detonates on 99 octane but runs perfectly on 100 octane, using 116

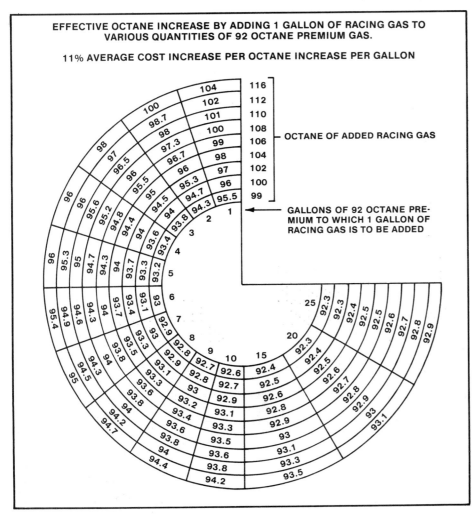

EFFECTIVE OCTANE INCREASE BY ADDING 1 GALLON OF RACING GAS TO VARIOUS QUANTITIES OF 92 OCTANE PREMIUM GAS.

11% AVERAGE COST INCREASE PER OCTANE INCREASE PER GALLON

OCTANE OF ADDED RACING GAS

GALLONS OF 92 OCTANE PREMIUM TO WHICH 1 GALLON OF RACING GAS IS TO BE ADDED

On the vertical scale locate the octane rating of the racing fuel; follow the circular scale to the octane value desired; then, read the value on the innermost scale. This is the number of gallons of 92-octane gas to which you must add one gallon of the racing fuel to obtain the desired octane value in the final mix.

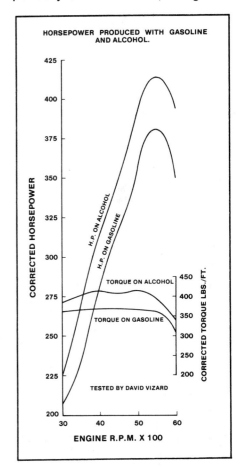

HORSEPOWER PRODUCED WITH GASOLINE AND ALCOHOL.

TESTED BY DAVID VIZARD

An interesting comparison of power output between gasoline and gasoline-alcohol is shown here. A "convertible" Holley from Internal Combustion Engineering was used on this modified street-type engine. Similar carbs are also manufactured by Braswell Carburetors.

octane gas is a total waste of money. You will not gain any more power from the added octane value.

Using racing gas on the street can be very expensive. The price of racing gas is between 50 and 200% more than ordinary gasolines. However, it is possible to mix a high-octane racing gasoline with ordinary service-station gas to come up with a "home-brew" high-octane. This will save a lot of the expense but still allow you to use a fuel with enough octane to prevent an engine with relatively high compression from detonating. The accompanying chart shows how the octane value of a service-station pump fuel can be improved by mixing it with a high-octane racing fuel.

Mixing two types of gas may or may not prove convenient. If a source for racing gas is not readily at hand, mixing your own blend is, at best, awkward. The high cost may also be a problem, but if you are willing to pay the price, you can buy or hand-blend gasoline with nearly any octane rating you desire (at least, up to a point). Once again, refer to the chart. This will show the typical price increase, per gallon, compared to the octane increase.

We must also point out that the method used to get high octane values from racing fuel is to use tetra-ethyl lead as an anti-detonant additive. Tetra-ethyl lead contaminates the catalyzing agent in a catalytic converter, so if you have a car with a catalytic converter and want the converter to remain operative, avoid using a blended fuel that contains a

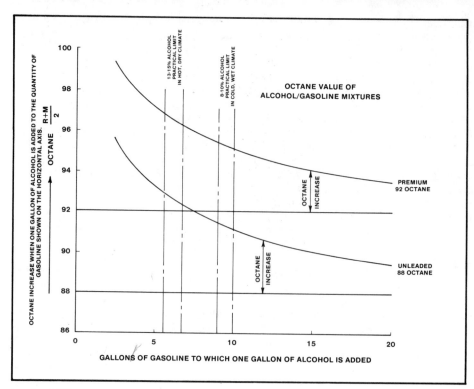

lead additive.

ALCOHOLS

Over the last few years, gasohol has been attracting more and more public interest. Gasohol is a combination of gasoline and alcohol. Unlike crude oil, alcohol is a replenishable natural source. The raw materials necessary to make alcohol can be cultivated as an ordinary agricultural crop. In countries that have an agricultural-based economy, alcohol can be a worthwhile alternative to fuels produced from crude oil. At the time of this writing, at least one country is already producing vehicles which run exclusively on alcohol-based fuels, but as with anything, there are pros and cons to alcohol.

Within the framework of performance with economy, the most important aspect of alcohol fuels is that they are highly resistant to detonation. As such, they can be effectively used as octane boosters. Basically, two forms of alcohol are generally avail-

Here we see a fuel mixture of 89% gasoline, 8.9% methanol, 1.8% acetone and 0.3% water. Note that everything has mixed and there is no phase separation.

A mixture of 87% gasoline, 8.7% methanol and 4.3% water produces separation at normal room temperatures. Close inspection shows three distinct layers. The gasoline is on top, then there is a layer of mixed gasoline, water and methanol and the bottom layer contains water that will not remain in solution.

able for this purpose: methanol and ethanol. Of the two, methanol is cheaper and more readily available, but using any type of alcohol as a motor fuel has serious limitations. However, let's first look at the plus side.

If you look at our graph, you will see just how much effect methanol has on the octane rating of a typical unleaded fuel. The horizontal scale represents gallons of gasoline. The vertical scale represents octane increase. The curved line shows the increase in octane typically achieved by adding one gallon of methanol to the baseline quantity of gasoline. In other words, point A is the octane figure achieved if you added one gallon of methanol to 35 gallons of 90-octane unleaded gasoline. As the amount of methanol is increased, the octane value goes up. At point B we have one gallon of methanol added to 9 gallons of unleaded gasoline to give a mixture of 10% methanol to 90% gasoline. At this point the average octane rating has gone up by 3.5 points.

As far as costs are concerned, we find that methanol is about 70% more expensive than gasoline, but cheaper than racing gasoline. Again, refer to the chart to see what cost increase, per gallon, is incurred for the increase in octane.

By comparison with a mix of racing gas and pump gas, we find that an alcohol blend does not cause dire problems with catalytic converters. And, it does not adversely affect emissions levels to a great extent. It helps

reduce some emissions, others it increases, but on balance, the addition of small quantities of alcohol to normal gasoline does not create any unforgivable emission problems.

On the debit side, mixing methanol with gasoline does have numerous problems, most of which can be minimized. *The first and foremost problem is that only a limited amount of methanol can be successfully dissolved in gasoline, and this amount is dependent upon the temperature of the fuels.* When the temperature is lower, less methanol can be dissolved in gasoline. In hot, dry climates, it is possible to use as much as 20% methanol in a gasoline blend without much likelihood of trouble. In cold, damp climates this ratio should be reduced to around 10%.

Also, methanol is hydroscopic. It attracts water. And, if water is allowed to enter an alcohol-based fuel, phase separation can occur. The water, methanol, and gasoline will separate into three distinct layers. Again, the more alcohol there is in the blend, the more likely this is to happen.

Another factor to be considered, especially in colder climates, is that methanol does not evaporate very easily and can cause cold-start problems. In hot climates the opposite problem can result. Methanol boils at a lower temperature than gasoline and vapor lock can result. To offset both phase separation and cold starting problems, it is possible to add 1 or 2% of methyl-ethyl-ketone or acetone to the blend. A useful side effect of

adding either of these compounds is that both help increase the octane value of the fuel slightly.

The next problem to consider is created only when the blend contains a relatively large percentage of methanol. The best air-fuel ratio for efficient combustion of methanol is different than gasoline. Methanol needs to be mixed at a ratio of 6.5lb of air to 1lb of methanol, whereas a chemically-correct mixture for gasoline combustion is typically around 15.5lb of air per 1lb of gasoline. As the percentage of methanol increases, the need to rejet the carburetor also becomes increasingly important. If the percentage of methanol is kept low enough, the need to rejet is, for all practical purposes, eliminated. The turning point is around 10%. This will vary from vehicle to vehicle (many factors affect the results) but, *generally speaking, blends of up to 10% methanol can be satisfactorily used without the necessity of recalibrating the carburetor.* This, of course, assumes that the carb was previously calibrated correctly for standard gasoline.

A problem that is not so easily solved, however, is corrosion. Most automotive fuel systems are constructed of components commonly made of lead, zinc, magnesium, copper and aluminum alloys. As it happens, most of these materials will corrode rapidly when they come in contact with methanol. Depending on the exact nature of the materials in the system, this can be a very severe problem. It can be minimized by keeping the

Here we see the result of a large quantity of alcohol and water in a gasohol mix. This mixture consists of 83.3% gasoline, 12.5% methanol and 4.2% water. The photo was taken before the undissolved methanol-water layer at the bottom of the jar settled completely, but the boundary between this mix and the top layer of gasoline is barely visible as a dark, fuzzy line around the edge of the container.

This is the same water-gasohol mix, except acetone has been added (2.5% by volume). There is still some separation existent but the volume of separated mix has reduced because the acetone helps the water-alcohol solution dissolve into the gasoline.

Temperature has a distinct effect on the phase separation of methanol-gasoline mixes. This mixture has been cooled to 30°F and separation is evident. The mixture contains acetone but it did not prevent phase separation at this temperature, but when the temperature was increased to 40°, the separated layers dissolved back into the mixture.

A "convertible" alcohol carb is a reasonable way to reliably gain extra power for weekend racing. Race-proven convertible and straight-alcohol carbs are offered by Braswell Carburetion, Internal Combustion Engineering and C&S Carbs.

methanol. This is because the fuel-air ratio required with ethanol is about 9.5:1, rather than the 6.5:1 of methanol.

CONVERTIBLE ALCOHOL CARB

Another way of achieving suitable performance with alcohol and saving some money is by using a convertible alcohol carburetor. A convertible alcohol carb can be used either on gasoline, for normal day-to-day use, or alcohol, for bracket racing, etc. *Merely switching to a properly calibrated alcohol delivery will give your engine between 13 and 23% more power. Yet, with a convertible system you can retain the economy of using normal pump gas during daily driving.*

To convert to alcohol delivery when you arrive at the strip, it's simply a matter of recalibrating the carb and switching to a secondary (alcohol) fuel source. If you are using a Holley carburetor the job is very straight-forward. All you need do is remove the standard float bowls and metering blocks and replace them with different bowls and blocks pre-calibrated for alcohol (if the standard bowls are already equipped with large inlet needle-and-seat assemblies, they may not have to be replaced). Then, you can connect the float bowls to a separate alcohol fuel line, pump and tank (mounted in the trunk), and go racing.

The nice thing about running alcohol is that, like nitrous-oxide injection, it will increase engine torque substantially, as the nearby graphs shows. This means it will also reduce quarter-mile times by a considerable amount. (Any time an engine produces more torque, the increase can be likened to adding extra cubic inches to the engine.) Once the bracket-racing session is over, it's a 10-minute job to replace the gasoline bowls and metering blocks, and reconnect the main gas tank.

concentrations of methanol low. Concentrations up to 10% do not seem to cause undue problems, even over a period of three or more years. From this it seems possible to conclude that 10% alcohol blends could be used with acceptable reliability for relatively long periods. *Nonetheless, when alcohol-based fuels are to be used in any standard automotive fuel system, all of the fuel-handling components should be inspected periodically.*

By comparison with its close relative, methanol, ethanol has far fewer problems associated with its use. The only real problem is that it is more expensive than methanol. However, it is less corrosive on fuel systems, it mixes more readily with gasoline, it is less sensitive to phase separation and it does not affect the jetting of the carburetor to the same extent as

OCTANE-BOOSTER ADDITIVES

As octane values at the service-station pumps fall, so the number of octane boosters on the market rise. Some are good; others are worthless. It's not practical to test every brand to see how effective each is, because if any factor changes, e.g., the quality of the base fuel, the results can differ. However, the author has had personal experience with three octane boosters that have proven their worth. These are the additives available from H & H Racing Fuels, Atlantic Coast Engine-

The biggest problem with alcohol carbs is supplying enough fuel to maintain proper air-fuel ratios. A lean alcohol mixture will burn down an engine just as swiftly as a lean gasoline mixture. Since such large quantities of fuel are required for an alcohol-carbureted engine, it is important to insure constant, sufficient fuel delivery to the main jets. On the I.C.E.-modified alcohol carb, the float bowls are "injected" with fuel from an auxiliary, micro-switch-controlled, high-pressure, fuel circuit. They claim this system can provide enough fuel flow to support 800hp.

With sufficient fuel in the float bowl, the next problem is to meter the fuel, again in sufficiently large and correctly proportioned quantities, into the engine. The screwdriver indicates the wide-open-throttle enrichment circuit (power-valve channel restriction) of the Holley carb. Note that this channel is substantially larger than stock, to provide the large quantities of enrichment alcohol needed during high-load/wide-open-throttle operation.

Most octane boosters act as anti-detonant agents and are generally not flammable. They can usually be stored and transported in relative safety. Weekend racers can easily add a dose of booster to the fuel tank and dial-in some additional initial ignition advance to increase track performance.

ering and Moroso Performance Sales.

Just how much these additives increase the octane rating depends on the octane of the original gasoline. If the base fuel already has a high octane rating, these additives will not increase the octane very much. On the other hand, if the octane of the base fuel is low, these additives can be a big help. *In some cases, when used in concentrations of 80-100:1 with a low-octane gasoline, they can increase the octane rating as much as four points.*

The advantage of carrying only a small quantity of octane booster, rather than a large quantity of alcohol or high-octane gas, is that it is not necessary to set aside a large space, either in the vehicle or in the garage, for storage. Storing combustible fuels is, at best, extremely dangerous. However, in comparison with conventional fuels, the volatility of most additives is relatively low. Therefore, it's inherently much safer. Carrying a quart, or even a gallon, in the trunk of your car involves a minimal fire risk, as compared to carrying a similar container of racing gasoline.

If you are shopping for octane boosters, make certain you check the price of all available brands. And, it is well worth the effort to do some experimenting. There is a big difference in the price, even among the most popular brands. If a cheaper additive will increase the octane enough to prevent detonation with your specific engine, buying one of the expensive additives will only increase your operating costs and not give any additional benefits.

While we are still concerned with cost, we must point out that one of the problems with octane boosters is that hot-rodders often insist on mixing them to higher concentrations than

The channel to the booster-discharge nozzle also needs to be enlarged to increase fuel flow. Only certain types of Holley boosters can be modified to provide enough fuel delivery for alcohol applications. This is critical for wide-open-throttle mixture control and if a restriction exists at this point, the engine may be damaged.

"Octane boosters" can be a valuable aid to performance and various types of additives are now available. The author has conducted tests on many brands. He has found that some are more effective than others, and the worst ones are virtually useless. The additive marketed by Atlantic Coast Engineering has proved to be among the best.

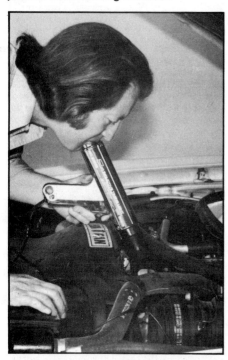

Boosting the fuel octane with an additive allows many late-model, emissions engines to be operated with more efficient ignition timing. Most engines produce maximum power with total ignition advance of 36-40°, but current production engines may have as little as 25° total advance. With better fuel, an additional 6-12° of advance can often be used, increasing power and economy. (Though, too much advance can hurt economy and power.)

recommended by the manufacturers. This is done, apparently, in the belief that high concentrations will give them a super-high octane rating and better performance. This is not so! Past a certain level, increasing the concentration will do very little, or nothing, to the octane values.

Moreover, it is worthwhile to explore the effects of concentrations less than that recommended. Very often an engine may need only a slight increase in fuel octane to eliminate detonation, and using less booster may raise the level enough, while also economizing on the use of the additive.

Adding a smaller concentration of octane booster does not necessarily mean a proportionally smaller octane increase. The most common ratio of additive to fuel is 80:1. This concentration may, as an example, increase the octane of the baseline fuel by four points. However, if the concentration

is reduced to 160:1, cutting the amount of additive in half, the octane could very well still be increased by three points. This may be enough to make your engine run like a top, but you'll wind up using half as much additive per tank of gas. The point to remember is, it is well worth the effort to do your own experimenting with smaller proportions of octane booster. *All you need is just enough to cure detonation after the ignition timing has been optimized.*

IGNITION TIMING & OCTANE

As octane values plummet, not only do usable compression ratios go down, but the maximum amount of ignition timing also changes. Late-model, emissions-tuned vehicles usually have ignition calibrations that reduce detonation (sometimes), but these same settings are far short of maximum-power tuning.

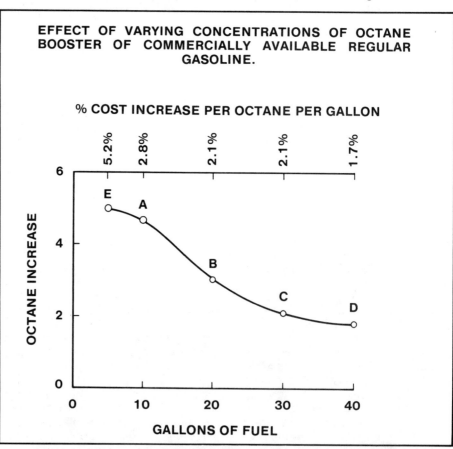

EFFECT OF VARYING CONCENTRATIONS OF OCTANE BOOSTER OF COMMERCIALLY AVAILABLE REGULAR GASOLINE.

% COST INCREASE PER OCTANE PER GALLON

This graph shows the approximate effect of various mixtures of octane booster and regular gas. In this test the octane booster was produced by Atlantic Coast Engineering (A.C.E.) and the base fuel was Texaco Regular. Points A and B were generated from an octane test engine. Points C, D and E were developed by running fuels of known octane through the engine and comparing the timing-induced knock level with that of the booster-treated fuel being tested. The point to note here is that adding booster past the recommended 80:1 ratio did not raise the octane value a significant amount. Note the cost increase (percentage per gallon) for each point of octane increase. The cost to boost the octane 1 or 2 points is a lot less, proportionally, than trying to gain 5 points. These calculations are based on the assumption that octane booster is typically 10.5 times the price (per gallon) of regular gasoline.

To give an example, let's look at the ever-popular smallblock Chevy. When this engine is operated under maximum-performance conditions (i.e., high compression and high-octane fuel), the best total ignition setting is almost always 36-38°. Any less or any more timing than this is likely to result in a loss of wide-open throttle power. But, on many late-model stock engines the total advance is restricted to 20°. If the ignition is advanced beyond this point, in an effort to increase the usable power, detonation becomes an immediate problem.

This seems strange because with lower compression the flame front in the combustion chamber is traveling more slowly. All things being equal, a low-compression engine should benefit from more advance than a high-compression engine. Offsetting this is the fact that many late-model emissions engines use a highly heated intake charge to counteract induction density changes. This decreases the average emissions produced throughout the operating cycle, but it reduces the amount of ignition advance that can be used at wide-open throttle.

Very often, if the octane rating of the fuel used in such an engine is increased through the use of an additive, the ignition can be advanced to the point where maximum performance and economy can be achieved without danger of creating detonation problems. However, if you have tuned the engine to operate efficiently on boosted fuel and for some reason you have to use low-octane fuel (perhaps you forgot to keep your supply of octane booster up to par), detonation may virtually hammer the engine to death when the throttle is opened even the slightest amount.

OCTANE BOOSTER COST EFFECTIVENESS

The primary reason we have been discussing high-octane fuels is to allow the use of high compression ratios. If the compression of an engine can be increased, it will produce more power and more economy. But, there is a bottom line question: if the octane-boosted fuel costs more, can we expect proportionally more mileage from the engine to offset this cost? In other words, if it costs 10 cents/gallon to boost the fuel octane, will the car get the equivalent of 10 cents more mileage from each gallon of boosted fuel?

Generally speaking, adding four points to the fuel-octane number will allow the compression to be increased by 1-2 points. Of course, such an

approximation is dependent on a number of factors, so it is difficult to be precise. But, if we assume some generally applicable numbers, we can determine a fairly valid answer.

Let's say we have an engine with a compression ratio of 8:1 and we are going to increase the compression by approximately 1.5 points to 9.5:1. Referring to the chart in the cylinder-head chapter that details the effect of compression ratio on power, we can see that raising the compression from 8:1 to 9.5:1 will typically result in a 3% gain in power and a 6-8% gain in economy. But, increasing the octane of a gallon of fuel by four points raises the fuel costs between 10 and 20%. From this standpoint, boosting the octane is not necessarily going to increase overall economy.

However, there are some other rather elusive factors we need to consider. First, if you also install a cam with a little more timing, increasing the compression will have a more pronounced effect. A camshaft design that will give power in the 5,000-6,000rpm range generally has more duration than a low-rpm, stock-type cam. This tends to reduce the "effective compression ratio." Under these circumstances, the increase in power and economy from raising compression will be more than that predicted. *Accordingly, if all other engine systems are thoughtfully brought to optimum conditions to complement the increased compression ratio, the benefits of high compression will be substantially greater, and the cost of adding octane booster can often be offset by the increased mileage gains.*

LUBRICANTS

One of the most significant technical achievements in recent years is the development of synthetic automotive lubricants. Exhaustive testing has shown that these oils provide many advantages over mineral-based oils. These oils last longer, giving between two and four times the mileage per oil change. They hold the desired viscosity over a much wider temperature range. And, they have better lubricating qualities than conventional oils.

As a result, they have many operational advantages. During a cold start, an appreciable amount of power is used to pump thick, cold oil through the engine. Synthetic oils are much less viscous when cold, so an engine is relieved of cold-start oil drag. The reduced internal friction brought about by use of synthetic oils also reduces wear and increases power

Extensive testing has shown that the increased lubricity of synthetic oils can produce measurable increases in economy. Admittedly, the gains are small, but in the overall picture small gains can add up to more money in your pocket. However, synthetic oils are still very expensive. In the future, as the cost of organic-based fuels continue to climb, synthetics will become much more practical. And, as an additional benefit, they will provide better engine protection over wider temperature ranges and longer operating periods.

and mileage.

Extensively documented tests of synthetic oils have shown them to be worth an average of 4.2% more miles per gallon during normal driving. The greater part of the mileage gains are accrued during a city-driving cycle when a cold-start is involved. Under these conditions synthetics have produced a typical mileage increase of as much as 6%.

When viewed in the light of the cost, synthetic lubricants don't look quite as good as these percentages suggest. To a large extent, what you may save on fuel is offset by the increased cost of the synthetic oil. To date, the cost of synthetic oil has been very high in relation to mineral-based oils, but as the cost of petroleum continues to climb, they will increasingly become a viable alternative. And, if you add to this the reduced wear on pistons, rings, bearings, valves, etc., that result from the use of a top-grade synthetic, the increased engine lifespan becomes an important part of the equation. If the engine makes more power over a longer usable lifespan, the average cost of operation goes down, and no matter how you look at it, economy goes up.

CHAPTER 16 INSTRUMENTS & DRIVING STYLE

- GAUGES TELL THE STORY
- DETECTING ENGINE LOSSES
- DRIVING STYLE

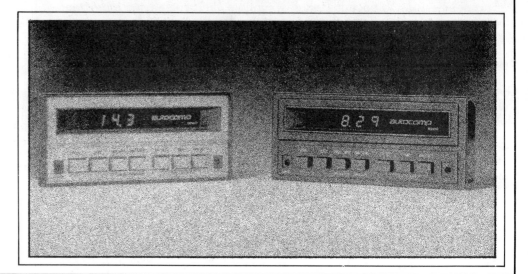

The last factor in the performance-with-economy picture is the driver. The best high-mileage technology is not going to produce satisfactory results if the driver isn't also "tuned" for economy. Most of us enjoy a bit of spirited driving, but if we practice sound high-mileage driving techniques in our day-to-day travels about town, the occasional night song of full-throttle temptation will be much less costly.

INSTRUMENTS & DRIVING CYCLES

Just because you have built a performance/economy engine, does not necessarily ensure that you will save money. Once the mechanical potential exists, it must be used economically. This is not to say that we have to drive like little old ladies all of the time, but if we gain maximum economy during normal driving and cruising, our wallets will hurt a lot less, even with those few times when we squeeze the throttle hard.

INSTRUMENTS

The more you step on the throttle pedal, the more gas you use. It's that simple. Any instrument that can help you monitor the throttle and use the pedal lightly will help fuel economy.

An age-old method of driving economically is to drive with a vacuum gauge. If a vacuum gauge is coupled to the intake manifold, it will show when the engine demand for air is increased. If the air demand goes up, so does the fuel demand. When you press the throttle, the vacuum in the manifold will decline. The more you press on the pedal, the more the vacuum drops.

One of the most useful economy instruments currently available is the trip computer. The computer monitors many aspects of operation, including speed and fuel flow to the carburetor, and presents a direct readout of instantaneous or average mileage.

And, the lower the vacuum is, the more air and fuel the engine is using.

By adding a vacuum gauge to the instrument panel and driving so the vacuum reading does not drop below a certain level, say, eight inches, fuel economy can be substantially improved. (The actual vacuum readings will vary from engine to engine, but eight inches is a good general minimum because most carburetors have power-valve systems that add fuel enrichment when the vacuum drops below about eight inches.) To see no less than eight inches on a vacuum gauge, you will have to accelerate from a standstill at every traffic light gently and not stab the throttle suddenly. Any quick acceleration will show up as a sudden drop of the needle on the vacuum gauge. If you ignore what the vacuum gauge tells you, there will be no mileage increase.

A more sophisticated development is the trip computer. This instrument electronically monitors many aspects of operation, including speed and fuel flow to the carburetor. As such, it can give a direct readout of vehicle economy, in terms of either average mpg or instantaneous mpg. This is probably the ultimate economy-monitoring device.

By utilizing one of these devices, and noting what it tells you, a substantial amount of fuel can be saved, but like the vacuum gauge, if you ignore what the instrument is telling you, you will save nothing. There are many examples that exemplify the benefits of sound driving technique, but none are more vivid than the personal experience of the author. Through the use

of a trip computer he was able to improve the mileage of a vehicle powered by a smallblock Chevy V8 from 15.8mpg to 20.2mpg during a typical commuter-type driving cycle.

This is a substantial savings, but not difficult if a trip computer is used to its fullest extent. But, apart from providing information that will allow you to drive economically, these trip computers can be a lot of fun to use. The more sophisticated models will keep track of the distance between two points, average mpg over this distance, total distance traveled during a trip, aver-

age time to travel that distance and several other functions that can make a long trip much more interesting. If you monitor one of these instruments carefully, you can learn quite a few small gas-saving tricks.

Speaking of long trips, cruise controls are often cited as economy devices. If you try very hard to drive at a steady speed, you can match and even exceed the mileage that a cruise control will give you. However, this requires concentration and becomes quite tiresome after awhile. The cruise control relieves the driver from this demand and prevents driving fatigue. Most drivers do not have the patience to maintain top driving standards for 500-600 miles at a stretch. If your normal driving often includes long trips, a cruise control is a worthwhile investment.

On smooth, level roads the cruise control will do a better job than all but the very best drivers, but on undulating roads an economical driver, operating the car in a sensible fashion, can beat the mileage of a cruise control. A cruise control cannot anticipate that the vehicle is approaching a hill. It only knows the hill exists by virtue of the fact that the car slows down. If the car slows down too abruptly, the throttle is opened sharply, bringing the accelerator pump into action and sending a big shot of fuel into the engine. This uses more fuel than if the driver had taken control of the situation and started to ease the throttle down slowly, well ahead of the approach to

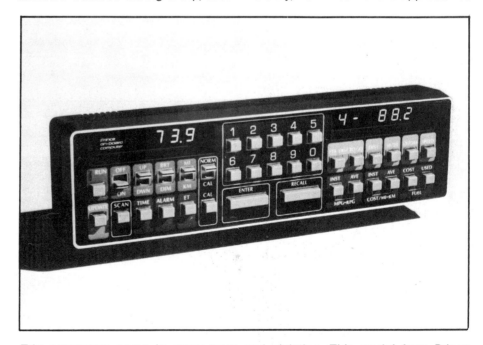

Trip computers come in many types and varieties. This model from Prince Corporation is one of the most interesting and sophisticated. Through application of state-of-the-art microprocessor technology it can monitor numerous functions and display a seemingly endless variety of time, distance, speed and mileage data.

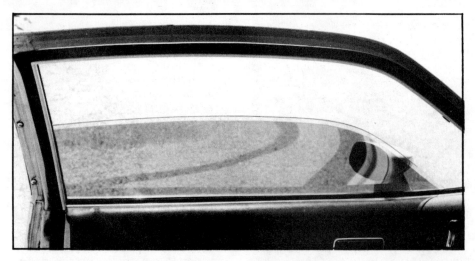

When an automotive air-conditioning system is operating, there is a marked reduction in engine economy and power. Heat-reflective film can be used on the windows to effectively lower interior temperature and reduce the desire and need to use the air conditioner. When reflective film was installed on the side windows of this car, the interior was considerably cooler, even on the hottest days.

sunlight on the occupants, but they allow more heat into the car than those window treatments that are afixed directly onto the glass. Remember, the object of the exercise is to prevent heat getting in the car, and an air space between the heat shield and the glass will allow heat to be trapped within the car instead of being reflected.

DRIVING STYLE

In the final analysis, the mileage achieved per gallon of fuel depends not only on the engine and the vehicle, but on the driver and the driving techniques he employs. The potential to save fuel is highest on short trips, such as the typical drive to work in the morning, so let's examine such a trip to see what can be done to improve economy.

the hill, to build speed slowly in anticipation of the hill. Most drivers use this technique without even thinking about it, but a cruise control cannot see down the road to anticipate conditions. It can only react after the car begins to lose speed.

ENGINE LOSSES

It's not commonly realized just how much power an automotive air conditioner uses. On a hot day an air conditioner running at full tilt will drop the engine output by 10-12%. This is power that would otherwise be used to propel the car down the road. If the demand placed on the air conditioning can be reduced, so will your fuel bill.

Much of the heat collected inside a car on a hot day is due to the "greenhouse effect" of the glass. Reflective coatings on the glass drastically reduce the sun load on the interior of the car. Using a louvred sun screen on cars that have a steeply raked rear window will also help. In hot, sunny climates, like the Southwest, it is possible to save as much as one mpg by treating the side windows with reflective coverings and by installing louvred rear window covering.

Some types of window coverings are not actually fixed to the glass. These coverings may prevent direct

Driving around town with the windows open, rather than running the air conditioner full blast, can improve economy considerably. Also, if the car has a steeply raked rear window, adding a louvered sun screen over the window will reflect heat and keep the interior cooler.

Though the price of gasoline has skyrocketed in recent years, car enthusiasts will always be able to enjoy days and nights on The Boulevard. Keeping your car in top condition and driving with an eye toward maximum "cruise" economy will stretch the most mileage from the least gas. All it takes is a little thought and attention to simple details.

The first fuel-saver is related to how you parked the car when you returned home. If possible, always park your car in a warm garage. When the car is warm in the morning, it will be easier to start and the choke will be engaged for a shorter period. Second, it is better to do start-and-stop maneuvering while the engine is warm. Therefore, if you have the choice of driving into the garage and backing out in the morning or backing in when you return and driving out in the morning, you should do the latter. If you back your car into the garage at night, when you start the engine in the morning, you can drive straight out without having to maneuver the car when the choke is fully engaged and the engine is burning fuel at a prodigious rate.

On a typical eight-mile trip into work, backing the car into the garage at night and driving away in the morning will add about one mpg to the average. The shorter the trip is, the more difference it makes. Again an example will serve to illustrate the point: in an experiment conducted by the author, backing the car out of a simulated garage and driving 600 yards gave an average fuel consumption of 5.5mpg. By backing the car into place and driving straight out (with the engine cold), the fuel consumption figure at the end of 600 yards was 10.9mpg. This is almost double the economy. Of course, the farther you drive the car, the less effect this short stretch has, but it's a simple trick and it does save fuel.

The next point to consider is how the car is driven the first few minutes you are on the road. If you accelerate too slowly while the choke is still engaged, insufficient air is drawn through the carb to "unload" the choke butterfly. This leaves the engine in a very inefficient mode of operation. When the engine is still cold and the choke is engaged you should try to

accelerate briskly (this doesn't mean stamping the throttle to the floor) to get the engine up to about 2000rpm relatively quickly. At this speed the engine needs less choke and the automatic mechanism will pull the butterfly open (technically, this is called unloading the choke). Once the car is up to 2000-2500rpm, try to maintain a steady cruise until the engine warms up and the choke is deactivated entirely.

Once the engine is up to normal operating temperature, it's time to consider the route you will take to your destination. Any time the car has to stop, energy that was used to accelerate the mass of the vehicle up to speed is lost when you have to apply the brakes. As a result, more energy is again required to reaccelerate the car to speed. To give you an idea of the mileage lost due to stops, three stop-and-start cycles from a typical urban highway speed is equal to one mile of steady-state driving. This means that when you plan your route to work, missing three traffic lights is equal to driving one mile farther. And, if four traffic lights are bypassed by a route that is one mile longer, you have saved fuel.

Of course, it's not possible to avoid all traffic lights. If you drive a route regularly, try to pace the speed of your car so you arrive at lights on green. This may mean lifting off the throttle quite some time before you arrive at a light. Watch down the road. If a light goes red, do not drive up to it. As soon as it turns red, take your foot off the throttle slowly. The trick is to let the car slow just enough so you don't have to apply the brakes while traffic clears ahead of you. Then, you can slowly apply the throttle to accelerate the car back to cruise speed. After a little practice you should be able to let the vehicle coast down at just the right speed so that the light is likely to change to green or the

traffic ahead clears by the time you get there.

The most difficult decision at traffic lights is, if they are already green, will they still be green by the time you get there? You should avoid as many stops as possible. If you think the light may turn red, but you can get to the light by opening the throttle a small amount (say, another half-inch), go for it. Less fuel will be used by building an extra 5 or even 10mph, than a restart from a dead stop. This does not mean you should floor the throttle to shoot through every stoplight. Always use a light throttle foot.

Learning the timing sequence of the traffic lights on streets you travel frequently will be a big help. In many cities the lights along major streets are timed so that traveling along the road at the proper speed (usually the posted speed limit) will allow you arrive at all the lights when the are green. However, not all cities have such a traffic light system.

Another area where potential fuel savings can be made is by selective use of the brakes. If you try to judge your braking distances so you do not have to touch the brakes until the car is under 30mph, a fuel saving will result. This involves anticipating what the car in front is going to do, or anticipating the road situation, so that if you have to slow down or stop, you can lift off the throttle and let the car coast down to about 30mph before gently applying the brakes.

If you have an automatic-transmission vehicle, avoid driving too slowly. Automatic transmissions have an inefficient speed range that varies depending on the stall speed of the torque converter and the weight of the car. Normally, this range is between approximately 20 and 30mph. If an auto-equipped car is driven too slowly, the engine is operating in an inefficient range and the torque converter is also slipping because the fluid pressure inside the converter is not sufficient to form an efficient fluid coupling. (Manual transmissions tend to be more economical at slower speeds, because they do not have low-speed slippage like a torque converter.)

If you have an automatic-transmission vehicle, when you leave a traffic

An automotive engine is not efficient when it is cold. Overall fuel use is reduced if minimum loads are imposed when it is cold and if it is not forced to idle for long periods with the choke activated. Rather than back out of the garage when the engine is cold, back-in when you park the car (and the engine is warm) and drive straight out in the morning when the engine is cold.

Reading the road ahead can conserve fuel. In this series of photos the driver is approaching an intersection, but he notes that the light is going to turn red before he arrives and he sees that he will have to come to a complete stop. But, rather than drive to the intersection at full speed and apply the brakes at the last second, he lifts his foot gently from the throttle and coasts slowly to the intersection. He gains the most distance for the least fuel, and uses the least amount of braking to reach a stop (which also extends the life of the brake linings). The idea is to use the least amount of braking and the least amount of throttle.

light, do so at a modest, but steady, pace. This will allow the transmission to shift into high gear relatively quickly. Then, try to do the majority of your accelerating up to speed in high gear. Under these conditions the engine operates in a higher efficiency range. Of course, you have to bear in mind that you must keep the throttle opening consistent with relatively high manifold-vacuum conditions. (For the type of engine that we are generally discussing in this book, eight inches of manifold vacuum is a good figure to consider as a minimum for good overall driving economy.)

When you arrive at work, again park your car in such a manner that you can drive straight out when you leave. If there is a big rush at the end of the day to go home, try to arrange to go home earlier, or if this is not possible, leave later so you do not have to spend time in a traffic jam with the engine wasting fuel. Remember, you do zero mpg when the engine is running but the car is stopped. If the choke is engaged, the engine is consuming fuel at the rate of 2-3 gallons per hour. If you spend five minutes in a traffic jam before getting away from your place of work, the fuel that is consumed during that time could well have propelled your car 3-4 miles down the road.

If you have a number of trips or errands to do, try to do them all at once. The engine can then be kept at the most efficient operating temperature for a longer period of time and you won't waste fuel warming the engine between each trip. Remember, most of the fuel consumed on short trips is used during the warmup time. If you can avoid numerous warmup cycles, fuel will be saved. And, during your short trips, if you have to leave your car in a parking lot, try to pick a spot where you can drive straight out when you leave.

All of these details may sound unimportant, but they add up. We all enjoy the performance of a finely-tuned engine, but if we drive economically on a day-to-day basis, we'll have more time and more money over the long run.

Here we have tried to represent a different situation. The driver is cruising down the road at the legal speed limit, but as he watches the road far ahead of the car, he anticipates that he will arrive when the traffic light is red if he maintains speed, but if he slows down, he can arrive when the light is green. He lifts his foot off the throttle slightly, but he tries to maintain as much speed as possible (so he will have to use less throttle to reaccelerate to cruise speed) to reach the intersection just as the light changes to green. In situations like this, it should be remembered that less fuel is needed to accelerate the car from 30 to 50mph than to accelerate from zero to 50mph.

CHAPTER 17 AVOIDING THE RIPOFF

- BUYER BEWARE!
- WORTHLESS GIMMICKS
- SPENDING MONEY WISELY

RIPOFFS

It is probably fair to say that there are more automotive ripoffs perpetrated under the guise of economy than anything else. Understandably, it is difficult for someone who is not an automotive engineer to differentiate between what is a genuine economy device and what is not. Certainly we can't make every reader an expert, but we will try to give some general guidance here to help the performance enthusiast recognize some of the obviously questionable "economy ripoffs."

The first rule is study the advertising for any product very carefully before you lay your money down. The advertising for suspicious "bolt-on mileage-makers" tends to appear in general do-it-yourself magazines, the sort of magazine that is aimed at a broadly-based population of casual readers, rather than a magazine that will appeal to knowledgeable automotive enthusiasts. The people who sell these things probably feel true enthusiasts know enough about automotive engineering to recognize a suspicious deal when they see it. But whatever the case may be, be wary of economy devices that are advertised exclusively in some non-automotive magazines.

Also, be wary of gaudy, high-key advertisements sprinkled with claims that seem too good to be true. If something sounds too good to be true, chances are it is! Very often such devices are proclaimed to be the latest that science can produce. Read these ads very carefully. Usually they are written in simple, but confusing, language. After you've read the entire ad, if you still don't have a clear-cut idea of how the product works, take a second, very cautious look.

Beware of statements that unilaterally condemn other devices or components. The typical line reads something like this: "When your carburetor runs into its inefficient range...," or words to that effect. Stop to think if such broadly formed criticism seems reasonable. In this case, consider that most modern automotive carburetors can be calibrated rather precisely to deliver as rich or lean a mixture as desired. The huckster would have you believe that all carburetors are badly designed and his product will correct all of the inherent ills of existing products. (Carburetor problems can exist, but generally they are created because the carb is being used on an unusual or non-standard application and the calibration is not optimum for the intended usage. However, all widely-used modern carburetors are based on proven engineering and design principles, and once they are properly calibrated, very little can be done to improve their overall performance.)

Whatever the device may be, ask yourself how it works and why should it give more economy. Applying cold logic in these situations can often be the basic undoing of such advertising methods. If you cannot reasonably visualize how the device works, be suspicious. The final test is to look at the actual numbers claimed. If the ad says "...up to 15%," bear in mind this means your gain could be anything from nothing to 15%. The key words are "up to."

Of course, the ad may attempt to substantiate claims by quoting what various "average" people have gained with the product in question. When you read these quotes, bear in mind that basic human psychology plays an important part in such advertising. When most people spend money for an economy device, they obviously do "wish" it to work, but average people are not trained to perform carefully controlled comparison tests. Very often a person will unknowingly change his style of driving after installing an economy-improving device, and any short-term gains may be the result of this subtle change and have nothing whatsoever to do with the product.

Even if you are wary of fraudulent claims, it's tough to sort through all of the economy products without becoming confused. Perhaps, a brief look at some of the common types of devices to avoid may help. This is not a condemnation of all products in these general categories, but if you learn to recognize some of the caution signs, hopefully, you can keep from wasting money on worthless doodads.

A popular gadget that has been around for years is the "super spark plug." Usually this type of device is either a surface-discharge or multi-electrode plug. They seem like useful products and they do work, but they are of dubious benefit in an ordinary automotive engine. Surface-discharge spark plugs have their uses in special applications, e.g., high-performance outboard marine engines, but they are designed specifically for applications that require a plug with a very low heat range. They do not operate effectively in the heat range typically required for street-driven or even high-performance automobile engines. For maximum efficiency they require a super high-powered ignition system and, even then, they are very susceptible to fouling.

What about triple-electrode spark plugs? On the surface this sounds like a good idea. Supposedly, this plug delivers three sparks, to three separate ground electrodes, instead of one. Unfortunately, a practical understanding of electricity reveals that this is not possible. In reality, the secondary high voltage will arc to only one ground electrode, the one that has the least electrical resistance (the smallest gap). No matter how many electrodes the plug has, only one spark will be generated when the voltage jumps to ground.

If all else remains constant, a multiple-electrode plug will probably operate as good as a standard plug, but not better. If there is an advantage to more than one electrode, it could be that the life of these plugs is slightly longer than conventional plugs. Since there are three electrodes available for the spark, the normal deterioration is spread over three, rather than one, electrode. The disadvantages of this type of plug are that the electrode gap cannot be simply and accurately adjusted, as on a conventional plug, and they are generally more expensive.

Another old-time favorite is the "ignition booster." This device is generally hooked into the ignition between the coil and the distributor secondary-voltage wire. It is supposed to give a "much bigger" spark. Most of these devices are essentially an air gap or a piece of carbon rod designed to increase resistance in the secondary system. (There are conventional spark plugs that work on a similar principle. They are called resistor plugs, and they have a built-in air gap along the center electrode.)

The function of the air gap is to create an intermediate block (resistance), causing the coil secondary voltage to build to a higher level. When the voltage reaches a certain level (determined by the degree of resistance), it bridges this intermediate resistance in a burst of energy. This surge of voltage then reaches the end of the center electrode and shoots across the normal plug gap. As a result, if the plug is worn or oily, the voltage surge should be better able to overcome this increased resistance and provide a suitable spark to initiate combustion.

When properly designed, ignition boosters, resistor plugs and specialty air-gap plugs can be helpful if your engine has an oiling problem, but if your engine is not oiling (and has an adequate ignition), these things won't help at all. On the other hand, if any of these devices are not properly designed, they can cause trouble. If the ignition is only providing a marginal spark and the spark booster has too much built-in resistance, the voltage may not be able to bridge the intermediate resistance, and a misfire is created.

If you have inadequate ignition, the best cure is to thoroughly check and overhaul the system, rather than trying to "band-aid" the problem with a makeshift device. If an engine oiling problem exists, there are two possible means of curing it. Either overhaul the engine, which is what you should be doing to get best mileage and power, or see if there is a standard resistor-type spark plug that can be installed in your engine. (A quick check in the Champion Spark Plug, or similar, catalog should reveal whether or not there is a plug suitable.) These plugs have a very limited amount of intermediate resistance and can be helpful in certain cases. They are by no means,

There is no substitution for thorough tuning and careful attention to operational conditions! It is certain that we all live within the constraints of the basic laws of physics and any "miracle mileage" claims should be viewed with skepticism.

The sure way to avoid ripoffs is to understand basic engine functioning and have an honest respect for your machinery. This 340 Mopar with triple Holley carbs has been updated to present-day standards and delivers astounding mileage at highway cruise speeds (when it is operating on only the primary Holley two-barrel carb). No "tricks" here, just sound basic mechanical principles, executed in a professional manner.

though, a "cure" for oiling, they can only be viewed as a temporary stopgap measure.

When you read some of the advertisements, "fuel atomizers" look like a good bet. These devices are generally installed between the carburetor and the manifold and they purport to increase the atomization of fuel.

What is often overlooked is that fuel being dumped into a high vacuum tends to vaporize much easier than fuel at normal air pressure. Remember, the boiling point of a liquid goes down as the air pressure drops. This means that at part throttle it's much easier to vaporize the fuel in the manifold. About the only phase of carburetion where reasonable atomization doesn't take place is during full-throttle, low-rpm conditions. At these times the "atomizer" may produce large droplets of fuel that could well do with further refinement.

Most atomizers resemble a screen-wire grid. The general idea seems to be based on the belief that fuel exiting the carburetor in the induction airstream hits the wire grid, breaks up and is re-introduced into the air in "better atomized" condition. In actuality, during part-throttle operation, very little re-introduction takes place because the fuel is already atomized, or vaporized, to a large extent by the time it reaches the atomizer. Under these conditions the performance difference is usually negligible. At full throttle the atomizer may help somewhat, however, it impedes the airflow so

much that, from this aspect, it tends to reduce power. On balance, it would appear to be of little proven value.

A rather unusual economy device popularized in the early Fifties and Sixties was the "tailpipe booster or extractor." These gadgets were supposed to suck the exhaust right out of the engine. Possibly, most of these things were sold on their aesthetic appeal rather than their functional value.

In fact, some tailpipe boosters have proven to work, but the economy gains are so small that it is unlikely you could ever recoup your investment over the normal lifespan of a car. Consider this: by the time the exhaust has reached the end of the tailpipe, it has gone through the worst obstructions possible. "Boosting" the exhaust at this point is a little late in the game. If possible, the effort would be much better spent up near the exhaust valve, not 10 feet away, at the end of the tailpipe!

However, inventors have tried every conceivable means to draw the exhaust out of the tailpipe. Some have tried to suck the exhaust out with small impellers. Usually it takes more power to turn these things, by one means or another, than the extra power they can possibly produce. Others have attached "extractor cones" and all sorts of weird things onto the end of the pipe. Usually these devices are designed to gather air flowing under the car and use it to draw the exhaust gas from the tailpipe. If anything can be said about

these bizarre festoons, it is that they successfully increase the overall aerodynamic drag of the car.

Our advice here is simple. Rather than spend your money on a tailpipe booster, spend it on a good, free-flowing muffler and exhaust system. You will gain much more.

One of the currently popular "tricks" is economy oil and/or fuel additives. Most of these chemical additives do nothing, or very little, for the performance of an engine. On numerous occasions the author has tested oil additives on an engine dynamometer. In a few cases, small power gains were recorded, but these gains were always so close to the threshhold of measuring accuracy, that it could not be said with certainty that the gains were due to the fuel or oil additives.

This doesn't mean that all additives are a waste of money; some of the additives available on the market do improve the durability of an engine oil and, as a result, are worthy of a place in a mechanic's tool box. However, the point to remember with additives, be they fuel or oil additives, is that their cost can seldom be justified in terms of actual economy or power gains. If an additive does reduce engine friction or give extra mileage, almost certainly the gain will be so small, in relation to cost, that it will remain a financially improbable proposition for quite some time.

Usually, if you examine the claims made by additive manufacturers with a skeptical eye, you can see that they are rather thinly clad. For instance, one particular brand of fuel additive claims a 30% increase in mileage. Some simple mathematics reveals that if this claim were true, the additive has approximately 26 times the energy, per pound, that gasoline contains. It would seem then, that pound-for-pound this additive is more powerful than nitroglycerine, which is commonly regarded as the most powerful general chemical reactant available.

Fortunately (?) for the consumer market, the Federal Trade Commission (F.T.C.) is beginning to realize that more and more fraudulent devices are going to be offered to the unsuspecting public. Slowly and with all-too-familiar bureaucratic fumbling, steps are being taken to ensure that all economy claims are backed up by tests from a reputable agency, such as the Environmental Protection Agency. It is a shame that the government has to increasingly take a Big Brother role in consumer affairs, but it's either this or every man for himself.

APPENDIX

ACCESSORIES/SERVICES

AIRFLOW RESEARCH
11754 Roscoe, Unit #6, Sun Valley, CA 91352
213-767-4270, Retail Catalog: None

H & H RACING GASOLINE
412 Marine Avenue, Wilmington, CA, 90744
213-518-6000, Retail Catalog: None

HEANY INDUSTRIES
P.O. Box 38, Fairview Drive, Scottsville, NY, 14546
716-889-2700, Retail Catalog: None

HEATHKIT TUNEUP INSTRUMENTS
Veritechnology Electronics, 330 E. Ball Road
Anaheim, CA, 92805
714-776-9420, Retail Catalog: Free

SPEARCO PERFORMANCE
7541 Woodman Place, Van Nuys, CA 91405
818-907-7851, Retail Catalog: Call

CAMS/VALVETRAIN

CAM DYNAMICS
530 Fentress Blvd., Daytona Beach, FL 32014
904-258-8845, Retail Catalog: $3.00

COMPETITION CAMS
3406 Democrat, Memphis TN 38118
901-795-2400, Retail Catalog: $5.00

CRANE CAMS
530 Fentress Blvd., Daytona Beach FL 32014
904-252-1151, Retail Catalog: $4.00

CROWER CAMS & EQUIPMENT
3333 Main Street, Chula Vista CA 92011
619-422-1191, Retail Catalog: $3.00

ENGLE RACING CAMS
1621 12th Street, Santa Monica CA 90404
213-450-0806—Order & Tech, Retail Catalog: $2.00

ERSON RACING CAMS INC.
550 Mallory Way, Carson City NV 89701
702-882-1622, Retail Catalog: $4

ISKENDERIAN RACING CAMS
16020 S. Broadway, Gardena CA 90248
213-770-0930, Retail Catalog: $3.00

LUNATI RACING CAMS
4770 Lamar Avenue, P.O. Box 18021
Memphis TN 38118
901-365-0950—Order & Tech, Retail Catalog: $3.00

RACER BROWN
12111-1/2 Brandford St., Bldg. C-4
Sun Valley CA 91352
818-897-4044, Newsletter: Free

CARBURETION/ FUEL INJECTION

B.A.P.
(Weber Carburetors)
3025 E. Victoria Street, Compton, CA, 90221
213-537-3130, Retail Catalog: Call

BRASWELL CARBURETION
1650 E. 18 Street, Unit P, Tucson AZ 85719
602-884-7282, Retail Catalog: None

CARTER AUTOMOTIVE CO. INC.
(Carter Carburetors)
9666 Olive Street Blvd., St. Louis MO 63132
314-997-7400, Retail Catalogs available at, Federal-Mogal dealers; for location, call above number.

FUEL INJECTION ENGINEERING
25891 Crown Valley Parkway, So. Laguna CA 92677
714-582-1170—Order & Tech, Retail Catalog: $2.50

HOLLEY REPLACEMENT PARTS DIV.
11955 E. Nine Mile Road, Warren MI 48089
For technical information, hard-to-get parts, and
literature, call: 615-859-4924, Retail Catalog: $3.00

MIKE JONES CARBURETION
7602 Talbert Avenue, #6
Huntington Beach CA 92647
714-848-5505—Order, 714-848-5500—Tech
Retail Catalog: $2.00

HEADERS

CYCLONE EXHAUST
19007 S. Reyes Ave., Compton CA 90221
213-639-6211, For Catalog: 216-398-8300, ext. 333
Catalog Price: $3.00

DOUG THORLEY HEADERS
1561 Commerce St., Corona CA 91720
714-735-7280, Retail Catalog: Free

EAGLE HEADERS
19007 S. Reyes Ave., Compton CA 90221
213-639-6211, For Catalog: 216-398-8300, ext. 333
Catalog Price: $3.00

HEADERS BY ED
2710-SA 16th Avenue S., Minneapolis MN 55407
612-729-2802, Header Catalog: $3.95, Header Parts
Catalog: $2.95

HEDMAN MFG.
9599 W. Jefferson Blvd., Culver City CA 93021
213-839-7581, Retail Catalog: $3.00

HOOKER HEADERS
1024 W. Brooks St., Ontario CA 91762
714-983-5871, Retail Catalog: $4.00

IGNITION

ACCEL IGNITION
Echlin Road, US Route 1, Branford CT 06405
203-481-5771—Order & Tech, Retail Catalog: $4.00

ALLISON AUTOMOTIVE
720 E. Cypress Ave., Monrovia CA 91016
818-303-3621—Order, 800-325-2159—US Tech
800-325-5864—CA Tech, Retail Catalog: $2.00

AUTOTRONIC CONTROLS CORP., MSD IGNITION
1490 Henry Brennan Dr., El Paso TX 79936
915-857-5200, Retail Catalog: $2.00

GENERAL NUCLEONICS, SPEEDATRON
2807 Metropolitan Place, Pomona CA 91767
714-593-4985, Retail Catalog: None

MALLORY IGNITION
550 Mallory Way, Carson City NV 89701
702-882-6600, Retail Catalog: $4.00

MANIFOLDS

CLIFFORD PERFORMANCE
500 West Harrington St., Unit H, Corona CA 91720
714-734-3310, Retail Catalog: $3.00

EDELBROCK CORPORATION
411 Coral Circle, El Segundo CA 90245
213-322-7310, Retail Catalog: $2.00

HOLLEY REPLACEMENT PARTS DIV.
11955 East 9-Mile Road, Warren MI 48090
For technical information, hard-to-get parts, and
literature, call: 615-859-4924, Retail Catalog: $3.00

OFFENHAUSER SALES CORP.
5232 Alhambra Ave., PO Box 32218
Los Angeles CA 90032
213-225-1307, Retail Catalog: $3.00

PACER PERFORMANCE PRODUCTS
5345 San Fernando Road West, Los Angeles CA 90039
213-245-3654, Retail Catalog: None

WEIAND AUTOMOTIVE INDUSTRIES
2316 San Fernando Road, PO Box 65977
Los Angeles CA 90065
213-225-4138, Retail Catalog: $3.00

PISTONS/ MAJOR ENGINE COMPONENTS

APT, Automotive Performance Technology
561 Iowa Avenue, Annex E, Riverside CA 92502
714-783-0344, Nitrous cams, pistons, rods, cylinder
heads, and other related parts

ARIAS INDUSTRIES INC.
13420 S. Normandie Avenue, Gardena CA 90249
213-770-0055—Order & Tech, 213-532-9737—Pistons
213-538-2505—Engines, Retail Catalog: $3.00

HANK THE CRANK INC.
7253 Lankershim Blvd., N. Hollywood CA 90241
818-765-3444—Order, 213-877-0347—Tech
Retail Catalog: $4.00

JE PISTONS
15681 Computer Lane, Huntington Beach CA 92649
714-898-9763—Order & Tech, Retail Catalog: $3.00

MANLEY PERFORMANCE PRODUCTS
13 Race Street, Bloomfield NJ 07003
201-743-6577—Tech
800-526-1362—Order (No direct sales)
Catalog: None

SPEED-O-MOTIVE INC.
12061 E. slauson Avenue, Santa Fe Springs, CA 90670
213-945-2758, Retail Catalog: #4.00

SPEED-PRO/SEALED POWER CORP.
100 Terrace Plaza, PO Box 299, Muskegon MI 49443
616-724-5011—Tech, 616-724-5266—Order
Retail Catalog: $3.00

TOTAL-SEAL PISTON RING CO.
2225 W. Mountain View, #17, Phoenix AZ 85021
602-242-9421, Retail Cagalog: Free

TRW PERFORMANCE PARTS
8001 East Pleasant Valley Rd, Cleveland OH 44131
Contact nearest TRW dealer to order.
800-352-2273—Tech, Ex Ohio
800-992-2273—Tech, Ohio
Retail Catalog: $5.00

There's A <u>How-To-Do-It Book</u> For You In Each Performance Series Below

ENGINE
5 Books

- Ford Performance
- Chevy Performance
- Mopar Performance
- V-6 Performance
- Engine Blueprinting

The S-A Design Engine Series has no equal in providing high-quality, high-performance information. Each book contains easy-to-read tech along with hundreds of photos, charts, and graphs. Our Engine Series gives you the information you'll need to build a reliable, high-horsepower engine for street, track, drag racing, or off-road use.

CARBURETION
2 Books

- Holley Carburetors
- Carter Carburetors

Cut through the black magic of selecting, tuning, modifying, and rebuilding Holley and Carter carburetors. The Carburetion Series has helped tens of thousands of enthusiasts get the most from their induction system. From selecting jets for more economy to modifying metering circuits for racing, you can count on our Carburetion Series: no magic here — just tested, accurate info.

SUPER INDUCTION

3 Books

- Nitrous-Oxide Injection
- Street Supercharging
- Superpower

If you're interested in real ground-pounding horsepower, the Super-Induction Series is what you're looking for. Everything from the subtleties of hidden nitrous-oxide injection, to outrageous belt-driven supercharging is explained in easy-to-read text. We show you how to avoid the pitfalls, select the system, bolt on the hardware, and get the most for your money.

EXPERT

2 Books

- Smokey Yunick's Power Secrets
- The Chevrolet Racing Engine

Ever wondered how top experts find more horsepower per cubic inch than many knowledgeable people thought was possible? The Expert Series gives you an inside look at the "secrets" of two of the country's most successful engine builders: Bill "Grumpy" Jenkins and Smokey Yunick. These two unique books reveal techniques and insights that you can use to build reliable stock or Pro-Stock horsepower into your engine.

* Available in 1988

BOLT-ON
5 Books

- Guide To Bolt-On Street Power
- Performance With Economy
- How To Build Horsepower*
- Hot Rodder's Handbook*
- Building The Smallblock Chevy*

The S-A Design Bolt-On Series will help you select everything from mufflers to manifolds, gear ratios to gear drives, and tires to tachometers. All written for easy reading, these books are the nuts and bolts of hot rodding, and they will become the most valuable references in your performance library. This series will help anyone understand the complex world of performance technology.

SUPERSTREET/ SUSPENSION
2 Books

- Building A SuperStreet Mopar
- Drag Racing Chassis & Suspension*

If you'd like to build a car that corners as fast as it accelerates, the SuperStreet/Suspension Series has it. If you just need guidelines for component selection, or if you're looking for in-depth information about suspension function and design, this series has the answers you want. Includes everything from selecting brake fluids to details about center-of-gravity, roll couple, plus engine building tips; all written in understandable terms. Find out how to make your car handle like a Porsche and run like a Musclecar. Look into the books in this series.

PAINTING BODYWORK
2 Books

- Custom Painting
- Basic Painting & Bodywork*

Reading the S-A Design Painting and Bodywork Series, can help you produce silk-smooth, factory-matched repaints or eye-popping custom paint tricks in your own driveway. Many enthusiasts believe that top-quality painting and bodywork can only be done by experts, and while it's true that experts have the know-how, the books in this series can show you the right way to start, help you while you practice, and have you doing "expert" work in short order.

ALTERNATE FUELS
1 Book

- Propane Conversions

Gasoline produces horsepower, but it also produces smog, increases ring and cylinder-bore wear, contaminates engine oil, promotes erratic running when cold, can "vapor lock" when hot, and more. The Alternate Fuels Series book Propane Conversions provides a fascinating look at the use of propane for street performance. Learn how a straightforward conversion to LPG or propane can nearly double engine life, increase performance, reduce emissions (to virtually nothing), and improve driveability!

We encourage individuals to purchase books from a local retailer. S-A Design Books are sold internationally in speed shops, book stores, and automotive parts outlets. However, if you cannot find our books locally, you may order direct from S-A Design by pre-paying $12.95 plus $2.00 (postage and handling) per copy (California residents add 78¢ tax each). Mail to S-A Design Order Desk, 515 West Lambert, Bldg. E, Brea, CA 92621-3991, or call 714-529-7999.

Join Our Book Users Group – It's FREE!

Join the S-A Design Book Users Group now! Just some of the benefits are:

- Free newsletter keeps you in contact with our authors and readers
- Special discounts on books
- Technical updates
- Info on latest publications
- Join BUG and stay in touch

YES! I would like to activate my membership in the S-A Design Book Users Group now!

Name _____

Address _____

City _____

State _____ Zip _____